To Travic

Thank you and hope you enjoy my ride

Uphill
An Inspirational story of suffering, greed, carnage, immense courage and gut-determination
All Rights Reserved.
Copyright © 2019 Geoffrey Bott
v3.0

Paperback ISBN: 978-0-578-21930-1
Hardback ISBN: 978-0-578-21931-8

Cover Photo © 2019 Mona Sanatgaran Neo Design. All rights reserved - used with permission.

Library of Congress, Certificate of Registration: TXu 2-129-280

PRINTED IN THE UNITED STATES OF AMERICA

Solihull Publishing

Acknowledgments

It would have been incredibly difficult, if even remotely possible, to have escaped hell without the assistance of others. I would be remise if I didn't acknowledge their divine efforts and unbridled commitment in their endeavors. There were others too but I will be forever indebted to the following:

Dr Bannar, whose courageous decision changed the course of my life. He unexpectedly passed away December 2018 and will be missed by many people.

Dr. Watson, who performed groundbreaking knee surgeries beyond anyone's imagination, with such dexterity and precision.

Chris Proctor, who dragged me back into physical therapy when I was contemplating walking away.

James Proctor, my lawyer and friend, who kept me going through immense, mind-boggling legal struggles.

Claire Fortier, a renowned editor and friend, who somehow managed to transform and massage my therapeutic but chaotic 110,000 word manuscript into a legible story.

Thank you with my unlimited gratitude.

Note from the Author

In order to escape the chaos, I was told to purge my head. I did and it just kept building. I couldn't stop myself. I would come home and keep writing. How do I write this, was the repeated question? Where do I start even?

It wasn't written to be a book. It was written to be a self-counseling exercise. To be a document on which I could leave the memories behind and allow myself to move forwards in life. I listened to professionals and took the manuscript, printed it out and compiled it into a story.

The story turned into my self-healing process and my self-imposed therapy.

I lay it all out there and don't sugar-coat anything. I create a character who is fallible and imperfect. He makes poor decisions and mistakes. We all do. It would not be interesting to read about how perfect someone is. Too many of those people already exist in this world. I was told the hardest subject to write about is one's self. I was about to write my first book on the most difficult subject there is. No pressure then. However, the details are graphic, intense and vivid. This is real life and not Hollywood. The character is left naked and exposed, not in the literal sense, but in his desire to write a shockingly true depiction of what he lived through.

My hope is it inspires and motivates others. I hope it helps people overcome their own demons, their own version of hell. The goals I set myself on my cycle were ridiculous, even for a fully abled person. But I wasn't going to be beaten down. I wasn't going to surrender. I wasn't going to give up.

Crying does not make a man weak but gives him strength. Many tears were spilled to finish this book. For those who encouraged and supported me, I owe a debt of gratitude. To my children, I love you.

Table of Contents

Preface i

Section 1
Chapter 1 3
Chapter 2 10
Chapter 3 14
Chapter 4 17
Chapter 5 20
Chapter 6 23
Chapter 7 26
Chapter 8 29
Chapter 9 35
Chapter 10 39
Chapter 11 45
Chapter 12 48
Chapter 13 51

Section 2
Chapter 14 65
Chapter 15 69
Chapter 16 83
Chapter 17 90
Chapter 18 97
Chapter 19 101
Chapter 20 111
Chapter 21 113

Section 3

Chapter 22 133
Chapter 23 137
Chapter 24 140
Chapter 25 145
Chapter 26 150
Chapter 27 153
Chapter 28 157
Chapter 29 170
Chapter 30 174
Chapter 31 178
Chapter 32 182
Chapter 33 190
Chapter 34 196

Section 4

Chapter 35 211
Chapter 36 219
Chapter 37 222
Chapter 38 225
Chapter 39 227
Chapter 40 229
Chapter 41 232
Chapter 42 236
Chapter 43 242
Chapter 44 244
Chapter 45 246
Chapter 46 251
Chapter 47 253
Chapter 48 256
Chapter 49 259
Chapter 50 262
Chapter 51 266

Section 5

Chapter 52 273
Chapter 53 275
Chapter 54 278
Chapter 55 280
Prologue.. 282

Preface

THE SUN HAD been beating down on me for more than nine hours. My sweat was evaporating in the scorching heat, leaving a sticky residue on my skin and clothing. The winds cascading around the mountains had blown dirt, debris and insects in my path. I was grimy and dirty. My stomach was screaming at me. I'd been burning calories and expelling essential nutrients at an alarming rate. My energy was depleting fast as I cycled up the seemingly endless mountain pass. My muscles were aching but all of that was overshadowed by the immense pain in my left knee.

If it wasn't for a surgical complication in April 2002, where I nearly lost the rear leg muscle, I would not be feeling much at all. But the intense pain in the rear of my knee was massive. It felt as if something was tearing apart. A tendon, a muscle, ligament, who knows? But the pain stabbed through each rotation and it got worse as the revolution extended my leg.

The indentation created from the surgery only a few years ago was also a problem. As the skin was being drawn into my knee joint, there was this intense pressure around that region as my skin was being dragged and stretched inwards. My body was aching, I was hungry, my stomach and muscles were yelling in unison but I cycled on.

The road was narrow, a typical two-lane mountain road twisting through a cavern formed from millions of years of erosion. On either side, the mountains jutted up, creating this incredible scenic route as the road traversed through the valley. Huge boulders lined the road.

Trees were sparse. Some vegetation was evident but the altitude and lack of summer rain precluded much from growing. The lack of vegetation and overhanging trees meant the sun perpetually seared the surface of my skin, now hot and burning after hours in the saddle. I could see the afternoon sun leaning towards the west, where storm clouds were generating.

As I pedaled up the mountain I knew I was within two miles of a rest stop. There I could feed my hunger, rest my muscles and relax the pain, long enough to gather the strength I needed to complete the final section of the fifth mountain pass of the day.

I pulled my bicycle into the rest station just east of Pickett's Junction in Alpine County, California and quickly downed a Coke. I am not a Coke fan but I needed to replenish the calories I was rapidly burning. I then ate nuts, banana, protein bars, peanut butter and jelly sandwich, anything really to fill my body with calories and nutrients, which my body was using up almost as quickly as I replenished them.

It was Saturday 12th July, 2008. It was my last stop before the 1,500 foot climb to the top of Carson Pass, elevation 8,580 feet.

I was on the final leg of the infamous Death Ride, one of cycling's most grueling endurance events. It was a one day ride of 129 miles, traversing 5 mountain passes and climbing 15,000 feet in an area known as the California Alps. The brochure I had picked up months before called it "a daunting feat." Daunting indeed! Fewer than 1,700 riders of the 2,700 cyclists that had signed up would go the distance

The ride was staggering. It was insanity for those with two functioning legs, but absolute madness for someone who was told he would never ride a bicycle again.

People thought I was crazy when I told them my plans. Perhaps I am.

Only a handful of people thought I could do it. I knew I had to.

As I stood there, in sight of the final pass, I looked at the hell facing me and actually felt pretty good. A hundred miles and four mountain passes were completed. I already climbed 13,500 vertical feet. This was it, the final climb.

I looked over at my bicycle, the bright yellow Giant TCR2 light-weight that seemed to carry the very soul of me. I purchased the barely-used road bike from a store in South Lake Tahoe where I had been living since 1999. I bought it in May 2004, shortly after my surgeons told me that my left knee was finished and I would never be able to ride again.

I carefully grabbed the handlebars and wheeled it free so I could climb on. With the bike on my left, I planted my right leg and swung the left over the bar. It was the only way I could get on my bicycle without my left knee collapsing completely. I secured the left foot in the pedal clips and took off, securing the right foot as I pedaled away.

I signaled to my girlfriend, Crystal, who with my son Michael, was following me in the black Toyota Highlander I had recently purchased. They were with me for emotional support, even though neither understood what I was doing or, more importantly, why.

At 7,000 feet in the Sierras, afternoon thunderstorms with lightning and sudden downpours are frequent. I could see the clouds amassing in the distance, heading toward me. This was going to be tough. At this altitude, rain is problematic. It is cold rain, quickly freezing exposed skin. That, I knew after four years of training, was never a good thing when screaming down mountain passes at high rates of speed. When mountains are steep, I must keep my brakes perpetually engaged to control speed so the bike remains manageable. That's a very difficult proposition with frozen fingers and wet brakes.

I started cycling west on Highway 88, passing Pickett's Junction, onto the final climb. I'd trained Carson Pass many times so was well aware of the road curves and the steep climbs facing me. I looked down at the cheap computer on my handlebars. Over a 100 miles so far today. I had been on the bike since 5:30 a.m. It was now pushing 4 p.m.

With dark clouds churning, I needed to move. I could see many riders ahead of me and a bunch behind. I gathered speed, the bike's computer reading over 25 mph. Behind me, I had gathered a small peloton of perhaps ten cyclists. They were following in my slipstream as I blocked the wind. At those speeds, one has a head wind no matter what. I kept cranking.

After a few miles I knew the road was going to bank to the right, at which time it would not be flat anymore. As I approached and the gradient changed, my speed dropped precipitously. In my condition, I didn't have the muscle to propel up mountain passes. As I reduced my speed, the small peloton behind me passed. The lead rider thanked me for the ride and appreciated the speed at which I had dragged them along. He had no idea what I had gone through to get there or how truly miraculous I felt to be able to bike at all.

The road became steep. I kept my head down, got into my rhythm and pushed up the mountain.

A few more twists and turns, a few more short climbs and I was closer to the top of Carson Pass. As I got nearer, I saw the right-hander that I knew would take me on the final climb. I gathered my thoughts, cleared my head and peddled on. It was steep but I knew it would get steeper still.

As I made the turn, the weather also took a turn. A massive gust of wind almost forced the long procession of cyclists in front of me to stop in their tracks. The storm was darkening the sky. The winds started to howl and the angry clouds finally burst their anxiety onto the masses below. It took some effort to control my bike. I was pedaling uphill into a monumental headwind. Not only was the rain cold, but it was blowing like a pressurized blaster against my exposed hands and face. Within minutes my cycling clothes became drenched and cold.

For that big day, I had chosen a special cycling kit hand carried from France. It was the AG2R pro-cycling team kit, which was sponsored partly by Rover/MG in England. I am a Rover enthusiast and a race car aficionado. But now my kit was soaked.

Another thing I learnt cycling in mountains is that sweat from climbing can be detrimental when it turns cold. Not only is it uncomfortable but it rapidly cools the body temperature.

Now my shoes were getting wet from the spray splashing up from the front tyres. This was not good either.

Some cyclists had stopped at the side of the road and pulled out their rain gear. They were obviously more prepared than I. Some had rain capes that covered them and the handlebars. "How nice," I thought, "No wet fingers that feel as if they are falling off. Hmm, I must be more prepared next time."

Next time!! I quickly purged that thought to deal with the current predicament. I had made a left turn as the road curved upwards and was now facing the top of the mountain pass. I could see the road snaking its way upwards. Sometimes the open face of a mountain pass can reveal how daunting a climb can be. There was a small portion where it got greater than 10% gradient. My muscles were already burning. But I vowed that a short gradient increase was not really a detriment--only a mile and a half to go now.

I passed the steeper gradient, and at this point the road narrowed and curved to the right around the mountain face. On my right was a perpendicular rock face. On my left, a majestic view down Hope Valley.

It was still raining hard, the wind was still blowing. There wasn't much protection at this height. Trees do not grow in rocks. The road curved around and the gradient decreased until, finally, it flattened out. I could see the green Carson Pass sign and knew I had conquered the fifth mountain pass of the day.

Passing the public viewing/rest area off to the left, the road now started to head downwards as it straightened out. I could see the staging area and rest stop for the cyclists about 100 yards in front of me. It was packed.

As I approached, my head began to spin. The DEATH RIDE. Few finish. Even fewer thought I could or I would. But there it was, the end of the hardest test of my life.

I had endured five major surgeries to rebuild my left knee, including numerous complications and rejections that required additional emergency surgeries. I had staggering pain that left me screaming, reducing me to a narcotics addiction that changed my personality. I spent eighteen months on crutches and two years in physical therapy, three days a week. Then there was the failure and rejection of the second knee rebuild. And more tears spilled as I endured emotional, psychological and physical devastation.

In May 2004, orthopedic surgeons told me my left knee was finished. I came out of the surgeons' offices with one thought: I am not finished yet. I will beat this.

I had no idea at the time what that would mean or what monumental drive it would require. I knew none of this when I started cycling again.

But now I stood on the top of Carson Pass, mountain climb number five of the infamous Death Ride, doing the one thing my surgeon said I would never do. Maybe that's why so many people thought I was crazy.

SECTION 1

Chapter 1

IT WAS THE Autumn 1980 in England, and I was in the fifth and final year of high school. I had just turned 17 and was one of the younger Upper Sixth Formers. I was studying mathematics, physics and chemistry before embarking on a university education whose location had yet to be determined. Malet Lambert High School was a mile from my home, located on the east side of Kingston Upon Hull.

Hull is on the north banks of the River Humber in northeast England. It's an historical town and used to house one of the largest fishing ports in Europe. But after my family moved there in 1968, the docks declined, costing thousands of jobs, all the fallout from misguided political decisions.

I was born into a middle class family, the youngest of five. My twin brother, Nicholas, and I were always told we were a mistake.

"The last time you told me you knew what you were doing, the twins arrive," my mother would often say to my father. It was funny, for the most part.

As children, we were to be seen and not heard. We were never told much and we didn't ask questions.

My father spent time in the British Navy during and after WWII, but he didn't talk about it. He was based on an aircraft carrier and visited Japan right after the tortuous hydrogen bombs were catastrophically dropped by the US military. He never discussed what he saw except on rare occasions, voicing "I never want to see that again."

My father left the military soon after the end of World War II to work as a fireman on Britain's steam railways. It must have been grueling shift work, moving coal into the boilers. He later left the railway and became a certified CPA. He was in and out of work as companies shut down or down-sized, which meant the family moved more than most people back in the '50s and '60s. We finally ended up in Hull, a weird place to me because the people who were born there mostly stayed there.

Before his huge stroke in 1982, my father worked at British Aerospace as an insurance manager. My mother, Muriel, used to work at the National Children's Home, a government facility to house unwanted, neglected and/or abandoned children. She worked there until she married my father and started having children.

My oldest brother John was perceived as an outcast, and still is. At times he did certain things just to wind our mother up, which he accomplished to perfection. Three years later came my brother, Chris, who went on to graduate with an engineering degree from University of Salford and made his life's focus to make money. Four years later came the only girl in the family, Jennifer, who went on to get an advanced computer programming degree. Four years behind her came Nick and me. Nick, like my father, went on to work at British Aerospace.

None of my siblings excelled in sports. Nick played football for the high school team until his life was nearly cut short in his mid-teens due to complications from an appendectomy.

But I was brilliant at most sports. I was fast and immensely competitive. I had the drive and desire to want to succeed. Challenging myself on the field, in a game or in a race, was at the very core of me. I wanted to win.

On that day in late September came one of the proudest days of my life. In my final year of high school, as I was sitting in the school assembly, I heard my name.

"Geoff Bott has been selected to represent Hull U19's Rugby in the forthcoming Hull and East Riding trials. It is an honour for Malet Lambert High School."

Rugby was not my primary sport. But only a week or so earlier I had failed in my bid to represent Hull U19 football as a goalkeeper, a significant failing that devastated me as I had gained some respect in the footballing world.

A few days after that failure, I had played one of my finest games ever, watched by several coaches of significance at my school. I pulled off a stunning save as I clawed away, full stretch, a ball heading into the top corner of the net. We ended up beating one of Hull's top teams from a private school 2-1. But the save didn't save my bid to represent my school.

Consequently, in the rugby trials, I took my anger and frustration out on Hull and East Riding's star winger, poor guy. I watched as he was coming towards me. The rugby ball was tightly wrapped in his left arm as he attempted to keep it away from me. He was fast but I doubted he was faster than me. I had become Hull School's 100m and 200m track and field champion that summer, so there was no way I was letting him passed me.

He was bigger, his shoulders broader, but that did not distract from my desire to take him down. He tried to side-step me and beat me on his outside as he gathered speed. I switched and pushed with the left leg so that I could change directions with him. The look of bewilderment and shock enveloped his face as I charged him at full speed. With my head down slightly and eyes focused only on him, I hit his chest hard with my right shoulder. As I did that, I secured both arms around his waist and pushed with momentum and power. Newton's First Law of Motion: a body continues in a straight line until acted upon by forces. He had no chance as I took him off the field. He buckled backwards beyond the touchline and over we went, the ball falling away from his tight grip and rolling on the ground.

I stood up and walked away but not before looking into his eyes. I just took out Hull and East Riding's star left winger. I wanted him to remember me.

But in the second half of the trials representing Hull U19's in October 1980, something happened that would leave me scarred for the rest of my life. I was heading into a tackle when I felt someone kick my left knee. It buckled slightly and I felt something give. After the tackle was made I looked down at the knee and saw blood pouring down the lower leg. I immediately signaled the coaches and jogged off the field. There was a bucket of water and a sponge which I grabbed in an attempt to ebb the flow and clean it up. I found a deep laceration which I thought required stitches but being a typical rugby player, I washed off the excess blood and ran back out onto the field. I had no idea what had just happened.

A few weeks later my knee gave way in the living room of my parent's home and I fell to the floor in agony, grasping it with both hands. In all my years of playing sports, this was something new. I had no idea how bad this would become.

The following morning, my knee had swelled. Swelling made it so uncomfortable I made an appointment with a local doctor. He was a general practice doctor, not a specialist, and rendered little in the way of support or advice for what might be happening. He examined the knee but did not elect to take x-rays. In fact he did none of the routine diagnostic tests that I now know were necessary.

In any event, I was given several possibilities as to why my knee collapsed, but no compelling evidence to prove much of anything. The doctor seemed to have little idea what was wrong with my knee. Since I found no real reason to prevent me from carrying on, I simply left the office and walked home.

I went back to my classes and continued excelling at sports. In the winter, I played football and rugby, but also elected to add badminton and squash to the sporting calendar of activities.

In late November, while I was playing badminton, it happened again. My left knee buckled and I collapsed, laying in a pile on the gymnasium floor. The pain was something unforgettable. It shot from the knee area straight up my back. After a few minutes, my knee settled down and the joint went back to normal. I lay on the floor for a while as people gathered around and then I got up. The knee was good so I carried on. I was too young, too naïve and too stupid to do anything else, so I continue playing.

When I finally did go back to the doctor, I ran into another problem: the British health care system. Mundane issues like bad joints, no matter how painful, get put on the back-burner. Deemed non-essential, they don't take precedence. I was put on a list and left there.

But the doctor did warn me that I was at risk for serious damage if I continued to play sports. It was advice I failed to heed.

This wasn't my first encounter with England's one-payer National Health System (NHS), which is free to everyone. But free doesn't always mean good.

When I was eight, I had severe stomach pains that wouldn't go away. I was kept away from school but they grew worse. Finally a doctor was called to my house. The doctor immediately requested an ambulance and I was whisked off to Hull Royal Infirmary. I didn't understand what was going on as I was being prepped for emergency appendectomy. I vaguely remember being on a gurney and being moved into a room with big round lights on the ceiling. I faded into oblivion as the anesthesia worked quickly.

Appendectomy is a simple, routine procedure and very common. However, I was very ill afterwards. The days dragged into weeks in hospital. This wasn't normal. I would be given a taste of food and immediately reject it. I could not stomach anything so was fed intravenously through a tube in the arm. This went on for nearly three weeks. Each day, my mother took two buses to be with me and I needed her help. The support staff at the hospital were not very attentive. It was Britain's NHS, after all.

Slowly, I recovered and started eating solid food. What I learned later was the surgical area had not been cleaned properly and I became sick from the toxins discharged by my appendix. This was the first surgical complication I had experienced, but it was far from the last.

In fact, my next surgery seven years later would scar me both outside and in, and it would impact my relationships with woman for years to come.

It was 1976 and I was 12. I was in my final year of Alderman Cogan Junior High School and my life was going great. I was strong, healthy and feeling good. Classes limped along. I was lazy at homework, but it got done, usually last minute late at night on a Sunday.

I had volunteered to play goalkeeper for the school's football team, my first year as a keeper. It was just an impulse decision, something I wanted to try, but in my first game, I saved a penalty taken by a Hull Schools player, a kick high and to the left. I scrambled, stretched and palmed it over the bar. It was a strong save and great start to a new season.

By the end of the season, I was selected by the players for "Player of the Year" Award. It remains my biggest football prize. I still have the medal.

When I left the junior high school for senior high, I continued advancing my goalkeeping skills. My sports were moving me forward. I was being noticed by the high school's football coaches. I showed promise and was being watched by rival coaches and teams.

I was now 15 and in high school's 5th Grade when the huge set back came out of nowhere. The school sponsored a random health screening. No problem for me, I thought, I would be ok. I was in great shape, fit and strong.

A week later, I was being wheeled into the Beverley Hospital surgery suite to undergo emergency testicular surgery. The exam showed my left testicle had not descended properly. The anomaly should have been corrected soon after I was born, but apparently no one noticed. This put me at risk for injury and testicular cancer.

My parents had a choice: Get emergency surgery after a serious injury on the sports field or get planned surgery immediately. My parents opted for the planned surgery. I was devastated. To this day, I cannot think of an operation more emotionally and psychologically damaging to a 15-year-old pre-sexually active boy.

I spent a week in hospital because the surgical site would not heal. The incision on the ball sack would not heal properly. The rough skin made it more difficult. I was on my back for the first five days with a metal frame over my groin to avoid inadvertent contact with bedding. My legs were kept bent and open because of the swelling. The pain was incredible and would not go away.

I was eventually discharged from the hospital and sent home to recover. I changed my own dressings but the surgical incision on the sack kept leaking and bleeding. It was another week before I could return to school. In the meantime, teachers and administrators described my surgery at school as a "private" operation. That just got me teased and ridiculed. At the time, I didn't understand what had happened and why. No one ever explained it to me. I only knew I had lost a lot of blood and my left testicle, although now dropped, had shrunken because of it.

For the next year, I would get stabbing pains in the testicular area. It would appear as a sharp pain but then disappear just as quickly. Finally, I did a self-examination of the incision area and found a sharp piece of plastic protruding from the skin. The scar had partly healed over it but enough was left for me to grab it and pull. Out it came and away went the stabbing pains.

The operation, however, haunted me for years as I felt un-whole and dysfunctional. I became an introvert. I had always liked girls, but after the surgery, I became afraid of them. Insecurity would overcome me.

It was many years later, when Lance Armstrong went public about his testicular cancer that I started to open up more about mine. He provided me that confidence. My years of hiding and embarrassment were over.

But long before Lance helped me make peace with my condition, I had my first sexual encounter, one that can only be described as disastrous.

Chapter 2

I MET LYNNE during my last two years in high school. She was tall with a medium build and thick, long, curly black hair. She was an art-disciplined student; played the violin and sang soprano in operas. She was very smart and exuded class. Being brilliant in English, coupled with an upper-class English accent, she was eloquent and lovely.

In my last year of school, as we approached Christmas 1980, I began to notice how Lynne was giving me more attention. I was a member of the bridge club, as she was, and we would stay after hours to play. But the more she paid attention to me, the more scared I became. My testicular surgery two years earlier left me very insecure and shy around girls. Girls, however, liked me. I was a gifted athlete, very smart (allegedly) and well liked in school. Those attributes attracted her to me.

Christmas arrived, a time I always enjoyed. Christmas parties, dancing with classmates were things I greatly looked forward to, so when the time came, I was out on the dance floor, doing my thing. As suddenly as before, my knee collapsed and locked, followed by spasming pain. This time it seemed everyone was watching. Lynne was there and helped me get up. She didn't know what was going on but she could clearly see the pain etched in my face as the tears rolled down. Finally, my knee settled down and I got up, one knee working and the other radiating pain. I went to the student cloak area and just started to cry. Something was clearly wrong and I had no idea what.

After the dance at Christmas, Lynne and I began to get closer.

Then one night in late February, I kissed her. She had warm, tender lips and it was lovely. After that kiss, we began to see each other more often. One day Lynne came up to me at school and said, "I just passed one of your buddies in the playground outside. As I walked past him, he told his friends, 'That's Bott's bit.'"

"Really? I am sorry," I said, failing to curtail my laughter.

"I didn't know I was Bott's bit," she said, also laughing.

With that, I had a girlfriend. She was kind, thoughtful and there for me when I had my first knee surgery. My parents loved her and her parents liked me. I was always a gentleman to her, never touching her inappropriately. Little did she know it was from my own fear of being intimate.

In the meantime, I was experiencing some setbacks with the knee, and the pain was intolerable. Finally, my father took notice. He, as an insurance manager for British Aerospace, had private health coverage known as BUPA, which I hadn't known. I was on a five-year waiting list through the NHS, so my father suggested I go see a specialist. I did and surgery was recommended.

In April 1981, I went into a private hospital for surgery without any clear expectation of what the surgeon would find. I remember vividly coming out of anesthesia in the recovery room. On the right side of the bed was a bedside cabinet and on top was an opaque glass jar with something pickling in it. It looked like liver or something sea-food. Definitely Y-shaped. When the surgeon came in to talk to me, he explained that the lateral meniscus had been split in two. It wasn't supposed to be Y-shaped, he said. It was supposed to be just a half moon. The Y portion was where it has been ripped in two. Menisci in the knee joints are integral pieces of tissue and required by the knee to keep functioning. Essentially they are the cushions between the tibia plateau and the femur ball joint.

At the time of my surgery in the '80s, it was common practice to remove damaged cartilage. That practice would end up being massively detrimental twenty years later, when I was told by a California surgeon that removal of menisci creates a 100% failure rate in knees.

After my surgery, all I could think about was the end of school. Oh, and the important A level exams before then. Classes ended in June, and a group of friends went to celebrate at the Lake District, a famous area in northern England, for a six-day holiday. A few days into the holiday, Lynne and I were on our own. We made excuses to our friends and stayed behind. Lynne sat next to me on the couch and we started making out. I had my hand up her shirt and she was beginning to move her hands towards my crotch.

After a few minutes we headed towards the room where Lynne was sleeping. Caught up in the moment, I had a temporary lapse of shyness, while Lynne unbuttoned my jeans, adjusted the zipper downwards and put her hand down my underwear. I had an erection but as she began to touch me, something snapped in me. I pushed myself away, moved over to the other end of the bed, curled up into the fetal position and started crying like a baby.

At first she did not understand and was worried. My reaction was so sudden. My first sexual encounter after testicular surgery was a monumental disaster. I was devastated. It was embarrassing and awful. A part of me was not whole and I felt ashamed. What a mess.

I composed myself and explained the surgery, the complications and the results of it all. She was surprisingly understanding. She said she loved me and said she would deal with whatever I had to deal with. I did not take note then that it really did not affect her. My insecurity over the complications seemed superficial and unimportant. My perceived aberration didn't phase her.

The following evening was very different as I made love to her for the very first time. It was wonderful. She was even more beautiful with no clothes on. Her youth, soft skin, supple breasts, pubic hair (yes, women had hair back then), all so exciting to caress and feel. I really had no idea what I was doing then, but I came and it felt overwhelming.

A couple of days later I was sitting on the couch next to Lynne and had my legs tucked underneath me. I moved a tad and the pain in the left knee shot up through my back to the head. I immediately screamed and leapt up off the couch. I dropped to the floor on my knees and doubled over grasping my left leg. Lynne must have wondered what the hell she was doing hanging around me, but she was never anything but concerned, honestly concerned. She came over, helped me up and sat me on the couch. She then sat next to me and placed her arm around my shoulders. She kissed me on the lips and told me she loved me. It was a tender moment with a wonderful lady. The pain from whatever happened dissipated as my mind focused on her and we headed back to her bedroom.

A few weeks later, I was in surgery for a second knee procedure. It was then the doctors discovered the dissolvable sutures from my first knee surgery had not dissolved. And thus started my pattern: injury, surgery, complication, surgery, injury and so forth.

Chapter 3

FOR MOST OF the final years in high school and the first two in college, I worked in a cycle shop in Hull. It was the thing that saved me. The testicular surgery turned me inside out and I could not escape the shell I had clamped myself into. Working in the cycle shop brought me out into the open because I had to deal with customers. I slowly, but surely, gained confidence in myself.

I worked on bikes owned by the poor and working-class clientele. Some were ancient and old (the bikes, not clientele). Occasionally someone would bring in an expensive road bike.

I had no money to buy anything. However, I was learning the business and I started to trade for things as I came across the opportunity. It was fascinating working out deals to upgrade my mode of transportation in high school. I had a group of friends who cycled everywhere. Hull was flat so cycling was how we kids got around. We went everywhere on a bike no matter the weather: sun (well, not very often in England back then), rain, clouds, cold, snow, sleet. It didn't matter the climate. We dressed warm and went everywhere.

I could not afford the expensive cycling clothing and monies required for the special shorts, shirts, gloves, helmets (not worn back in those days), shoes, etc were far-fetched. I cycled in school uniform or jeans and jackets most of the time.

But my love for cycling was born one Christmas when my parents bought my twin brother and me each a used three-speed bike. I loved the thing. I dismantled it, stripped the paint, sprayed it yellow and mastered my own decals. I put some black mud guards on, modified other aspects and even built a brake light that operated when the brakes were activated.

It was pretty cool but I wanted something else, something better. I wanted a racing bike. My good friend Mark had a bright purple, ten-speed racing bike, and I envied him. Mark knew someone selling a yellow ten speed. I somehow raised 10 pounds to buy it and then sold the three speed. So began my lifelong passion with buying and trading bicycles and cycle parts.

The store sold Puck cycles and, as part of my duties, I would remove them from their shipping boxes and build them up to sell on the floor. I remember the damn boxes being heavy and I had to drag them down from upstairs. These were steel ten-speed sport bikes made for an average cyclist. I would get them ready for resale but would also have to do a safety inspection before one ever sold.

I remember taking a light green ten speed out of its box and loving it. I wanted one. I worked something out with the manager, who had become my friend, and he sold my yellow bike in part exchange for a green Puck ten speed. I had just purchased my first brand new bike.

This is when I really started to get into cycling. This green beauty was easier to pedal than all the earlier bikes.

Then the store manager wanted to sell his lightweight Viking racing bike and had put it on the shop floor. It was a beauty, with much better components than my Puck. I traded up again, and got this beautiful blue Viking road bike. My green Puck was sold partly used. I was now in fat city. I ended up buying a woolen Viking team jersey worn by the professional team, which I still have. It was the first proper clothing for cycling I ever bought.

Some months later someone came into the cycle shop carrying a frame. He wanted to know the cost of building that frame into a complete bike. The manager looked at it, as did I. It was a hand-built English frame made by S.M. Woodrup. There were a few boutique cycle manufacturers dotted around Britain and this was one such manufacturer. The frame was a little bigger than my Viking. Back then I wasn't into the science of frame size and the difference it makes to cycling.

The manager and I looked at each other and then looked at the customer. We explained the frame would require higher-end components in order to build an operational bike. It would be expensive, we advised. He traded the frame for a brand new Puck off the floor, having zero interest in spending the kind of money required to build it up.

I bought the frame and, again, still own it today. I paid the shop the trade-in value of 20 pounds, took it home and transferred all the components from the Viking onto this S.M. Woodrup frame. But not before I painted the scratched-up frame red and added my own decals.

Years later when I was given five minutes to get out of my house during a nightmare divorce, I grabbed this bike, along with a few other things that I could cram into my Range Rover. It had the same red paint and custom black/white graphics from decades ago.

That summer of 1982, after my first year in college had ended, the owner sacked the manager and asked me to run the shop for the three months. I needed work and I accepted the challenge. I never thought the days in the cycle shop, with all the deals to upgrade my bike, would expand into what I did in 2004 and beyond.

Chapter 4

MY RELATIONSHIP WITH Lynne fizzled out towards the end of my third year at the University of Sheffield. My final year in college just happened to be one of my happiest.

Unfortunately, I was lazy at school and university. I did what I needed to do to pass. That was it. I had continued playing squash and badminton but also got involved with the electronic/electrical engineering football team that winter and acquired a name for myself. It was all good. And I was on top of my game.

In the summer of 1983, along with two friends, I purchased a three-story townhouse up on Broomhill Road, Sheffield, for 11,000 pounds. The house was nothing special, but it had a lot of rooms and an empty loft area. It had potential. My friend, Steve, organized the purchase and mortgage since he seemed to be the one most adapted to the task. He was well organized and disciplined. John was a friend who played badminton and squash for Merseyside and with whom I played racquet sports a lot. Steve set about converting the loft into two bedrooms. We then converted the front living room into a bedroom. The kitchen was large enough for a dining area.

Now we were equipped with two additional rooms, which we easily rented out to students. The income from that paid the mortgage and I lived my final university year rent free. Towards the end of the final term at university, one of the girls renting a room left and we needed a replacement. Then one afternoon, a knock on the door would change my life. A gorgeous young lady was standing there. She was so beautiful.

"Hello, my name is Julie. You have a room to rent?" she asked with an intoxicating smile.

"Yes, please come in and I will show you it," I replied. "I am Geoff. Nice to meet you."

We went upstairs and I showed her the bigger room in the loft area. I just happened to be living in the small room adjacent to that one. I was still shy with women but she was really friendly.

"I am leaving my boyfriend and I need to find another place," she said.

"Sorry to hear that," I offered my condolences.

She was taller than me, even more so aided by high heeled black shoes. Her long, straight dark brown hair was parted on the side and flowed down one side of her face. She kept having to flick the hair out her beautiful green eyes. The maneuver was so cute. She was slender with beautiful skin and a lovely chest. Later I learned she was 21, one year older than me. Her smile and bubbly personality were mesmerizing.

Julie liked the house and the room, but I did not care much about that. She was making me feel very secure and comfortable around her, which made me a tad nervous. Obviously she had no idea. How could she?

Once I had shown her the room, we continued talking and I asked her to go for a drink. To my surprise, she said yes. She was funny, entertaining and really outgoing. But, importantly, she made me comfortable and relaxed.

After we got to know each other in the bar, I invited her back to the house. My heart was beating fast. She was dressed very nicely, in a white blouse and calf-length dark grey skirt. The skirt, as it turned out, had a hidden slit that one could only observe under certain conditions.

I put on some music as we continued talking. We were very comfortable. Then she lay on her back and put her gorgeous long, slender, perfect legs up the wall. That is when the skirt revealed the slit. My oh my, now I had a partial view of her white French panties. Was this heaven?

I invited Julie to stay the night and so she did. We removed most of our clothing as we continued talking and then climbed into bed. I had seen her perfect breasts and I was throbbing. She wanted to make love to me that night but I wanted to show her some respect so declined. I don't know if I was naïve, stupid and/or ignorant. Likely all three, but she later told me I impressed her with that decision.

I snuggled up behind and wrapped my arms around her. We spent the next day together and that night I made up for my strange decision.

After some extended cuddling and foreplay, I removed her panties and saw the tuft of hair covering her vagina. I removed my underwear and I had an erection that seemed to make her smile. We climbed on the bed and I explained that she is only the second woman I have made love to. I was extremely nervous which I dealt with very well somehow, but not knowing how. I climbed on top of her and slowly slipped inside her delicious, model-type body. She felt warm and wet. After I came, I slowly climbed down and made her climax with my tongue.

"That is the best orgasm I have ever had," she proclaimed, totally spent.

Julie didn't rent the room. She ended up living with me for my final days in Sheffield.

Julie dressed like no one I had ever seen or dated before. She was exotic and erotic. She always wore high heel shoes that matched what she wore that day. She had this lovely short denim skirt I liked. One day she wore the skirt over some tiny red panties. She had a matching red T-shirt along with red shoes. We went out for lunch to a bar and I remember very vividly her sitting on a chair in front of me as we talked. I could see a red triangle patch of her panties as she sat with her legs bent, knees together and feet on the floor. She was sexy, pulsating and had this amazing charisma and provocative charm about her. Men were captivated by her presence.

Chapter 5

JULIE FIRST MET my parents at college graduation, two summers after my father suffered a massive stroke.

For years, my father had been threatening to leave my mother as soon as his youngest children, my twin brother and I, were on our way to adulthood. In the summer of 1982, he made good on his threat and took off. No one really knew where he was or why. He took the family caravan and was apparently living in it. At least, that's what everyone presumed. Much about my father could probably be explained by his early life. He never knew his father, who died when he was two. His mother passed away when he was sixteen, leaving him an orphan. He was then raised by his auntie. Presumably, soon after high school, he entered the British Royal Navy to escape his poor childhood. It would make sense but nothing was ever discussed or brought up with my parents.

For my mother, his leaving was devastating. She was heartbroken. She didn't sleep much and would be up early, cleaning and vacuuming just to occupy her mind. She could not believe him, even if he had been declaring his intention to leave for years. She just chose to brush off his threats and was stunned when he did leave.

Then in August, only a few months after his leaving, came the phone call. Our mother explained, "Your father has had a massive stroke," she told my sister, my twin Nick and me. "He's in a very bad way according to the hospital. I knew he was sick. I knew he was going to have a heart attack or a stroke. That's why he left. He was sick.

I knew it," she said with conviction, as she was trying to justify his decision.

My father had high blood pressure. Heart disease was prevalent in his family. His only brother died at age forty five. High blood pressure is something he passed on to me.

She rushed to hospital to see him. Seeing him in the hospital was awful. My mother was a mess.

"He is in a bad way. He will not fully recover from this and will be partially paralyzed for the rest of his life," she said. "He has been hit on the right side of the brain which affects the left side of the body. He will recover his speech but the left side will be paralyzed."

She was struggling and tears were flowing down her face.

The days dragged into weeks, then months. Physical therapy was required to adjust to the massive change that he now faced. It never occurred to me then what battle he was facing. Not only a physical battle, but he faced a deep mental abyss. This great struggle never struck any chords in me until twenty years later when I faced the abyss of physical limitations and the toll it takes on your body and mind.

My mother took my father back home when he was released by the hospital. My sister was not pleased with that decision as she was worried about our mother, not the man who left her and his family. Our mother pointed out that he needed serious care. "Who was going to do that? The woman he left his wife and family for isn't" she said.

My mother wanted him back home. She could not envision a life without him. She was also concerned that no women, especially the one he left the family for, would be interested in a disabled man after his stroke. My father would have ended up in a home if our mother had not have made that courageous decision.

I would later learn that not many marriages survive when serious health issues prevail. The human body is exposed and left naked for others to prod and poke during health crises. Not necessarily physically naked, but the psychological and mental barriers are torn to pieces for all to see. A lot of people cannot handle that and fall. Our mother's decision saved a man's life, our father's life, and likely her own along with it.

In the end my mother knew just one thing: "He is the only man I ever wanted. I waited on him until he returned from the British Navy," she said and with surprising candor. "I liked it when we cuddled at night."

She took him back and she never took money from the government to take care of him.

Two years later, when Julie met my parents at my graduation in Sheffield, I wasn't confident that my mother would approve but I knew my father would. Even after his stroke, confined to a wheelchair, he was a handsome man who dressed with style. I hardly ever saw him in jeans and he always wore a suit and tie for work. He was always liked by the ladies, knew how to flirt with them and make them laugh. When it came to Julie, I was confident he thought I was thinking with the little head despite any pleas I would have made to the contrary.

Julie and I drove back to Hull for a few days after the graduation ceremony. Much to my mother's disappointment, we would not stay. We were moving to Manchester. I was stepping away from my childhood and friends I had made in Sheffield. I was moving forward, a move that changed my professional career.

Chapter 6

JULIE AND I packed our bags and tossed them in my Cortina. It was summer 1984 and Julie and I were moving. I navigated through Sheffield and grabbed the A57, known as the Snake Pass, and headed north. It was a gorgeous two-lane highway that traversed beautiful, rolling English countryside known as the Pennines.

We had been to Manchester a few times and had already secured living quarters. The old brick, three-story semi-detached house belonged to a friend of my oldest brother. The couple who owned it were young but not married. They purchased the home to convert into single-room apartments. We had a room on the second floor.

When I graduated I was going to quickly find a job and change the world. That's what I thought. Well, it did not quite work out that way. I could not find work for three months. During those empty months we learnt Julie was pregnant. Now the pressure to find work, any work, was intense.

I went to an employment agency in Manchester and met up with a lovely, kind lady. She took down the pertinent credentials and started finding me job interviews. I was asked to head down to Cheadle, just south of Stockport to a small private environmental company needing an electronic test engineer. The salary being advertised was low but I needed the experience and I needed the job.

The company made environmental control units for big commercial buildings. Six women built various circuit boards for the control units. There were different models depending on the application, and four test engineers had to make sure they worked correctly after the manufacturing process. Circuit boards that failed at remote customer installations were also repaired and tested by these four engineers. Well, three, as it turned out. They were interviewing me for the fourth position.

The engineer desks were lined up against a wall, one behind the other and the supervisor sat front left so he could see all of them. Each desk had its own test equipment, soldering station and other pertinent electronic devices to satisfy the job requirements. It looked intimidating. The area was separated by shelving and then off to the left was the manufacturing area. Six ladies were arranged three rows of two and they also had their own supervisor. I was informed about the working conditions because these ladies were unionized.

With my first interview complete, I was transferred to an upper manager and entered his private office upstairs. He was VP, or COO, something like that. The title I cannot recall but I do remember him being arrogant. I explained the situation that my girlfriend was pregnant and I needed to support her. He looked at me.

"Would you work for this amount?"

His offer was less than was being promoted and less than I had already been told.

"Yes," I did not hesitate. "When can I start?"

It was my first foray into the corporate world, and I knew I would not be there long. I just needed six months experience under my belt.

It was also the first time that I had worked around union people. Each day we had to start at a specific time, then a ten-minute morning tea break, then lunch, then ten-minute afternoon tea break. At first, I thought it was great. However, it became very irritating. I would be in the middle of testing circuit boards or diagnosing faulty ones and it was tea-break time. I had to stop, have tea and then start the thought process all over again. Ten minutes invariably turned into fifteen, sometimes twenty minutes.

Towards the end of my six-month tenure there, I started to ignore the tea breaks. This labeled me as a management boy but I wasn't really. I just needed to learn. The union people hated me but I did not care.

It was also during those six months Julie and I realized it was time to get a home of our own. Julie and I were expecting a child and needed the space and privacy. I now had an income, so it was time. We found a Barrett home in North Reddish: A two-bedroom, one-bath, two-story townhouse. We had our first home.

Chapter 7

IT WAS AUGUST 1984 and Nick and I were approaching our 21st birthdays. Those birthdays are big events in England and it is customary on such occasions to have big family gathering. So that's what my mother planned. Invitations were sent out to relatives spread around Northern England. Nick worked in Germany at the time and would return for the party.

Julie and I had found out weeks earlier that she was pregnant and I was very worried about telling my parents. They were religious and believed in the sanctity of marriage. Pregnancy outside of marriage would be the first in my immediate family so this was new ground. I was putting off telling my mother until the right time came, I had convinced myself, not really knowing when that would be.

The party was great and a lot of people showed up. We saw family members that we had not seen for several years. Julie was enjoying herself but she wasn't drinking. She wasn't showing at all in her dress. We stayed on for a few days afterwards to visit and then headed back to Manchester.

My father was still recovering and I could see the changes in him. He was learning to walk again with a cane and had some mobility. Their bedroom was upstairs and every night he made the slow, painful ascent to the bedroom. And each night he did with attitude and determination.

Attitude and determination are major keys in the recovery process as I would learn later. My father was trying really hard but I could tell he got frustrated and irritated at times. He was determined to show us what he could do. Our mother didn't have a lot of patience, which likely helped in this case. He was forced, presumably, to do things for himself. Tough-love they call it. He had always been independent, but the stroke meant he had to rely on others for many things. It was a battle he would wage for the rest of his life. Being dependent was a huge psychological blow, along with the obvious physical and emotional ones.

Seeing him climb the stairs one at a time showed his courage and determination. He had guts. He always seemed to hide his depressive state and constantly laughed and joked. He showed his strength and hid the psychological destruction really well.

When Julie and I got back home, I felt we had managed to keep our secret. Then a letter arrived and my perception of 'doing ok' suddenly got corrected.

"When is the baby due?" my mother wrote. "If you need help or support, then let us know."

That part of the letter surprised me. She not only knew about the pregnancy but she was offering her support. I took a few days to compose myself and then called home.

"Hello Mum, it is me," knowing she knew my voice.

"How are you doing? How is Julie? How far along is she?....."

She had a whole list of nice questions to ask me.

"How did you know she was pregnant?" I asked her.

"She had a small stomach and she wasn't drinking. Those are tell-tale signs," she said.

Of course they were. And of course my mother would know. In addition to having children of her own, she had worked in a home for unwanted, orphaned and/or neglected children before she got married. Of course she would know. What was I thinking to believe otherwise?

When we came home again for that Christmas, we were given a bed together. My sister was very surprised, as we were, but my mother explained that I could not do any more damage than I already had. Fair point but it went totally against her values and the way she lived her life. Sharing a sofa-bed with Julie at my parent's home blew my mind. The only answer is she thought I would do the right thing. I was working hard and providing a living, which I had learnt from our father. I was supporting her and what she wanted to do. I was preparing for our baby being born. I was doing everything my parents and society had taught me, except I wasn't married.

I believe in the end the question of how mother would react came down to two alternatives: she could support us in this decision or lose a son. She also wanted to see her grandchild being born. I am confident that was the overwhelming decision behind composing the letter and going against every value she held in high regard.

Chapter 8

SIX MONTHS AT the new job and I was bored. I was pretty good at it now and most faults had become common and easily repaired. But I hated the job and needed to move on.

Then in March 1985, I got paged. On the phone was the lovely lady from the employment agency in Manchester. She surprised me.

"Hello Geoff, I hear you are not very happy at work", is all she said.

Ignoring the 'how did she know' question, I replied,

"No, I am not. I hate this job".

"I have an interview lined up for you already. The company is in Wythenshawe. It manufactures mass spectrometers and is looking for installation engineers".

That phone conversation changed my professional life.

I had little knowledge of mass spectrometers. I thought they were little boxes that sat on benches. When I walked into the building for my interview, my mouth dropped when I saw how big these instruments were.

The company was VG Analytical, Ltd, one of the top four mass spectrometer companies in the world. The interviews went very well as I was passed from department manager to department manager. I was just baffled by the size and scope of the machines. How was I going to learn these things? They were huge and very complex.

The Installation Manager explained that they would be implementing a new training program. For the new engineers, each would spend some time in electronic test, then clean assembly area, floor test area and out into the world to install them. The position, I learned, would require extensive world-wide travel.

The following day I got a call from the employment agency. I was offered the job. The base salary was a little higher than I was making now but it was irrelevant. Travel would incorporate bonuses and expenses as well as per diems.

It was the international travel part that had me going. It was the opportunity of a lifetime.

I started working for VG Analytical, Ltd in April 1985. What I did not know at the time was installing big mass spectrometers required a lot of heavy moving and lifting. That, and extensive travel, would lead to the demise of my knee, as well as my relationship.

I was the first engineer to be put through a new training program. I spent approximately six weeks in electronic test, six weeks in clean assembly (where they built the mechanical housings, lenses and sources comprising a mass spectrometer), six weeks in wiring and fabrication and then six weeks on the shop floor testing finished products. I also traveled to some sites in England as part of the training. It was fascinating work and I was getting to know the instrumentation inside and out.

Mass spectrometers operate under high vacuum. The models I was involved with used diffusion pumps for this purpose. Essentially they heat up special Santovac 5 oil which then evaporates. At the top of these tall pumps are cooling pipes which then condenses the oil vapours. As the oil vapours fall, the air gets sucked out of the vacuum chambers.

They get very hot. One day I was working around one of these pumps and I smell something burning. A second or two later I feel the pain. The smell apparently was my left arm. Hmm.... I did not know flesh smelt like that nor did I know the pain from burning.

When I moved to Manchester, I was invited to play for Sale Rugby Club. Rugby Union was an amateur sport back then but Sale was one of the top clubs in Britain. It had international players in its camps.

Training mid-week evenings was always hard work but always inevitably ended in the bar. One evening, after a tough session, we all sat down on Sale's rugby field, catching a breather. A minute or two later Steve Smith came and sat next to me. I could not believe it. I had seen him on television playing number nine for England. He was brilliant, fast and agile. He was England's captain. We said a few pleasantries before we continued in our quest to beat the living shit out of our bodies.

I was new in the club so had to start at the bottom. I did get selected to play for their fourth team, which actually was an honour I failed to recognize at the time. At the start of the season I scored the first three of four tries. I had power, agility and fitness coupled with tremendous short-burst speed. The knee was doing really well and it didn't bother me at all.

By now I was working for VG and excessive travel was about to prohibit any social life at home. In September, my boss asked me if I wanted to go to Moscow to help do an installation. I was told it would be part of my training and I would be going with another engineer. Of course I volunteered. Russia at the time was deeply segregated from the rest of humanity. What an experience this would be. It would be my first excursion outside of the British Isles without my parents. And it was the adventure of a lifetime.

It took several weeks to procure our USSR visas but in early October I was off. We were installing a 70E-HF mass spectrometer at a scientific institute. Each morning the same driver would show up at the hotel to greet us and take us to the destination. Each day the same low-fuel light was illuminated. Perhaps the government was concerned over the driver taking off. The institute buildings were essentially nondescript but the scientists were friendly. They were excited to see the installation of their mass spectrometer because it would allow them to develop their research.

Unknown to many, some phenomenal scientific discoveries have emerged out of Russia. As an example, one prominent scientist formulated the Periodic Law and created his own version of the periodic table of elements. It is viewed as the most significant contribution to material chemistry and the table is used in my line of work. Working with these Russian scientists was an honour and a privilege bestowed on so few at the time.

The interesting part of this installation was the American DEC computer had not been shipped with it. It was technology not allowed in the Soviet Union so we were left to use photographic paper and hand calculations. The computer would show up after we left, I speculated.

It turned out to be a three-week trip. During the second week, the engineer traveling with me and I were sitting in the hotel bar when I noticed these Russian ladies staring at us. They were beautiful, all of them. Naturally, I thought it was my charm, personality and good looks that had them spellbound.

When the engineer accompanying me disappeared to the bathroom, one of the ladies came over. "You can have me if you want" she said, telling me the price for which she would make her services available. That quickly dispelled my theory of why they were staring. Later I learned that in Moscow there were specific hotels for foreigners only. The only Russians allowed in were workers and prostitutes.

When the engineer returned, I told him of the offer. Cheap, he replied. I had no idea and was about to enter a world I knew nothing about.

In anyone's life, there comes a T-intersection where a decision has to be made: turn left or turn right. One of those choices can be a good one and the other can be of questionable origin. This was a T-intersection that had inexplicably presented itself from a questionable source. I was happy. Julie was beautiful and we had a son together. Work was going well and a dream job that would require international travel. I was determined and motivated. Unfortunately, I felt something was missing. Testicular surgery had removed something. I was incredibly insecure and had avoided women as a consequence. The result was this introvert, shy, quiet guy who was afraid.

I had missed my adolescence and sexual awakening in high school. No one had helped me through this period. Children were to be seen and not heard. I struggled on my own with this immense belief I was not a whole man. I had been teased in school which made matters worse. I had other attributes but being physically scarred was a serious psychological problem.

A T-intersection arrived in my life and I had a decision to make. I was sitting in a bar in the Union of Soviet Socialist Republics. With an absurd and incredibly naïve understanding of what I was about to do, the Russian lady ordered a taxi and we took off to her apartment. It was a decision based on questionable origins for sure and one that would haunt me years later. I also didn't understand the damage I was about to inflict on Julie and our son. However, decades later, I would reflect on my decision made in that bar on a very dark, very cold October night in Moscow. The immensely poor behavior would drive me through another crossroad-in-life where I would have two more children to try and protect. I would make a much better and more informed decision when that time came.

The woman who took an interest in me lived in an apartment across the city so we took a taxi there the first time. The other times we met, I took the underground metro and then a bus. I am not sure if a KGB Officer ever followed me but I am sure someone must have.

I would spend the next two weekends with her. She taught me many things, but the two I remember and still use in the day-to-day life are tipping and how to dress.

Britain was not a tipping culture and people were paid to do a job. Arriving in Moscow, we were left to our own devices in the evenings. Service was a problem because it was a communist country and no one cared if you were served. The Russian lady showed me how it was done. I was asked to give a dollar bill to the gentleman who hung our coats at the restaurant, a dollar bill to the lady who seated us and a dollar bill to the server. This changed the experience totally. Suddenly, as if by magic, quality service was incorporated into our evening's entertainment.

I had never met anyone who wore expensive clothing before until I met her. I didn't even know how different they were. She was truly glamorous. She wore fashionable and elegant clothing and looked really good doing so. I took that lesson to heart and to this day buy clothing based on the quality and looks. A high-stakes Russian call girl taught me that clothes could make the woman, which I transposed into meaning the man also. Unknown to me, it would be critical when I was attracting my future wife, and not in a beneficial way.

I returned home from Russia, explained to Julie my poor indiscretion only to fly out a week later. This time to Bologna, Italy to work on a project that turned out to be a disaster. Two weeks later, after their lab was still not properly prepared, I flew home.

My relationship with Julie was already strained. My compensation from travel had not yet been paid. I knew Julie was getting money from the government. We were not married so she had some assistance as a single mother. But I did not know just how dire her situation had become, our situation had become.

The problem with our relationship was my inability to communicate. My childhood really did not help that fact. We never had family discussions and we never saw our parents discussing anything together. The art of communication, required in all facets of life, was not there. It was missing. Julie and I needed to talk about serious issues but I didn't know how to. I had not been taught.

The other serious problem was my trip to Russia. I returned a changed man. I saw and experienced a different life, if only temporarily, but I was captivated by it. The glamour, excitement, international travel, the Playboy image, the expensive clothing, all of it jangled a nerve in the brain. I had just seen it all and I saw first-hand what that did to a person. How the Russian lady behaved and dressed made her stunning and the image blanketed my mind. I learnt also that her interest was based solely on wanting me to marry her and take her away from the USSR. That was her driving force.

Unfortunately, I was to leave again. This time for America in January 1986, a trip that would change my life completely.

Chapter 9

I HAD BEEN to America twice. In 1973, my uncle had moved his family from Burnley to just north of the Boston area. We flew into New York from London a year later and then on up to Boston and spent three weeks enjoying a totally different world and culture. It blew my mind.

In August 1979, we spent three weeks in California visiting my older brother who had moved there to work for McDonnell Douglas in Long Beach. We traveled all over the state and adjacent areas. It was an incredible holiday.

So I was ecstatic on that cold December day in 1985, when the VG Installation Manager told me that I would be installing an instrument at Hoffman La Roche in Nutley, New Jersey. It would also be the first test since Italy and the first installation I would be doing on my own.

I purchased a suit in England for twenty pounds but it was thin and not very warm. When I arrived at the hotel via taxi from Kennedy Airport, New York I ventured straight over to the pharmaceutical facility to meet the clients and assess the site for installation. I wore the suit but it was seventeen below outside. I froze to death, but looked good doing so. Even the client got a chuckle but it broke the relationship ice between client and engineer.

I would end up spending eight weeks in Nutley, New Jersey, a small city just fifteen miles west of New York City. The instrument, as it turned out, was going to be installed on the fourteenth floor of a fifteen-story building. From that vantage, I could see the skyline of New York City. It was pretty exciting.

The instrument I was asked to start installing was full of options and had many extraneous specification requirements for it to be classified as 'signed off.' I found this out when I arrived on-site. I was still new and very green but the performance criteria for any instrument had to be proven to the operator and/or laboratory manager before the equipment could be categorized as 'installed.' Specification sheets were provided and each one had to be initialed and signed when completed. Typically there were funds remaining on the invoice so completing installations was crucial. Once completed, a one-year warranty period commenced.

I had been told to do what I could and return to Manchester. No one expected me to complete the installation, but that was precisely what I did. I worked with an incredible instrument operator, Vance, who had years of experience operating these types of instruments. I worked incredibly hard and Vance provided the knowledge and experience to help me.

His laboratory manager was a hardened German and I was warned he could be strict and difficult. One frightfully cold morning Vance and I came in after a night of heavy drinking and I just sat by the instrument with my head on the desk. I could not move. The lab manager walked in, took one look, turned around and departed back to his office. Vance just laughed but the German knew nothing much was going to get achieved that day. I was told he had mellowed, which was fortuitous for me. It was exciting to be in a foreign country working like this and not as a tourist. Those were incredible weeks and I worked and played really hard.

I learnt that VG had an office up the road in Stamford, Connecticut and I had to communicate with them on occasion to get parts shipped. I learnt they were looking for a service engineer to work and I decided I wanted to move to America.

One weekend I rented a car and drove up to the Stamford office. The job would require extensive travel, but I got lost driving to the interview. I was an hour late arriving at the bar/restaurant I was supposed to meet my contact. Yes, an interview in a bar, with my future manager. It was pretty casual. We talked for a while, drank beer, ate lunch and I headed back to Nutley. I got offered the job, but I had to finish working for the UK company first. As the signing-off period drew near for my Nutley project, my boss in England contacted me. The factory wanted more work from me.

During those eight weeks, I had been calling Julie often. I even talked with a neighbour she had made friends with. The conversations were good but I could tell something wasn't right. She wanted me home and I didn't understand. It never occurred to me she needed help. I was lost in my own world.

I had put pressure on myself to complete the installation in New Jersey but it was taking significantly more time than we had planned. I was only expected to be gone two to three weeks. There was no way Julie and I had planned for an extended term being away. Her patience was fraying and she needed help. I was three thousand miles away.

After I had finished in New Jersey, I really should have gone home. Unfortunately, I had already received news in early March from the factory that Julie had gone back to London with our son. She called my manager and told him. Our communications dropped off but we agreed to get back together when I returned home.

At the time, I did not understand exactly why she had left me. Decades later, I found out that she had no money and could not support herself and our son with me on the road. Money was something Julie and I never talked about, any more than my parents had when I was growing up. The notion of having a conversation about money was ridiculed and just never existed. I was beginning to get paid for all the travel I was doing but she didn't know that. The money was just beginning to be transferred into my account. But by then it was too late.

I stayed on in America for another two months, installing instruments and finishing off other installations. I flew down to Birmingham,

Alabama (which was like a different country), up to Rochester in Upstate New York, back to New Jersey and then five weeks in Cambridge, just outside Boston. When I returned in late April, Julie came up for a few days to see me. I felt distant and not the same. Months of travel and the lifestyle that went with it--hotels, eating out every night, drinking, meeting people, developing my career--had taken a toll on my ability to communicate. Those months working in a stressful environment had exhausted me. My brain was fried. I returned home with no energy. We made love a few times, but Julie said it was not the same. "You used to be good," she said after making out in the living room.

She did not understand nor appreciate how tired I was, and to defend her perhaps I did not convey it too well. My communication skills in the relationship were lacking. Perhaps I was selfish now that I had been offered a job in the US. Once again, I had entered a new world. I was living a different life that gradually took me over. She left back to London with our son, and I would never see them again.

Many years later, through Facebook, I would learn Julie did try to contact me once when she found out I was married. In late 1987 my wife received a letter while I was away. My wife was clearly upset when she read the letter to me. Basically Julie was asking me what I intended to do about our son and what her place in my life was now that I had married. Then my wife read her reply which she intended sending without my approval. What she read to me then was only part of the letter she actually had written to Julie. The letter scared Julie apparently and she went into hiding. It told her to stay away, that my wife's family had money and if she continued to try and contact me, I would take my son away from her. My wife also wrote along the lines of me not wanting anything to do with her. My wife's letter was shocking in the extreme. I tried to find Julie for some years after that, but came up empty. I had one picture of our son which I kept for many years. I ended up losing his picture in my divorce.

Chapter 10

AS JULIE LEFT Manchester, so did I. I had one final four-week installation in Winnipeg, Canada, returning for my sister's wedding before I could take up my new position. My employers in Manchester were not happy that I was leaving for the US. A lot of time and money had been spent on the factory training and they were hugely disappointed. But I was excited at moving. I put the house up for sale, sold the BMW, grabbed what was left and flew to Los Angeles in June 1986.

My boss gave me a few weeks to organize myself and get sorted out. I lived with my brother in Orange County and I needed time to obtain a social security card and an American Driver's license.

I found America a strange place at first, and I was having some financial difficulties. Banks were not allowed to cross state lines. I could open a bank account in California in 1986 but I could not access money from anywhere other than California. It was pure madness. So, traveling the country was really problematic, made worse because the company that relocated me was slow at paying expenses. I needed cash when I traveled because many places did not take American Express, the card of choice for the corporate world.

Before moving to the US, I had asked my future manager what company car I was going to get. I had owned two V8 Rovers in England (but lost those in my oldest brother's bankruptcy – his landlord took them) and was currently driving a 1974 BMW 528 I had purchased cheap in an auction. I explained that I preferred to drive something with an American V8 motor in it. I asked him, therefore, if

VG could buy something used with the same money they were going to spend on a new car. One doesn't get anything unless one asks for it, I remembered from somewhere. To my surprise, he told me it was ok so I went looking for American muscle and finally found a Z28 that I loved. American V8 muscle was revered in Europe. I was in heaven now but I worked hard for this privilege. I repaid my boss with substantial work ethics.

It was in this Z28, my new company car, when I arrived in Las Vegas in late August 1986 to work on a triple-sector mass spectrometer. These were unique instruments. Software had not been written yet to operate the third sector. But I had quickly diagnosed and fixed it, having never worked on one of these before. I have an ability to work out faults very fast once electronic circuit diagrams and wiring schedules were presented to me. I was beginning to appreciate that even a 10-cent diode could take out a three-quarters of a million-dollar instrument.

Las Vegas was wild and the Z28 was incredibly well suited to the Las Vegas lifestyle. I was living a dream and it was time to enjoy it. I put on white trousers, a nice t-shirt and walked into the elevator in the Flamingo Hilton Hotel on the strip.

As I stepped out of the elevator, a beautiful young African American lady walked towards me.

"Are you looking for a date?"

How did she know I was a visitor, I thought. It was obvious, you idiot!!

"Well, that would be nice but I cannot access money. This country is madness and I have California bank accounts and no way to access them."

"Do you have a credit card?" she responded, seemingly anxious to sort out my financial predicament.

"Of course, but it is from England. I cannot use it here." I replied, sounding frustrated.

"No problem. This is Las Vegas. Follow me."

I followed her to one of the casino cashier's window.

"This gentleman has a British credit card and needs to get cash," she told the lady, then looked at me, smiling. My oh my, she was very pretty. How much did she say? Did it really matter? I thought. Not really.

"Do you have identification?" the cashier asked.

I passed to her my British passport and a few minutes later I was presented with the cash. Wow, I guess Las Vegas knows how to manipulate the system, even if I am not losing it gambling. Well, a different kind of gambling as it turns out.

The lady smiled, grabbed my hand and walked me back through the casino floor to the elevator. I pressed the appropriate button and up we went. We stepped into the room, then talked and laughed for a little bit. I gave her the money and she went to the bathroom.

She came back wearing just her red panties. She was lovely, her body was fit and real. Nothing fake there. I was naked at this point, showing signs of enjoyment. She played with me for a while with her hands while talking. She then slipped a condom on me and gave me a nice blow job before allowing me to climb on top of her. Once inside her delicious body, I hardened even further and climaxed soon after.

She cleaned me up and then both of us lay on the bed talking about life and our experiences. It was a fascinating encounter. It was companionship and that was important to me.

I was traveling alone all the time and had dinner on my own most evenings. I shared a bed with no one. The glamour lifestyle was not all that it was cracked up to be. Some locations, some sites, some cities were awful, depressing even, affording no enjoyment or entertainment. Some sites were all work and no play. Some places I did not want to do anything except do my work and leave as soon as possible.

Not here. After, we said our pleasantries and she departed the room. No drama, no small talk, no pretense, no expensive gifts. It was just genuine enlightenment and enjoyment from both parties. I thanked her for a great time.

A few days later, having finished my work, I was heading north on I15 and then east across the Colorado Rocky Mountains on I70. I was headed to Boulder, Colorado and my new home. The mountains were spectacular. I decided Grand Junction was the best place to stop for the night. What I was not expecting were the incredible vistas surrounding the city once the morning sun had risen above the skyline. It seemed to be in a big gorge surrounded by stunning majestic scenery. I was gob-smacked. It was spectacular.

Arriving in Boulder, I quickly found a nice two bedroom apartment on the outskirts of the city. It occupied the top two floors of a four-story apartment complex. It was much too big for just me, but I wanted somewhere to call home with all the traveling I was beginning to do.

I was learning fast and really enjoying flying around the US, solving scientists' instrument problems. It was all fascinating to me and I loved it. But the flying was getting crazy. Within a few months I had been upgraded on United Airlines' frequent flyer program twice.

Then an invitation to a Christmas Party changed my idea of home forever.

In November 1986, my friend, Tom, at Chevron Research Centre in Richmond, California invited me to the Chevron Christmas party.

VG delayed sending me to Chevron because they were a big client and I was an inexperienced service engineer. My boss, Ian, thought the scientists there, who were world-renowned for research and development, would chew me to pieces. This was one of the first laboratories in the world to hook up a computerized data acquisition system to a mass spectrometer. Before then data was hand-drawn by plotting chromatograms.

Tom made a request for a service visit through VG Instruments, the American subsidiary and the company I now worked for, and asked that I be the engineer to perform that service. With that I had the pass to go, so Tom's invitation to the Chevron Christmas party was great. But I didn't want to go on my own.

"Ok," Tom said. "I will ask my wife and get back to you."

His wife had asked a close friend if she would be interested in meeting me and she was. Now I had my date. I flew to Oakland Airport, walked over to the Hertz Car Rental counter and asked the lady for a sports car. I was meeting a beautiful lady so needed something special, I explained. I was anticipating something good since this is California.

"Well Mr. Bott, we have a teal Pontiac Sunbird or a silver Mercury Cougar."

Clearly she missed the point of a sports car. These were not sports cars. I just laughed. The mid '80s were not kind to the American auto industry.

"Well, err, thank you. I did say a sports car," I said, trying to make her laugh. The English accent always helped.

"Sorry," she said chuckling. "That is all we have."

"Ok, I will take the Pontiac Sunbird. Does it come with a bag to put over my head so no one can see me?" I added, with a big grin.

Gosh. Meeting my date in this thing would not go down well. I had already been told she owned a new bright red Toyota MR2. I performed the service work as requested by the scientists at Chevron and I was ready for the evening ahead. It was a Friday in early December.

Another engineer I knew from Finnigan MAT was working at Chevron that week, so before we left to meet our dates, Mark asked if we wanted to join him for a beer. Mark bought the first round as Tom and I found a table. When he returned, he had three pitchers of beer and three glasses. His idea of a round was much different than mine. Hmm, this is going to be interesting. Those three pitchers were quickly consumed, and then he asked if we wanted another round. Of course, came the reply but I honestly did not expect the same thing. Back he returned carrying three more pitchers.

We were already getting late and Tom needed to reassure my blind date that we were coming. He made several calls that night but obviously neglected to reference the amount of alcohol we were consuming. It evidently wasn't real beer because the effect it had was negligible. I was staying in the motel adjacent to the bar so Tom and I went to my room to get changed. Once my Italian suit was donned, we ventured over to a restaurant in the Hill Top Mall area of Pinole. I wasn't feeling too hot driving a Pontiac Sunbird, but the teal color made it much worse. It was dark outside the restaurant when we arrived, which helped, a little. It afforded plenty of camouflage and I parked it in a secluded area of the parking lot. We walked into the restaurant and found Tom's wife and my date.

When I saw her, my mouth dropped to the floor. I knew she was Lebanese but her beauty had not been sufficiently conveyed to me. When she stood, she was roughly my height, her skin was Arabic dark and smooth. Her eyes were a lovely brown and her dark brown hair was long and straight with bangs. She was very slender, less than 110 pounds, and the way she was dressed knocked me over. She wore a knee-length, dark purple silk dress that fit her perfect body like a glove. Pantyhose and high heels finished the stunning look. She could have been a model with grace and elegance. The memory of how the lady in Moscow looked came flooding back. I was immediately drawn to her beauty and how she dressed.

Tom made the introductions as I stuck out my hand,

"I am Geoff and really pleased to meet you." I said in a strong English accent.

"I am Marina." She replied, in a Middle Eastern accent.

She was gorgeous and the evening was wonderful.

Chapter 11

FOUR MONTHS AFTER meeting Marina, I was preparing to fly to San Francisco to ask her to marry me. Things had progressed and we were enjoying our relationship. During the four-month courtship, I would finish work somewhere in the country and fly to San Francisco for the weekend. I did this twice a month. This particular night, I had researched the best restaurant to propose in and found a converted sailboat moored on San Francisco's famous waterfront. Perfect. I called for reservations and told the head manager what I was trying to do.

"When you arrive in the area, drop by the restaurant and give me the ring," he said. "I will have the flowers ordered and then once they are delivered, I will have the ring placed in them. A bottle of champagne will be on ice. I will arrange to have the flowers and the ring delivered at the appropriate time during dinner."

I thanked him profusely. I then reserved a room in Corte Madera. It was half way between Novato, where Marina lived, and San Francisco, located in beautiful Marin County just the north side of the Golden Gate Bridge.

I told Marina I was flying in for the weekend and said I would buy her a new dress for our dinner in San Francisco. Then I drove to Stapleton Airport in Denver and took the two-hour flight to San Francisco. I was on a mission. I picked up the wallowing boat-like Lincoln Town Car at the rental counter and drove to the restaurant at the pier. I met with the manager and handed over the engagement ring. I drove over the Golden Gate Bridge and checked into the Corte

Madera Inn. I then called Marina and we met at the Corte Madera Mall complex where she bought a nice dress. Everything was now in place, and she did not suspect a thing. A few hours later she arrived at the Inn and we drove to San Francisco. She looked beautiful.

The converted boat on a pier in San Francisco was an incredible location for what was about to unfold. Dinner went well. When it was time for dessert, the flowers, along with the ring, were carried to the table. The champagne enhanced the arrangement. When Marina took the flowers and found the ring, she was shocked. She had not anticipated this at all. The patrons and working staff all started clapping. It was an incredible moment. I was engaged to a Lebanese beauty queen.

A few weeks earlier, I had asked her father for his daughter's hand, an honourable and respectful thing to do in a lot of cultures, including Britain. It was an interesting encounter with her father because a few months before he had kicked me out of their home one weekend. Arabic women were not allowed to date. They had to be engaged to be married to see men alone. But despite being kicked to the curb because of her father and brother's objections, I continued seeing Marina. Her mother liked me and knew about our encounters. Sometimes she accompanied us to visit other family members that also had accepted me. My future mother-in-law was so sweet.

With her father's blessing, our wedding was planned for 5th September, 1987. It would turn out to be a poignant moment in the Bott family's history. My wedding was the last time we were ever together as a whole family.

The wedding took place in the Catholic Church in Novato, California. My twin brother Nick flew in from Sweden. My sister and her husband and my brother, John, all flew in from England. Chris, his wife and two children flew in from Southern California. An auntie and uncle came in from the Boston area and my best friend, Jean, came in from New York.

My parents were the first to arrive and they came in a week early to get to know my future wife. They were apprehensive at meeting my future in-laws. I am not sure if they had ever been around Middle Eastern people before. My future mother-in-law was wonderful and made a large spread of food for our arrival. My father did not want to eat at first because he was very picky. It may have been that after his stroke, he was uncomfortable around people he did not know. However, those feelings were dispensed with, ignored or forgotten once he started digging into the wonderful Mediterranean spread laid out on the table.

On my wedding day, when I saw Marina coming down the aisle in her lovely wedding gown, I was stunned. She was absolutely gorgeous.

That Christmas Eve in 1987, we purchased our first home together. It was a typical 1,600-square-foot ranch-style California house with three bedrooms and two bathrooms, nestled in a suburb of Novato in Marin County. I had moved there from Colorado soon after we were engaged because I thought it would be best if I lived where my fiancée did.

I had just flown back from the east coast on Christmas Eve so Marina was already in our home when I arrived. There wasn't much in it but it was a start, the start of our lives together.

Chapter 12

WORKING HARD, I was learning my trade quickly and getting very good and very fast at solving instrument problems. I was becoming a popular engineer, sought after by clients across the country. That meant a lot of travel. It was becoming difficult to keep up because of the vastness of the country. Red-eye flights were common, allowing me the only time I really had to sleep.

One of the craziest weeks I remember happened soon after the Chevron party. It was the week before Christmas 1986. That Sunday I flew from Denver to San Francisco, then drove to Marin County to see Marina for a few hours. I took a quick flight down to Los Angeles and drove the 405 and then 91 to Riverside. I spent that Monday at the University of California's Department of Chemistry and then drove back to Irvine. Tuesday, I spent the day working at Allergan Pharmaceuticals in Irvine, then drove back to LA and took two short two-hour red-eye flights through Denver to Houston. I arrived in Houston early Wednesday morning, I drove the 75 miles to Freeport, Texas to work at Dow Chemical. Finishing there Wednesday afternoon, I drove back to Houston to work at Shell on Thursday. A two-hour flight back Thursday night to Denver, and the final hour drive to Boulder. On Friday, I was working at the University of Colorado's Health Sciences Centre. Saturday, I took a morning flight to New York and drove to VG Instrument's office in Stamford, Connecticut for a meeting. That night there is a party at my friend Vance' home in New Jersey. And the week ended with a flight to England on the Sunday to go home for Christmas.

I did not sleep much when I was traveling. Four hours seemed to be normal because I was energized. I was always flying somewhere. I tried to make sure I stayed in hotels with a workout area or access to an off-site fitness facility. I worked out often where travel allowed.

Sometimes the travel got to me. I was physically and mentally exhausted. Once I flew into Detroit without hotel reservations. It was late at night and I had no idea where I was going except to work at Detroit Edison the following morning. I eventually found a hotel, checked in and collapsed. In the morning I had no idea where I was, which town I was in. I panicked a tad before regaining my composure. It was the first time I experienced that kind of anxiety but it was not the last. Another time I am sitting at the busy gate area in Columbus, Ohio ready to board a flight to Philadelphia through Pittsburgh. I went comatose and when I awoke the terminal was empty. I missed boarding the flight and the chaos associated with it. It was madness.

The work itself could be grueling. I worked with big, heavy instrumentation, some weighing as much as 15,000 pounds. Unfortunately I wasn't aware of the perpetual damage I was doing to the left knee, nor to the rest of my body for that matter. I was on such physical and mental highs, everything else was secondary. Nothing could stop me, or so I thought.

When I moved to America, I left my road bike behind. I thought I would buy a better one there. But the price for road bikes was mind-boggling. Since I had not used up all of the moving allowance, I had my SM Woodrup shipped to the US. I had been poor in England so hadn't had the money to purchase correct cycling clothes nor was I aware of why cycling clothes were designed the way they are. Once the bike arrived, I purchase some correct clothing. I hadn't done any significant long distances on rides either. Instead I had kept my routine to short, fast, powerful sprints.

As I found out, there are two basic classes of cyclists: sprinters and climbers. They are different cyclists even on major pro tours. Sprinters have massive leg muscles and are generally bigger cyclists with added weight. Climbers are skinny and lightweight, but powerful. My thighs were large simply from me doing these fast, short sprints. Where I lived in Boulder, there was this short hill climb straight out of the road by the apartment. On days I managed to get home, I cycled up this short five-mile hill. When I lived in Sheffield, I would do a six-mile hill climb close to where I lived that would take me right out of the city limits.

When I moved to an apartment in Marin County in the summer of 1987, I found a huge cycling community. I simply had no idea. Mountain bikes were developed in Marin, I found out. Marin was full of rolling hills.

As fun as it was to cycle up those rolling hills, it was hard work for me. I didn't realize that my knee was deteriorating and my bones were just grinding on each other. All I knew was that I could not stand up on the bike nor could I push very hard for very long. I was strong and I just couldn't grasp what was going on. Time and hard work were not improving my condition. I got frustrated and would come home incredibly tired and in pain. I kept my rides short and fast but I really wanted to climb the hills. At the time I had no idea why I could not.

Chapter 13

IN MARCH 1988, things changed dramatically. I had a meeting with my newly appointed boss in Boston and he fired me right there. I got fired from the job I came to America to do. They had removed bonuses for engineers in January, which meant a 50% pay cut for some of us working all hours. I was taking red-eye flights to the East Coast so I could arrive at customer sites in the mornings. I was then taking late night flights to other sites or home so I could still put in full days. I wasn't given bonuses. I earned them. I worked incredibly hard. But that didn't change the outcome. I was fired because a 50% pay cut changed my attitude. I needed to find another way to make a living.

I could see potential in a third-party service and support company other than from the OEM (original equipment manufacturer). Customers with these instruments built in Manchester, England had no alternative resources for service and maintenance, parts and support. But what did I know about running a business? Absolutely nothing.

GB Scientific, Inc was founded end of March 1988. Marina offered her support and she thought it was a good idea. We had potential. She had a job which helped alleviate the financial stresses. Just one small problem in all this: We had no money.

The Director of Service at VG/Fisons agreed to sell me the Camaro Z28 I was driving, so that was good. A few weeks into my new venture, my wife came home and found me completing an immense detailing job on the car. I had clayed and waxed the entire paint, installed new blue striping along the bottom and painted the rims black where they needed to be black. It looked new from the factory. Unfortunately, a happy wife leads to a happy life, and she wasn't happy.

"What are you doing? Have you done any work yet? Talked to any new clients?" came the first round of questions.

My car looked beautiful. It did, there wasn't a scratch on it. That didn't impress her much for some reason and she stormed off into the home. Hmm, I realized I needed to work on this.

Out of the blue in April came a call from a professor at the University of California in Berkeley. She had heard I was fired so called me. The factory was installing a brand new ZAB2-EQ, which was a large instrument. The Q portion was new in the field and she wanted someone to run it. I was an engineer and good at problem-solving, but I had never run a mass spectrometer from an operator's standpoint. I needed work and I needed that experience. This was a dream. The money she was offering did not even pay the mortgage but it did not matter. That part was irrelevant. A UC Berkeley professor, Julie, hired me part-time as I built up my new company.

I worked at UC Berkeley for eighteen months. My first scientific publication originated from work in that lab. I had electronically modified the instrument so that it was capable of doing something no one had ever done before anywhere in the world. I had coupled the collision energy reference voltage to a probe ramp reference voltage which allowed collision energy in the quad gas cell to be ramped during acquisition. To this day, it is a feature on every MS/MS mass spectrometer. Julie wrote the scientific paper and put my name as the main author.

In 1990 I got a call from Stanford University. "Hello Geoff, this is Kym." He said in his Australian accent. "I am moving to UCLA and want you to move my ZAB-E."

A ZAB-E is a huge instrument and weighs around 15,000 lbs. I had never moved one before, but that never stopped me in the past. I did not mention that to Kym because I wanted the challenge. What could possibly go wrong with moving something one has never moved before? I knew instrumentation very well. This was just on a larger scale. I was sure I could do it.

I went down to view the instrument prior to quoting. It was large. I looked at how is was put together and looked at where the securing bolts were for dismantling the various assemblies. It was the first extended geometry ZAB VG had ever made, and the first one delivered in the world.

Moving scientific instruments, particularly ones of this magnitude, took a toll on my knee. Removal of the lateral meniscus back in the spring of 1981 had, in essence, removed the cushion between the bones in the outside compartment of the knee. As I perpetually crawled around the floor, moved heavy equipment, as well as traveling extensively and all my other activities, the inevitable was taking place. My leg was slowly buckling inwards at the knee as the gap between the bones began to collapse. The gap was narrowing and I began getting stabbing pains that went straight up my back into my head. I would have to stop what I was doing momentarily until it subsided. I had no idea that the bones were grinding together and I was destroying my knee.

In the summer of 1990, Marina picked me up from San Francisco Airport one Saturday after a work trip to Las Vegas. We had just purchased my dream automobile: a Euro specification grey market import 1986 BMW M635CSi. Marina wore a short skirt and nice top. She was gorgeous. She slid over to the front passenger seat as I climbed into the driver's seat. I told her when we opened the company that the first car I want to buy when it is doing well is a BMW M6. The North American model entered the shores in 1987 but departed in 1988. A very rare automobile. I found this Euro spec version a few miles from where we lived in Novato.

When we got home, it was clear Marina wanted to make love to me. With her clinging clothes I could see her body was changing shape. I made a mental note but did not say anything.

She moved off into the bedroom and I followed her. I watched as she lay on the bed and shifted her legs to a slightly open position. I had a clear view right up her white skirt. What a beautiful picture.

She was beautiful.

I climbed onto the bottom of the bed and crawled on all fours slowly towards her body. I felt myself getting hard as my heart beat fast. She could do that to me. I started with her feet which I began to caress with my hands as I licked them with the tongue. I could feel her body take notice as I began to pleasure her. I moved slowly and methodically upwards as the tongue and hands carefully manipulated her gorgeous shaped legs. Slowly pushing her skirt upwards, I revealed more of her incredible upper thighs and white panties. She knew I loved white on her which contrasted with her golden olive skin.

After making love she told me something:

"Geoff, I have something to tell you. I am pregnant."

She looked happy. She had stopped smoking so that we could have a child. Now she was pregnant. I could see her hips had changed a little (not difficult to notice with a body like hers) and her breasts were enlarging a tad. We were happy.

Michelle was born in April 1991, after over 24 hours of labour. A day later I drove down to the Sterling dealership in Marin and traded in the Camaro Z28 for a British four-door Rover sedan. I was a family man now.

A little over two years later, in August 1993, Michael was born. This was a much simpler affair and labour was short. We had our girl and boy family. Life was good. The business was successful, we were living a good life and everything was great.

My 21st birthday, family photo. This was two years after my father's massive stroke. My mother looked after him until his death in March 2001

Mum and Dad after my father was forced to retire after his stroke

Mum and Dad at my sister's wedding, May 1986

Me and my three brother's at my wedding September 1987

Red Square, circa 1985

In the foreground is Ivan the Great Bell Tower located inside the Kremlin

St. Basil's Cathedral.

The Kremlin and St. Basil's Cathedral

Gum Mall, the largest indoor mall at that time

Me modeling in Colorado, Spring 1987

My US company car

Michelle and Michael

SECTION 2

Chapter 14

"GEOFF, YOUR KNEE is shot. There is nothing I can do. There is too much damage and it's beyond repair."

It was July 2001. The words came from my surgeon, Dr. Terrence Orr. I was in the recovery room at Barton Hospital in South Lake Tahoe, California.

Two years earlier, I had moved to the "Jewel of the Sierras" with my wife and our two children because we wanted to enjoy life. My company was becoming successful and I wanted to live to work but not work to live. We had just purchased a huge home with an indoor pool. We both drove Range Rovers. Business was good. Life was great.

I had made some nice friends and started to play football (soccer) again. One Sunday in late summer of 2000, I was invited to play at a local field. At the end of the game, I did not feel good. The following morning, my knee had swollen like a balloon. I had never seen it swell like that before. I headed back to see the same surgeon in Novato that I had seen during the '90s. I was on my way to do some work at Stanford University in the South Bay but I had to sort out the swelling because fluid on the knee was excessive and incredibly painful.

When I arrived at the surgeon's office, I found my old doctor had retired and a new surgeon had taken his place. The office walls were now lined with signed photos of the San Jose Sharks, a professional ice hockey team. Being an avid Sharks fan since the franchise started in 1991, I was excited and hopeful that I would be seen by one of their surgeons.

Unfortunately, the surgeon didn't share the same excitement about my knee. He would try to fix it, he said, but there were no guarantees. Looking at my history, the doctor advised I get a clean-out of the joint. In January 2001 I went in for the fifth knee surgery. It was performed at the Novato Hospital using a local anesthetic known as an epidural. I would never again elect a surgery where I would remain wide awake. It was awful, but the news about my knee made the experience even worse.

"Geoff, you need to find a surgeon in Tahoe because you will need help," he said. "The only knees I have seen as bad as yours belong to professional hockey players."

But it wasn't until July that I really understood what he meant.

Dr. Orr, who lived at Lake Tahoe, was one of the best orthopedic surgeons in the country. He was the US Olympic Ski and Snowboard team surgeon and had the expertise to fix anything, I was told. I was optimistic that Dr. Orr could fix me, but much too optimistic as it turns out.

"Your knee is shot."

Those words just ricocheted against the walls of my brain. That cannot be true, I thought, I am only 37 years old. How could my knee be shot?!

In the recovery room, the first tears ran down my face and onto the pillow. Just a short flow but it would be the first of bucket loads in the coming years. I was entering a nightmare that would rattle anyone's soul. When my wife picked me up from the hospital, I was in a state of shock. The surgery was minor but the findings were horrific.

Then my depression started sinking in. I stayed in my bedroom most days. I became socially troubled, an introvert and extremely quiet. While my pain was not extreme, I felt the need to take the narcotics I had been prescribed in order to escape the world I had been thrust into.

"Your knee is shot!" Words I will never forget!!

Dr. Orr advised I visit Dr. Steven Bannar, another well-respected and admired Tahoe orthopedist who did knee replacements. Still in shock I went to see him. It was approaching 24th August, 2001, which would be my 38th birthday. How did my knee wear out so soon? The reason, as it turned out, was removing 70% of the lateral meniscus when I was 17 years old. The surgeon back then had told me it was a big surgery but no one knew the consequences. It had created a gap between the tibia plateau and the ball of the femur. After years of excessive activity, my knee had progressively buckled inwards as the gap created from the meniscus removal had closed. Evidently the gap between the bones in the lateral (outer) compartment of the knee had disappeared and they were now grinding against each other. This was not a condition conducive to comfort and longevity apparently.

The first surgeon in Novato, who had done surgeries number three and four during the 90's (removal of a lose body – bone tissue – and a clean-out), told my wife that I would be in trouble with each passing year, something she failed to tell me until much later. She certainly did not bring it up when we moved our office from Novato to South Lake Tahoe, a move that required moving tons of scientific equipment and took ten years off the life of my knee I am sure.

The only option was to replace the knee. However, replacing my knee would be a big problem because of my age, Dr. Bannar cautioned. At the time, replacements only lasted ten years or so. The younger the person, and the more active, the quicker the knee would wear out. Back then, a surgeon would drill holes through the length of the bones to secure the knee. Once the first knee wore out, the surgeon would drill slightly larger holes to accommodate the second replacement. This practice limited the number of drillings to two. If I replace the knee, chances are very high I would require another one 10 years later. I would be just 48. The second replacement would then have to last the rest of my life.

My insurance requested a second opinion so I scheduled a visit with a specialist in Sacramento for 12th September 2001. The day before John, my oldest brother, had called early in the morning and told me to turn on the news. He said World War III is starting. The first World Trade Centre tower had already collapsed and the second one was billowing smoke. I was gob-smacked. The towers were massive. I was at the top of those in early 1986 and I remember being awestruck by the sheer magnitude of the two structures. They were so tall, they moved with the wind and my legs shuck when I stared down from the top. How could buildings that big collapse? I spent the rest of that day, along with the rest of the world, glued to the TV set.

The next day, I drove to see a specialist in Sacramento. I learned that my knee never had a chance after the meniscus was removed in 1981. Nowadays, a meniscus could be trimmed or stitched together. But back then, they were removed and that meant a 100% failure rate for the poor souls who had menisci taken out. My knee was finished, basically. The various options included compartmental replacement (replacing the lateral portion), full replacement or osteotomy. Whatever the decision, it would change how I would live from here on out.

The specialist in Sacramento concluded that knee replacement was, at the time, the best option and so, after conferring with Dr. Bannar, it was scheduled for late January 2002.

Unfortunately, this presented a huge dilemma. Knee replacement would change how I live. I would have to change what I did for a living. But how?

Chapter 15

ELI LILLY IN Indianapolis was donating a 70VSE mass spectrometer to the University of Illinois in Urbana/Champaign. We were contracted to move and install the equipment. The first week after New Year, just weeks before I faced surgery, I flew to Indianapolis and found out the sprawling pharmaceutical complex was adjacent to downtown. It took a couple of days to dismantle the mass spectrometer. New labs had been added and the existing facilities had been upgraded over the years. This meant the laboratory doorways were not built large enough to remove the instrument. I had to remove sections that were not designed to be removed. Crawling on the floor, twisting the body inside the bowels of the instrument, I was trying to extract pieces that were not supposed to be extracted. The distraction was good since I was preoccupied and my head was not straight. The instrument was loaded and I left Indianapolis heading to Champaign.

It wasn't a long drive but I was crying a lot as I drove. I was greatly concerned about what my future would be. How could I continue to work like that?

In late January 2002, I was scheduled for my first knee replacement, on Thursday 24th. However, first thing Monday morning after I returned from Indianapolis, Dr. Bannar called, "I have cancelled knee replacement surgery Geoff. You are too young and I have serious concerns".

I had spent several weeks prior to surgery trying to cope with the emotional and psychological magnitude of losing the knee. I had not come to grips with it and had failed in the preparatory mental requirements for such a life-changing procedure. The telephone call that Monday morning shuck me up because it came out of the blue.

Adjusting to the new developments and the courageous decision the surgeon was making, Dr. Bannar advised an appointment had been made with Dr. Randy Watson. He was another renowned Tahoe surgeon who used to partner with the orthopedist Dr. Richard Steadman before Dr. Steadman opened his world-renowned clinic in Vail, Colorado. I was told Dr. Watson conducted surgeries other doctors cannot or would not do. He specialized on cases that have been turned down or have escalated into critical problems. Mine had now been categorized as a special case.

Sometime in February, I went to see Dr. Watson for the first time. I had no idea that six years later we would be hugging each other on a dance floor, not once but twice.

I awoke in Barton Hospital on an April afternoon in 2002. The pain was staggering. I was dehydrated and felt incredibly uncomfortable. My leg was bandaged extensively and had a huge covering on it.

Dr. Watson had just performed Femoral Osteotomy. He had concluded during the first office visit in February that this procedure would be the best option. He was very optimistic and exuded this amazing confidence when discussing how the knee could be saved. Essentially the lateral area of the left knee would be sliced open vertically with a ten-inch cut and my skin peeled back to expose the complete joint. Then the femur would be hacksawed in two just above the ball and set on an outward angle.

The knee has two critical compartments; the medial (inner) and lateral (outer). Mine had collapsed in the outer compartment which meant the leg had buckled inwards. By setting the femur on an angle, the leg would be bent (buckled) outwards. This would create a gap in the lateral compartment. The medial compartment was not damaged and would support the weight of the body during the healing process, with the aid of crutches at first. The angled femur would be held together with a huge titanium plate screwed to the bones. The gap where it was hacksawed would be stuffed with cadaver bone graft from a donated body.

Once the femur had healed securely and correctly, a cadaver meniscus would be found to implant into the gap the femoral osteotomy had created in the lateral compartment. This would be the second scheduled surgical procedure. In other words, I knew I was in for two big surgeries if, presumably, the hardware was removed at the time of cadaver implant.

I later learnt femoral osteotomy corrections are angled at eight degrees. My knee was so bad, the bones had been grinding for so long, Dr. Watson had to angle my femur at fifteen degrees to create a sufficient gap. It was at that time the largest correction he had ever performed, and likely still is.

I did not research femoral osteotomy before the surgery. Had I done so, I would have been more prepared. But the reality should have dawned on me when I was talking to a local anesthesiologist I knew as we watched our sons play baseball.

"How are you Geoff? What is new?"

"I am doing ok except I have major knee surgery this coming Thursday. I am having femoral osteotomy on the left knee".

"That is incredibly painful," he replied.

And that is all I knew as I was prepped for surgery. Waking up in agony, I saw my wife come into the recovery room. She told me that Dr. Watson was happy with the surgery and I should be good for recovery. Later, when Dr. Bannar looked in on me at the hospital, he shook his head and said he just didn't do those kind of surgeries. It was a very intensive procedure that took over four hours.

But God, the pain. The nurse attached a morphine drip into my arm. I had never had morphine before and this stuff was weird. A press of the button released morphine into my body from a dispenser bolted and padlocked to a stand at the side of the bed. It felt like cold water was being infused into my blood. The blood cooled as the morphine spread around my body. It felt bizarre. But I had read enough Vietnam War books to know it should kill the pain and make me comfortable. I tried to push the button again. Nothing. I wanted more but nothing happened. The medicine was timed, so I remained in agony. The pain was excruciating.

The knee was intensely uncomfortable and I could hardly move my leg. All I saw was the huge bandages. I wanted to tear them off to observe the nightmare underneath. I could not move. I kept telling the nursing staff "I need more morphine" but no one seemed to understand.

"We need to have you try and move the leg. It is very important after surgery," one of the nurses said.

"I cannot get comfortable. When I move the leg, the pain intensifies. The knee throbs."

"That is expected, sir." I hated being called sir. "Let me see you move it please," the nurse quietly and kindly continued.

I took deep breathes and then clenched for what was surely going to be a screaming moment. I slowly elevated the leg but the intense pressure around the surgical incision and the joint catapulted electrical pain signals through my body which were detected by the brain. I managed to control myself vocally but I quickly lowered the leg, taking controlled deep breathes as I did so. Jesus!

At the nurse's request, I repeated the seemingly futile exercise a few more times. Each time the pain level was bringing further tears to my eyes. I found out these are important exercises because the medical staff is determining the extent of any post-surgical complications and problems, if any. I was asked to see how much I could bend the leg but oh my God. I was struggling and I thought I could handle pain.

I stayed in hospital for two days before Marina was allowed to take me home. I was given a CPM (Continuous Passive Motion) machine that I would need extensively. CPM keeps the knee in motion to prevent stiffness and scar tissue from inhibiting its movement. I would end up using this a lot over the next eighteen months.

When I got home, I was placed on one of our sofa beds in the living room. One of us needed sleep so my wife slept on our California

King bed in the master suite. The mattress on the sofa bed was old and thin and incredibly uncomfortable. I could feel the springs underneath and my condition amplified the discomfort ten-fold. After we got home from the hospital, my wife left to see a friend, leaving me unable to get water or food. I became agitated, angry and frustrated. Eventually, four hours later, she returned. She had been drinking and found it funny I was thirsty and irritable, irrespective of the intense pain I was experiencing. I was pissed off.

For my recovery, I had been prescribed Percocet and Vicodin in limited quantities. I had never tried Percocet before but I knew Vicodin well and I knew I was going to get into narcotic trouble. Just from the level of pain I was experiencing alone I knew I would need copious amounts of medication. I hated those things and already knew what they would do to me.

My first foray into problematic narcotic trouble was after Dr. Orr's surgery in July 2001. It wasn't the level of pain back then but the words 'your knee is shot' reverberating around my head. I was depressed, seriously depressed, and I needed the drowsy-effect of Vicodin to take me away. To send me to another place I preferred to be. They did aid in my need to sleep but the drug-induced hangovers the morning after were terrible. I don't recall back then having to recover from withdrawals so I must have disciplined myself, or perhaps I just ran out of the drug.

After femoral osteotomy, I needed the medication. The surgery was massive and I was in chronic pain. I was struggling immensely with the level of pain. I started on one pill every four hours. Even the pills didn't alleviate the pain level. I was crying every night from pain, but not until my family went to sleep. I could not let them see me this way. I didn't want to appear weak and vulnerable in their eyes.

The first and only time I downed a Percocet, it sent me delirious. I wasn't sleeping at all so I decided to try one. As I lay on my back (the only way I could sleep after surgery), it felt like I was elevated four feet above the bed. I stayed awake because I was afraid to move in case I fell off the bed. The floating sensation scared the crap out of me and I never took another Percocet.

The following Tuesday, I had a post-surgical doctor's visit. My wife and children drove me there. That's where they stayed, in the car. I used the crutches the hospital gave me to maneuver into the office. As I walked from the waiting room area into the examination room, I walked through the x-ray area. I looked at the boxes and saw two x-rays of someone's left knee. There was no name attached to them. I stared as I walked past. Holy shit, the knee had this huge plate attached to the outside of it which was held there with about eight large screws. The screws were longer in the femur ball. My heart went out to the poor bastard who had that done.

Dr. Watson walked in the exam room with a big smile on his face. He was a tall, slender, older gentleman. He was very affable and caring. When I first met him he was very optimistic and exuded this confidence that the knee could be saved. He had ideas and solutions which made me feel very comfortable. I was stoked walking out of his office for the first time.

With this recent surgical procedure, he was so optimistic. He motioned me to follow him to the x-ray screens. When he pointed out the x-rays I had been staring at as I walked in, my heart sank. I nearly buckled and collapsed. Holy shit. Even though he had briefly described what he was going to do, it never occurred to me those were my x-rays. Wow. I worked hard to hold back tears.

For the first time I realized recovery was going to be a significant undertaking and I still had another surgery to go. A femoral osteotomy was a massive procedure. I was numb-struck at the x-rays. Back in the examination room he peeled away the bandages and surgical gauze. It was a knee I did not recognize. It was a bulb with no shape, except round. The surgery was so invasive, the swelling was huge. I watched as he removed the last of the gauzes to reveal the incision. It was long and I was surprised not to see the usual array of sutures all in a row.

"I used nylon stitching underneath the skin", he explained. "A long single stitch that looped in and out of the scar half way down. All I will need to do when the time comes is to cut the middle and slide them out of the flesh. No surface intrusion".

His work was impressive. The cut was clean despite its' length. He must have used a ruler, I thought. But a scar ten inches long presents problems of its own, I would learn quickly enough.

I told Dr. Watson that I was in incredible pain. He brushed it off as being typical for the procedure. The pain was behind the knee though, I pointed out. He said it was post-surgical trauma and not unusual.

My knee was cleaned up, dry blood removed and then it was dressed with new sanitized bandaging materials. Grabbing my crutches, I left the office, climbed into the back of my wife's white Range Rover and I hid from my family the fact I was crying the whole way home. I reached a new low point in my life.

Every night I would wait until my family had gone to bed before I allowed myself to cry. I was in agony. But I felt my children did not need to see their father in serious difficulty. For four weeks, I took pain medication and cried every night. Four very intense weeks!! I had delayed work at Lockheed Missile and Space in Palo Alto, California but I had to further postpone the site visit. I just could not function.

The weeks dragged on and on. I used the CPM machine to keep the knee in motion so it did not seize or generate problematic scar tissue. It was hard work. My knee could only flex and bend a certain amount. I was still sleeping on the uncomfortable sofa bed just big enough for me without the CPM machine on it. With the machine, there was no comfort to be had. Along with the perpetual pain, I did not sleep much at all.

I started physical therapy again, as I had for each surgery since Novato. Chris Proctor was the head of physical therapy at the location I was recommended. We had worked together after my surgery with Dr. Orr the prior year. He knew me and knew I worked hard. But this time I could not do it. The pain of moving and bending the knee was excruciating and debilitating. I tried but failed every time.

One day, four weeks after the surgery, I walk into my office and the office manager told me I didn't look good. I sure as hell did not feel good, but no one was listening. I had lost 20 pounds in four weeks, which was noticeable since I was not a fat person. I was losing weight fast and my face was turning white.

When I drove over to physical therapy that day, the young lady behind the front desk told me the exact same thing. "Geoff, you don't look good," she said with deep concern. I wasn't sure why people hadn't noticed before. It was as if someone had painted my face white all of a sudden.

I went home that afternoon and called Dr. Watson's office. The following morning Dr. Watson took one look at me and said I didn't look good. I had been telling people I was in pain for four weeks. Finally they were beginning to take notice. Then things happened quickly. If it was a blood clot, Dr. Watson said, it could kill me. Immediately scheduled were a bone scan, an MRI and a physical stress test.

The bone scan was interesting because I saw the negative of what the scan should be. Normally the good areas would show up white and bad areas would show up black. However, I saw the opposite, meaning the white areas were now the bad bones or areas experiencing some trauma. In my case, the left knee looked like a light bulb. It lit up like a bloody light bulb.

In the end, a blood clot was ruled out and nothing untoward showed up. But I was still in agony and losing weight. Consequently, the decision was quickly made to perform an emergency surgery for early June 2002.

The week leading up to the emergency surgery could not come fast enough. The pain was unbearable and I had lost significant weight. Finally the medical profession believed me. I knew my body and knew it well. I observed that using the CPM machine made the pain worse, but I had to keep using it. Not being able to do physical therapy those four weeks also set me back considerably. I had lost significant muscle strength from atrophy. There were practically no left leg muscles, which would make climbing out of this surgery so much harder.

Surgery number eight was done by Dr. Watson. My wife was there as I woke up in the recovery area. She was vague but mentioned I nearly lost the rear leg muscle.

I had no idea what had happened until I went to Dr. Watson's office for the post-surgical appointment five days later. I was right, there was a complication and it was pretty serious. Congealed blood had fused the IT band and rear leg muscle together. The doctor had never seen anything like it before. Had we waited any longer, he said, I would have lost the rear leg muscle. That explained the pain when using the CPM machine because the IT band and leg muscle likely wanted to go opposite directions. The huge ten-inch scar would have to be opened up again and Dr. Watson would literally have to rip apart the band and muscle. He just shook his head as he explained all this.

After the surgery, I was anxious to look at the scar so I had removed the bandages before I went to the post-surgical appointment. Dr. Watson had stitched using the same technique plastic surgeons used. He did an absolutely magnificent job. The huge scar was clean as the nylon stitch was weaved under the skin. It was cleaned up remarkably well. Too bad all that work would have to come apart again.

The recovery process from this surgery was becoming difficult, weird and unlike anything I had previously experienced. I was having serious problems recovering mentally. My head felt different. When I went back to work the following Monday, I picked up the phone to call a client I had worked with for nine years and could not remember his telephone number. I would dial someone's number and not remember who it was I was calling. I would have to ask them when they picked up the phone. I would also get into conversations and then stop mid-sentence as I desperately searched for the word I needed to use. I really did not know what was going on, but anesthesia and two big surgical procedures so close together had damaged my head. I was experiencing a partial memory loss and it was scaring the crap out of me.

Scheduled to visit Lockheed Missile and Space in Palo Alto for their training class, I headed down to the Bay Area about two weeks after surgery. I arrived in the lab but could not remember what I was supposed to be doing. I did not even know how to operate the mass spectrometer I was going to train them on. It was as if part of my memory had been erased. Anesthesia had wiped it out. Luckily, I mean luckily, the personnel at Lockheed had important meetings that day so I could not do the training. So I spent time training myself how to operate the instrument and reprogram that portion of my memory.

I was getting scared now. I was good at this stuff. My memory had been impeccable over the years as I built my company and my reputation. I could remember names and telephone numbers without writing them down. I could just pick up a phone and dial. I was also very good at multi-tasking. It was easy for me to do many things at once. All of a sudden, those abilities were lost. Part of my brain's capacity was wiped out just like that. If I was talking, and my wife was around when my mouth stopped, she would fill in the word I was looking for. With no one else around, it was completely daunting. I worked with some of the most educated people in the world. Now I sounded like some weird guy off the streets, instead of someone highly educated and well versed in the scientific field.

I was involved in most aspects of day-to-day business from running the laboratory samples, to finding parts, telephonic and email problem diagnosis, quotations. No one in the office had the technical knowledge to help me. Now, I would easily get distracted as a telephone call came in say and directed my attention somewhere else. I would forget what I was doing as I got dragged away. I could not control my head to perform different tasks at the same time. This was all new and baffling. I was brilliant at multi-tasking, or used to be. Not anymore it seems. That ability disappeared after knee surgery number eight.

It was scary but I told no one.

I had to start therapy again and got my head wrapped around that task. In the five week delay, my leg muscles had almost disappeared so I needed to work hard. Physical therapy started in earnest, two/three days a week. Chris and the other therapists worked very hard but I was always in incredible pain. Some of the exercises brought tears to my eyes. I had to stand for some but my knee could not take weight. The idea behind the therapy was to push and push so that I could increase the flexion and extension angles and increase muscle strength. However, unendurable therapy was always accompanied by chronic joint pain, which was exacerbated by stress from exercise. A real Catch 22. The throbbing, burning, crippling, acute, inflamed joint was suffering. But the worst part was the end when ice packs were placed on my knee. The skin around the scar was sensitive to the cold. That just sent me through the roof.

Dr. Watson had also performed Z-Plasty. I would end up having this procedure done a number of times. The iliotibial (IT) band was stretched and it needed to be lengthened to release some strain. This is a tough ligament to handle. One could hang a heavy weight on it and it would not stretch. Z-Plasty is done by cutting a Z into the band and then connecting the two pointed ends of the band together. Part of therapy required me laying down with the left leg on a foam roller. I had to lift my body up and roll the leg along the roller, along the length of the ten inch scar. The pain emanating during that exercise always brought tears. The idea was to stretch or loosen the strained band.

A few weeks after the corrective surgery, I bolt upright in bed in the middle of the night. What the hell was that? It felt as if I had been electrocuted and stabbed with a big needle at the same time. It was around the scar area. It had woken me from a rare deep sleep as the narcotics were working miracles that night.

At my next visit, I asked Dr. Watson what was going on.

"I sliced through nerves when I cut the flesh open," he explained. "Now they are trying to repair themselves. They send signals looking for the other end of the nerve. The sharp stabbing pain is what you are experiencing."

Holy shit, it was a perpetual process after each time the big scar was sliced open. They occurred at random times but the pain was incredible, like someone poking me with a huge blunt needle.

It would take months of physical therapy before I could bend my knee about 100 degrees to rotate on a stationary bike. Months and months of arduous, pain-induced pushing and pushing. The hard work was sometimes soul-destroying. I remained on crutches because the joint would not support my weight yet. However, I had done away with the hospital-supplied contraptions and found a pair of crutches that were supported by the lower arm. I could not tolerate the ones that fit under the armpits any longer.

I still had to focus on my company whilst this was going on. To this day, I am not sure how I dealt with it.

In August 2002, Marina conspired with one of her sisters to go on a Caribbean cruise with both families. I was still in massive pain and was dosed up on narcotics. How could this possibly be a good idea? How could getting around a cruise ship with a crutch be a good idea?

Marina's family was large. Her parents were from Palestine and were told to move by the Arabs in 1948, with the promise of a return to Paradise. They lived in Beirut, and after spending five years in the religiously incited civil war between majority Muslims and the minority Christians who were running the country, the family moved to America. The Arabic promise of Paradise went unfulfilled.

She had six sisters and one brother. The oldest already lived in the San Francisco area. She and her husband sponsored each sibling as they were forced to leave their home in Beirut. Political refugees is what I imagine, but the war was rarely discussed and I did not question too frequently. I learnt from an occasional comment that life when the war started was not very good and many things changed, including family, people and friends.

Four of Marina's sisters and her brother were older, separated by a few years. They mostly lived in Marin County, but the youngest two resided elsewhere in California. They were a close family but arguments often ensued, big at times. I was always impressed with how they managed to make up somehow. Resentments did not spill over into long periods of non-communication. The sister Marina was closest to was also close in age. Her husband and I would end up doing long charity cycle rides together.

It was Marina and her sister who booked the cruise, which left from New Orleans and included port-of-calls in Jamaica, Grand Cayman and Cozumel, Mexico. This would present some real obstacles as I was only supporting myself with one crutch at this point.

The cruise ship was huge. For someone with two perfectly good legs, it was fine. For someone in my predicament, it meant long walks. Walking any distance was troubling, tiring and painful. My knee could not bear full weight and the muscles were still small.

Each evening I took a Vicodin and just crawled into bed with my knee throbbing. Excursions were excruciating. Even the buffet lines were a challenge. Lying in the sun was fine, except for the people shocked by my massive red scar. I was ready for home. That cruise altered my thinking because my back was having problems accommodating the one crutch. I flew home and immediately grabbed a second crutch. For the next fourteen months, two crutches were the norm.

Soon after the cruise I was invited to Vancouver Island, Canada. We had a client in Sidney, which was located just north of Victoria. The 9/11 attack had drastically changed the travel industry and the joys of flying no longer existed, courtesy of the US government. It was a whole-day travel event. Getting through airports, changing terminals in San Francisco, going through Immigration and Customs in Vancouver and then changing terminals again for the flight to Victoria, just beat me up.

As soon as I entered my hotel in Sidney, the client called. He had just been fired from his job but he wanted to meet me for dinner nonetheless. He would bring along a friend. My knee throbbed from the long day. I was prepared to just order food at the hotel and go to sleep. Instead, ignoring the pain and immediate hunger, I agreed to meet Dave and his friend, Patrick, at a very nice restaurant by the water in Victoria. Dave had invited me to fix some equipment at the company where, up until only a few hours ago, he was CEO.

The dinner turned out to be the first meeting with two of my future environmental laboratory partners. I listened to what they had to say and then I offered a proposal they did not expect. I wanted to be part of this new venture and I proposed supplying the first two instruments. After dinner, I drove back to the hotel and took a Vicodin before collapsing in bed.

Chapter 16

SINCE THE CORRECTIVE surgery in June 2002, I had been working extremely hard at physical therapy. It was the only way to make my knee work again. But sometimes, it felt like I could hardly work. The pain was enormous. Then I started to see muscle growth. When a region of the body senses pain and trauma, it tells the brain to shut down that part of the body. In essence my brain was trying to shut down my knee and the muscles around it. But I was fighting that decision. Muscle growth was encouraging and kept me motivated, and motivation to enter therapy three times a week for months on end was definitely required. Motivation was a driving force.

Attitude was next. If one has a poor attitude, then motivation is pointless. Critical was a desire to keep moving forward. Inspiration from others was very important to me. Seeing other people's great pains and sorrows and how they pushed forward, always forward. This was mind-numbing stuff. Looking back, this is what my father must have dealt with after his stroke. Only his was a more serious life-changing event.

At night, things were different. I did not sleep much but I needed to. During the day I was busy at work or busy with the CPM machine and could catch a few winks of sleep here and there. I was beginning to become addicted to Vicodin now, which also was a new experience. The pain was horrendous so I had to have Vicodin. By this time, I had reduced my intake to only one at night prior to my search for sleep. Trying to function during the day on Vicodin was impossible so

I had to stop. I could not function with the drowsiness and the drug-induced hangover. It impaired my driving ability so I endured the pain and stopped taking the narcotic.

The memory loss from the anesthesia turned my head upside down. Life was different now. Memory loss was a massive detriment. I had a partial loss of vocabulary and was scared to talk to people. I had anxiety from just talking because if I lost focus or a particular word, I would panic. It was common for me to lose track of thought as I spoke and I would fight to find a word that was lost. I fought the inability to multi-task. I became rather easily distracted and forgot what I was doing. I fought an inability to remember names and numbers, which I was brilliant at remembering before the damage from anesthesia. I was beginning to notice something else also. People's names would go in one ear and out the other just as fast. The ability to store names was blurred and damaged. I would forget parts of the past and as soon as something or someone reminded me, the memories came back. It was like a software glitch where one would have to re-load software. I started to read a lot again so that I could re-program my brain with words I had lost. The impact of all this was huge and something I still struggle with.

The end of 2002 was approaching and although my muscles had improved in strength, something was changing. I was still on crutches eight months into this rebuild process. That was really getting me depressed. By the end of October, I just started to bend the knee far enough to get on the stationary cycle, which I thought would be the beginning of recovery. But that did not happen.

At beginning of November, I flew down to a client in Carlsbad, just north of San Diego. Getting around the airport on crutches, renting a car, stuffing luggage into the trunk of the Mustang Hertz had rented me -- everything required significant more work and energy. By the time I checked into the hotel, I was physically and mentally exhausted.

I had flown down to move an instrument. How does one physically move an instrument weighing around 5,000 lbs while hobbling on crutches? Not only that, the machine was on air mounts, or anti-vibration cushions as they were sometimes called, so the instrument had to be jacked up to remove those from underneath. An engine hoist had to be deployed to lift up another piece. I placed the crutches away from the work area and hobbled around whilst dismantling, moving and re-installing the equipment.

It was four days of sheer hell and agony. Every night I dosed up on Vicodin and every morning I woke up with a hangover from the medication. That trip was so physically debilitating that I vowed afterwards I would drive anywhere if the trip was within around a 500-mile radius of my home. It was so much easier than trying to navigate long airport halls and ridiculous security screening:

Screener: "Can we screen the crutches?"

Me: "No, how do I walk?"

Screener: "Can you walk without them?"

Me: "Yes, of course, I am only on crutches for attention and I don't really need them!!"

Screener: "Can we pat down your leg because x-rays show metal in that area?"

Me: "Of course there is metal. I have a bloody great titanium plate with screws holding my knee in place."

Screener: "Does it hurt?"

Me: "No, why would a huge titanium plate with screws hurt?"

Screener: "I will pat gently."

Me: "Ok."

Me: "What the hell? That wasn't gently."

And so it went, passing through long terminals, getting rental cars, traveling through crowded airplanes. It was staggering work, requiring energy I did not possess. I also quickly determined that driving would significantly reduce the wear and tear on the knee.

Towards the end of 2002, something was noticeably changing. When I felt my knee, I noticed some of the screw heads were being pushed towards the skin. I was also beginning to hobble a lot worse and my leg muscles were beginning to retract. Despite being able to work out on the stationary bike, my strength was diminishing. I could physically see the muscles getting smaller. It was an enormously depressing sight after working so hard in therapy. As the holiday period approached, the screw heads were pushed further against the skin and were now clearly forcing the skin outwards.

Christmas came and I was clearly deteriorating. We spent Christmas at my in-laws' home and the video taken of us opening presents shows how badly I was hobbling around. I was seen smiling, joking and being happy. That was a front, perhaps an aberration, for what I was feeling inside. I did not want others to see me suffering so I kept in a positive mood. At night I was continuing with the Vicodin.

In early January 2003, I was a mess. I went to physical therapy but Chris was not around so I left and didn't return. A few days later, he called me because I had not been to therapy all week. I started to cry over the phone. The screw heads were clearly showing through the skin at this point and I could not walk. The pain was crazy.

"I am a mess Chris," I said, trying to gather myself as tears were running down my face. I was so emotional because he was reaching out to me. He cared.

I went to see him and he could clearly see my issues. I called Dr. Watson's office and went to see him the next day. I was always grateful they cared. I was given priority because of my history.

I had x-rays immediately. I walked back to the examination room and waited for Dr. Watson. He walked in, only this time his demeanor had changed. He did not say anything but motioned me to follow him. This must be bad as I walked over to the x-ray boxes.

There it was. I had learnt to read x-rays over time and I could see an immediate problem. The area where the bone was hacksawed during femoral osteotomy was dark. It was a black line. The femur and the ball were detached essentially. Not only that but the screws were being pushed out. They were being rejected by my body so the plate holding the femur ball to the femur bone was becoming loose. Detachment was 100%. Basically the knee was falling to pieces. In medical terminology, it was known as a non-union. In my terminology, it meant I was screwed and in trouble.

My heart sank. I did not know what to say. I was heartbroken but I kept positive. I felt I always had to keep positive in front of Dr. Watson. He could not see me falter. He could not see me lose hope. He could not see me lose motivation. He could not see me give up. I had to remain positive despite the appalling circumstances.

"You have dissolved the cadaver bone graft and your body is rejecting the screws I put in to hold the titanium plate," Dr. Watson explained. I could see the torment on his face too. He was such a good man.

"We need to do this all over again," he said.

I just stood there for a moment whilst I tried to digest the implication of doing this all again. I felt my body drain of everything and was lucky the crutches were there to hold me upright. I now knew what femoral osteotomy was and I needed to do a second one.

"Can we do it quickly?" I asked. "Because this hurts."

His office called over to Dr. Bannar's office and I headed over there. I loved the fact that these world-class doctors were taking care of me. They showed so much empathy.

I was sent back to Dr. Bannar's examination room and waited. I had been told to prepare for more x-rays so I did. I walked into the room and got talking to the x-ray technician. He was funny. I was laughing trying to keep a positive attitude and camouflaging how torn to pieces I was. This guy also played rugby and so we got talking about rugby as he took various shots of the knee.

Then, after some silence, he said, "I used to be a hooker".

I had momentarily forgotten about the subject we were talking about.

"I used to be a gigolo," I replied, realizing too late he was still talking about rugby. The conversation was light and funny, but that all changed when he saw the x-rays. His face went serious, and he showed me back to the examination room without adding a single word. Dr. Bannar walked in, just as serious.

"Aren't you in considerable pain?" is all he said.

My body slumped into the back of the chair and tears started rolling down my face.

"Actually," I replied, "Yes I am."

I had to do the femoral osteotomy again, only this time I knew what that meant. I now knew how big the surgery was and I now knew the recovery process and how long it would take. Shit....

Dr. Watson had explained that my knee was lost. The first osteotomy was history. The second osteotomy was needed to attach the bones so that I could replace my knee. This time the cadaver bone graft would come from my hip. I seemed to be rejecting everything foreign put into the body. He would use larger screws. Larger screws, I thought!! I did not know that was even remotely possible.

I walked into my house and sat on the sofa dejected. I explained to my wife that I need to do this all again. I told her I had lost the knee and just sat and cried. She came and sat next to me, she tried to show some comfort. I had been on crutches nine months already and I knew I had at least another six coming up. I knew it would be another six months of physical therapy before I could get the knee bent enough to rotate on a cycle.

It was the end of January 2003 when I finally got rolled in. The huge 10" scar had to be sliced open for the third time in nine months. This time bone graft was removed from my hip, scarring the left side of my lower body which was almost mirror image to the one from the appendectomy years earlier. Once again I hated the anesthesia. Once again recovery was terrible. I was lost at sea. The pain, the trauma, the intrusion to the joint, the drugs, the devastating psychological effects of going through surgery after surgery. But the pain. Oh God, the pain! I was depressed. I knew what was coming now. Six more months of therapy and crutches before the knee could be replaced. It was a living nightmare.

However, I got a very different perspective one Saturday morning. The space shuttle Columbia was supposed to be landing in Florida. The TV was turned on but I had not bothered with the volume control.

I could not hear any of the reports but the pictures being repeatedly portrayed were those of the shuttle breaking into pieces. The astronauts had no chance of surviving. These images perpetually played out as I sat in a hospital bed recovering from the second massive osteotomy. But those poor astronauts had all lost their lives. I had to put things into perspective. I was not in good shape but I had no choice but to deal with it. As the TV demonstrated, life could be gone in an instant.

Chapter 17

MY SECOND OSTEOTOMY in late January 2003 was a turning point and I had seen the x-rays during the post-surgical office visit. This time the screws were longer, thicker and as wide as the ball joint. Shit! Dr. Watson had used the same long plate as before. I had to do this a second time in order to attach the femur so I could then replace the now-lost knee. It was an emotional, psychological and physical disaster because I knew it would be six more arduous months of crutches and physical therapy. But oh my God, the pain. Once again I got addicted to Vicodin as I attempted to escape the looming abyss.

Physical therapy sessions continued two to three times per week, work-travel permitting.

I did get a surprise a few weeks into recovery when my brother Chris told me he would come and visit. He told me he would bring his wife and daughter with him on an excursion across the country. They would drive a Sterling 827SLi someone in the Carolinas had given me. They were now living in Atlanta and had been for some time. This was a departure of significance since I could now be distracted for a few days. It could perhaps drag me out of my depressive state, even if it was only temporary. I needed something. Anything!

When Chris, his wife and daughter finally arrived, our office manager, Julie, got ski tickets to Heavenly Ski Resort at Lake Tahoe, a lovely gesture on her part. Chris and his family spent the day skiing and my wife and I drove over to meet them for lunch.

I thought I would be happy and distracted, but it did not work. It did not make me feel good watching others enjoying physical activity, especially since I had been told that my knee was a lost cause. I was devastated and miserable. After lunch I turned away with tears in my eyes. Crying was common at this point. The escalating emotional scars would take a long time to heal, if they ever would.

Chris and his family stayed with us for five days. On the last night, he spent a long time upstairs. He had come to visit me but seemed distant and really didn't show much care at all. He was pre-occupied with his own life and my state seemed superfluous and insignificant. His personality was incredibly similar to my wife's. The visit just dragged me further into the abyss. I had entered a bottomless dark pit.

Sometime in April I went to see Dr. Watson.

"We are going to do the cadaver meniscus next," he said with a beaming smile.

"What do you mean? I thought I was finished."

"No," he replied, "We have found a cadaver meniscus for you. It will be implanted after the osteotomy has healed."

Holy smoke, this wasn't the end after all. Now I had something to work towards. The knee isn't a lost cause and I was beginning to lose count how many times I had been told it was by various doctors.

Two months later, I was getting my blood withdrawn for pre-surgical tests. Early one morning in June, I am being prepped for surgery. This was it. I was finally getting the meniscus implanted and life would be good after it. Another four hour plus surgery. More anesthesia to recover from. More pain pills, more therapy, more crutches, but I was nearing the end. There appeared to be light in the tunnel.

When I woke up in the recovery room, something wasn't right. It took a few minutes to figure out what it was. Then I realized I couldn't feel my leg. The bandage was on there, but there was no feeling. My leg was completely numb.

I was taken home. I dragged myself to the bedroom and just collapsed on the bed.

I had moved back into the bedroom I used to share with my wife. No more awful sofa bed in the living room. She had moved to the bedroom suite upstairs because she needed sleep and my sleep did not exist anymore. The CPM machine was now a permanent fixture on the large king-size bed because I had been using it sometimes 20 hours a day just to keep the leg moving and my mind occupied. The CPM machine gave me a distraction.

The day after surgery, I had an appointment with Dr. Watson at his medical office in Incline Village, a curvy, hilly drive halfway around Lake Tahoe. I was beginning to feel the numbness wearing off. My wife drove me over there in her black 1982 Rolls Royce Silver Spur (a beautiful automobile if one likes repairing hydraulic leaks). I was laid out on the back seat as the plush ride took us east on Highway 50 through the city and then north on Highway 28.

Suddenly I was beginning to get some feeling again, but something seemed odd. As the numbness wore off, a burning, searing, fiery pain enveloped the whole of my lower leg.

"Sorry Geoff," my surgeon said. "I was adding extra stitches to make sure the meniscus stayed in place and I accidentally punctured the main nerve with the needle."

After each surgery I was given a video recording so that I could observe what was going on. During one of the recordings I had heard Dr. Watson talk about 'finding the main nerve' before anything else was done. Now, as my numbness wore off, I was learning the importance of locating it and protecting it. Holy shit, the pain was overwhelming.

"It hurts. It feels like my leg is on fire."

"Nerve damage is equivalent to pouring gasoline on one's leg and setting fire to it. As the skin melts and falls off, it exposes the nerves. This is the level of pain you are experiencing," Dr. Watson said.

I had pain when I burnt my arm in England which required hospital treatment. As it turned out, what I thought was only a surface burn had gone deep below the skin. This pain was considerably different.

It wasn't just the burning sensation but it affected movement also. Now I had to think before moving the leg. I had lost some kind of sensory motion. Sometimes I just could not move it at all. I would try but it would not move. Sometimes I would have to stop and put all the thought energy into the sensory actions required to move the leg where I wanted it to go. It was bizarre and troubling, but the pain. I had never felt pain that bad before.

"Geoff, I am going to send you over to a doctor in South Lake Tahoe who will take a look and prescribe appropriate medications and measures."

We drove back to the South Shore and to my office. As I was sitting in the leather chair at my desk, I read some email messages from the Rover-800 friends in England. I had to sit on a 45 degree angle to the right and a 45 degree angle backwards in order to be comfortable. I was laughing at some jokes but really I was not in good shape. My wife returned with Michelle to pick me up. They waited outside but I could not move. I was stuck. My leg would not move anymore. Even when I was telling my brain I want to move, it failed to send the appropriate control signals. I sat helpless on this weird angle. After a short period, I somehow managed to extract the phone headset from its cradle and dial upstairs for someone to help me. My wife came in soon after and helped me sit up properly, but the searing, fiery pain was unbelievable.

I staggered outside on the crutches and climbed onto the back seat of the Rolls.

In the 14 months I had been going through this ordeal, I had been successful at hiding pain and tears from my family. I did not want them to witness how I was struggling. This time though, as I climbed onto the seat, I screamed in agony and started to cry. I had never experienced pain of this magnitude before. I saw Michelle look at me in horror but I could not hide it anymore.

We got home and I sat on the edge of the bed. Marina grabbed the underneath of the lower left leg in order to assist lifting it up.

"Please let go of the leg," I begged. She did not understand and tried to help me.

"Please let go of the leg," I said in a more elevated voice but still composed, kind of. The pain was planted on my face.

She finally realized I was being serious and promptly let go. She was trying to help for once, but it did not work. It was like she grabbed an open wound and put my leg over a wood-burning fire.

A day or two later I went to see the nerve doctor recommended to me, and as I walked up, I noticed he was a psychiatrist. Oh great, I thought, after so many years of being told I need to see one. Perhaps he can fix the other problems people tell me I have. I entered the examination room and laid out on a bench with both legs stretched out and straight. Mandatory questions were asked and answered.

"I am going to perform some tests to see how bad the reactional delay is. I want to see how deep the damage is," he said. "I will be sticking pins in the skin so do not be alarmed."

The meniscal implant surgery had added two more long incisions and they cut down the lower portion of the knee, slightly on an angle. The leg was looking like railroad tracks. The two new incisions ran parallel to each other but of unequal length. The shorter one appeared more at the back and left of the knee. The longer one intersected the big scar on a forty five degree angle, right at the lower apex of it. In any event, they were bright red. All three were bright red because they were pretty fresh. The point I am labouring to make is the doctor could not miss them if he was blind.

He proceeded sticking needles into the right leg at various points along its length. He wrote down notes based on my reaction. I thought he was perhaps going to compare the reaction of the right with the potential damaged, slower reaction to the left. No, that did not happen.

"Well, it looks like there is no damage to reaction responses. That is good."

"You did the right leg doctor. The nerve damage is in the left leg."

"Oh."

Damn, even under searing pain, I managed to laugh. That was hilarious.

The left leg was tested and it came back negative. There was no noticeable or detrimental difference in reaction responses, which I guessed was positive.

He then prescribed Elavil to help alleviate the chronic burning but that just added to the demise of sleep patterns. As each day passed, the time I fell asleep got worse. I would fall asleep one day at midnight, the next day 1 a.m., the following day 2 a.m. When it got to 5 a.m. I had to stop taking the pills. The side effects were awful. Not only did they increase my sleep deprivation, but caused me more anxiety, double vision, disturbed concentration, and increased my agitation levels, which were already skyrocketing out of control. And it really did not aid in the pain symptoms. Those just gradually subsided.

I went back to the doctor for advice and he told me my body just needed to adjust to the medication. I was told to keep taking the drug. I did not keep taking the drug. The side effects were worse than the burning pain. Screaming in agony was much better than that stuff. I tossed the drugs and kept screaming instead.

The sensation eventually subsided after about a week. It became more tolerable, but that was speaking in relative terms. It had subsided enough to reduce the scream level to almost zero but the burning, tingling sensation was still evident. I likely was taking Vicodin also which will have compounded the side effects of the drug. It did not matter. I hated the drug.

I was back in physical therapy two to three days per week once the nerve pain settled down. It took me perhaps a month or two to get the flexion big enough to spin on the bike, but I don't really recall exactly when. Some things were just a blur. The hardware had not been removed so I knew I had to go in hospital again to have it taken out. My body seemed to hate the hardware. I remained on crutches. I could never seem to be able to support myself without them. It was just never ending but, I hoped for an end in sight this time, perhaps. I had to build up strength one more time in order to prepare for the last surgery.

I worked hard and I saw my leg muscles increase slowly. They are a large muscle group and the hardest to build strength in. It takes an inordinate amount of energy, resources, time and patience to build leg muscles in a healthy, abled person. Imagine the additional energy and resources required for me to build mine. It was a mental and psychological battle waged between the head and body. A battle the head would not always win.

Chapter 18

OCTOBER 2003, I was back in Barton Hospital. This time Dr. Watson was removing the hardware. Things were looking up. After immense work in physical therapy, I was heading in the right direction. I was still reeling from the nerve damage in June but nothing I could do about it now. The tingling sensation persisted (and continues to this day) but the abhorrent burning sensation had diminished remarkably. I arrived in the surgical waiting area early that morning. Hopefully, this surgery was for all the right reasons. Five surgeries with five different anesthesiologists over an incredibly difficult and disastrous eighteen month period.

This time the anesthesiologist for this surgery I already knew.

"Good morning Geoff. What are you having done today?"

"Dr. Watson is finally removing some hardware from the knee."

During that period I had been all around our small town in Lake Tahoe, hobbling on crutches.

During the past winter I was entering a local eatery establishment when I saw out of the corner of my eye a guy on crutches heading towards me. I turned towards a beaming smile.

"Hey, are you in the Special Olympics?" he asked.

"No," I said.

We chatted some more. I could see he had one leg missing. Suddenly my long stint on crutches seemed not so very long. He would always be on them but at some point I would discard mine, hopefully.

Countless times I would be in physical therapy and would hear people complain about crutches.

"How long have you been on them?" I would inquire.

"Four weeks," one guy replied.

"Is that all?" I retorted.

Sometimes I had to put things into perspective for me as well as others. It helped me too because at some point early on I had stopped complaining about them. The adage 'there is always someone worse off than you' is worth pondering during difficult times like these. Complaing about the crutches really presented no point in the end. I was on them, period. I needed them to aid walking, period. I had no choice, period. Complaining about them, therefore, was an exercise in futility and served no purpose. I had learnt to live with them.

I was prepped for the anesthesia drip and wheeled into the operating room. I saw my x-rays clipped to the light box hanging on the wall. The plate, pins (added to secure the cadaver meniscus during June's surgery) and screws all evident. I looked over to the anesthetist and saw his mouth drop.

"Some hardware?" he said, with an obviously shocked expression. My predicament did that to people, even in the medical profession. After my first encounter with the x-rays, I gradually stopped wanting to throw up every time I saw them.

I was transferred to the operating table and my left leg was being put onto a stirrup just as the suspend-from-death chemicals took hold.

From this surgery, I recovered very quickly, even though it was the 4th time the 10" scar had been opened. This time only one half of the nylon stitch came out. The other half got stuck in the mangled mess of skin and scar tissue manifesting under the surface. Portions of it still remain visible but nothing can be done about it short of digging it out. It remains a remarkable scar considering what it was subjected to. The visible nylon sutra is testament to the battle that was waged.

Within a week I was rotating on a stationary bike and finally, I mean finally, after 18 months, the crutches were tossed into a closet. I was off them and recovering. Most people would have tossed them off a cliff.

Back in my office a week later, I got an email from a friend in Phoenix. Judy had introduced me to a Rover Chat Group the previous year, based out of England. We had previously talked over the phone when Omar, now my closest friend in Sacramento, told me about a green Sterling 827SLi she was selling and advised I call her. I was a big Rover automobile enthusiast and already owned a limited edition silver '90 827SLi -- one of 11 "Silver Bullets" imported from England. Omar owns an identical Silver Bullet, which is how we became close friends.

However, a Rover, or any high-end British marque for that matter, in green was something to clamor after. Later Judy retracted the listing after finding this internet group and she received a lot of help fixing the problems on "Puck," as she called her car. She invited me onto the Rover-800 chat group, which I loved. People were friggin funny. That connection opened up some really bad days with shear laughter. I had never interacted on an open forum. I initially thought LOL meant Log Off Loser. Dosed up on Vicodin since April 2002, it apparently made my English humour funnier. That was the only positive side effect of the drugs, by the way. I was invited to be the US Moderator for the group, which indeed was a privilege.

A day prior to Judy's email, I receive an email from another friend of the group, saying that it was a shame about Judy. I did not know what he was talking about until I opened Judy's email. As I read it, tears poured over the key board. She had just been diagnosed with Stage IV lung cancer and it would be terminal. They had given her only six months to live.

My own health problems and the surgeries had made me very emotional. My body chemistry had been altered and I could not control my tears at times. Judy's plight put my knee issues into perspective. Despite the battles and chronic pain I had endured, my condition was not terminal. I was not going to die from having a bad knee, although anything can happen during surgery. Judy's email shook me up.

The letter continued:

"I have discussed with my husband and daughter and would like to give you Puck. I know you will look after her and restore it to original condition."

I had not even met her. It was an amazing gesture. I was speechless.

A few months later, my family flew down for a weekend to meet them. We could see she was not in good shape. We felt for her husband who would have to deal with her demise. He was a good guy and we liked them both. It was a hard trip but it very much put life into perspective.

As the end of the year approached, I continued pushing and pushing in therapy. For the first time since April 2002 I was off crutches and enjoying the new found freedoms that entailed. They were so intrusive to life's normal existence. I guess I had somehow adjusted to them and managed to live with the damn things strapped to my lower arms. People were shocked. One therapist I had met during some of my sessions saw me one day at a local Tahoe event.

"Wow, Geoff. I didn't recognize you. You look to be walking normally."

Christmas 2003 without crutches was something to savour. I was building strength on the spinner and I could see small positive changes to muscle growth. My knee was still a weird shape. It had lost some of the architecture associated with a normal structure but that was ok. I had survived some formidable odds to get this far.

Chapter 19

I ENTERED 2004 feeling very good. Physical therapy was increasing my muscle size and shape, and the stationary cycle was working wonders. But suddenly things started to change. I once again witnessed my leg muscles getting smaller. In addition, the knee was acting funny and the joint was getting worse. I went back to Dr. Watson and Dr. Bannar.

My physical therapist, Chris, had already seen this happen and had growing concerns. The news wasn't good. They diagnosed that my knee was failing again and now a lost cause. My knee was done!!

In May, I just walked out on physical therapy, not because I was finished, but because I was finished. I had been doing physical therapy constantly since April 2002 and I had simply had enough. It was depressing and mind numbing to keep doing repetitive exercises for two years. What made the predicament worse was seeing all the hard work deteriorate as the muscles got smaller. It was heart-breaking, a punch in the face.

But in late May, after walking out of Dr. Bannar's office, I became even more determined not to give up. I got on my bike, admittedly partly out of exasperation, frustration, anger, depression, irritation (the adjectives are limitless) and did a short, flat ride. I wasn't quite sure what I expected but I just wanted to ride. In an astonishing revelation, I felt no pain in the joint. I felt really good.

Five days later, after hosting a corporate booth at a scientific conference in Nashville, I drove to a local bike store, looking for a used road bike. Outside the store was this magnificent lightweight yellow Giant TCR2. The wheels had been upgraded to Spinergy Xaero Lites. It had an upgraded saddle, aero bars, which I had never used before, and a small computer mounted on the handlebars. All these added to an amazing package. The bike looked good in its shiny yellow paint and contrasting grey/black/white decals. This was the real deal. Remembering my days in the cycle shop in England, I could not believe what I was looking at. The store owner let me take it for a test run. It was really comfortable. Actually, the cycling motion was much easier than with the classic Cinelli I had been using. I paid $1,200 and went home.

Even with a different bike, I wondered how I would do in reality. Memories of a training ride in England came flooding back. After my meniscus was removed in April 1981, I went back to the surgeon for a post-surgical visit. After discussing the surgery, he asked me if I cycle.

"Yes. I cycle everywhere." I replied.

"You need to build up strength in the leg muscles. The knee requires strength in the muscles to help keep it together," he said.

I wanted to try out his theory by embarking on an early morning training regiment. One morning, soon after the alarm went off at 5:30am, I looked outside and it was typical Hull spring weather. Kingston upon Hull was very close to the North Sea coast and that often brought cold, damp, misty conditions as the winds swept inwards from the sea. I saw the mist and drizzle as I tried to gather my enthusiasm to cycle. I put on a normal tracksuit and a waterproof jacket. I didn't have correct cycle clothing to speak of. I had nothing.

I decided I was going to go east on Holderness Road a few miles and then turn around and come back. A pretty short but simple ride. Hull was flat so didn't require much thought on where to avoid. There was traffic and narrow streets, and those were impossible to avoid in England. Holderness Road was a four lane road where I had elected to cycle mitigating some of the dangers.

I was doing ok but it was bitterly cold. The mist, drizzle and condensation just cut through my body as the freezing humidity drenched me. A few miles in, I had a puncture in the rear tyre. Brilliant! Just what I needed. I didn't know how to cycle back then and wasn't aware of what to carry in case of a puncture. So every five minutes I dismounted the bike, grabbed the tyre pump and flushed air into the damaged tube. After doing that twice, I was done with the ride. I promptly turned around and headed home, having to pump up the tyre as I did so. I got home freezing. My fingers were about to fall off and I was miserable. It was an exercise in futility and I never did continue on.

Now, 10 knee surgeries later, I was considering my next cycling training program. I started out pretty flat, doing eight-to-ten-mile circuits and then 12, building up mile by mile.

In June, Lake Tahoe hosted the Most Beautiful Bike Ride in America, a charity ride around the 72-mile lake. Thousands of cyclists from all over the country, and some from overseas, show up each June to ride it. That June, shortly into my cycling program, I stood at the finish line, watching the participating cyclists ride the home stretch. I looked over at one participant who had just finished to see his computer. It was showing 4:45. He had been on his bike for four hours forty five minutes. Wow, what an alien concept.

Then, just as suddenly, another alien concept floated into my head. I thought I can do that. I can cycle around the lake. That would be my goal. I could do this. I would do this. It was utter stupidity on any level but I needed something to motivate me. I needed a goal, a challenge, a reason. I needed something, no matter how irrational it was.

In September, there was to be another ride around the lake known as the Tour de Tahoe. That's where I took aim. I had no friggin idea how. I had never cycled up mountains. I had never cycled 72 miles in one day. But now motivated, I got going on my bike. I started to build muscle. Slowly what was a bulbous mound started to take shape in the form of a knee. The leg started to gain strength. I remained on the relatively flat portion of road for several weeks but I started to elongate the route and add miles as I felt stronger.

Highway 89 was close to my house. Once I had gained sufficient strength and confidence I started down that route. It would lead to Luther Pass. I had cycled down Highway 89 and it banked left. When I made the turn, I was staring right at the start of a steep climb up the mountain. My heart sank. Holy shit. The road seemed to go straight up, winding up the steep pass for hundreds of vertical feet. I pushed on and managed to make it a mile up the climb. I stopped and turned around. I did not have the muscle strength for such climbs. I wasn't a climber. I had no idea how I was going to figure it out. Undeterred, I tried again a few days later. This time I reached a mile and a half. Now I was gaining something. I was learning very quickly that, for me, it wasn't just muscle and strength but a mindset that had to be right to reach the top of the mountain. On the third attempt I reached a midway point three miles up where the gradient decreased.

It was enough to stimulate my head and carry on. I had no idea the first two miles were the hardest where the gradient approached 10%. Once I got passed that, I was able to climb the rest of the way since the latter three miles were 5-6% gradient. Luther Pass ended up being a six-mile climb with a vertical gain of 1,600 feet. It was a gorge that had been cut through the mountains. At the very top of the pass was this green sign screwed to a wooden 4x4 post cemented in the soil: Luther Pass 7740 feet.

I could not believe I had made it. The endorphins had kicked in. Endorphins are peptide hormones that bind to opiate receptors in the brain. They help to make a person happy and reduced my pain level considerably. I wasn't feeling pain at this point. My muscles ached but the polypeptides were masking any pain. I was numb. I had never experienced such an overwhelming feeling in all my life.

I cycled quickly back down the mountain so that I could tell my wife about this massive accomplishment. She wasn't home.

The following day, my elation was still prevalent as I went to physical therapy to let everyone know. It was only the first step toward the Tour de Tahoe ride just four months away. I was feeling and looking much better. I had changed. I quickly made an appointment to see Dr.

Watson. No one knew that I was cycling. I showed up on my bike, wearing a cycling outfit. Their shock was instant. I wasn't unhappy, I wasn't on crutches, I walked properly, I was looking good. Dr. Watson was shocked. No one had expected such a turn of events in such a short time-frame.

The last time Dr. Watson saw me at the end of May, we were writing off my knee as a lost cause, lost beyond any hope. Now, things were much different. He could not believe it. I was placed on a table and then markings were put on both legs to measure muscle size. Obviously the muscle circumferences on the right leg were considerably larger than the corresponding measurements on the left. That scenario would never change no matter how much cycling I eventually accomplished.

As I worked on my cycling regiment, I conquered Luther Pass north face, but now I needed to go down the other side to Pickett's Junction and Hope Valley. What I never did was survey the roads in the car before cycling down them. I just kept adjusting and adding miles.

I had purchased the Giant bicycle but had not had it measured to see if it was the correct size. I loved it, loved the colour and bought it on impulse. I did not know how important it was to get it measured for my comfort and endurance. I started to get aches and pains in areas I did not even know one could. I was not doing enough miles to work this out correctly. It would be thousands of miles later and an agonizingly painful, long charity ride that drew my attention to things I needed to learn, adjust and correct. For now, I needed to ride, put miles on the legs and do as much climbing as possible. I did not really appreciate how far 72 miles around the lake would be. It was my head pushing, the desire to achieve something special, and the serious need to put behind me those fucking awful surgeries. Being naïve about what the task truly entailed was an attribute I would feed on.

I successfully navigated the south face of Luther Pass down to Pickett's Junction and back up. This would be a 25-mile return ride from home. After covering this a few times, I went on to include

Carson Pass which was long and steep. Then I made a valiant attempt at completing three passes one Saturday morning (I was a mile from the summit of the Carson Pass) and decided to sign up for Tour de Tahoe the next month. I felt confident.

Now Chris was getting excited. My knee was turning into a knee. Muscle strength was gaining pretty rapidly. I was changing not just physically but mentally, psychologically and emotionally as well. The change was staggering. People in the medical profession could not believe what they were witnessing. Where there is hope, miracles do happen.

As Tour de Tahoe approached, Chris contacted a friend at the local newspaper. I went over for an interview late morning two weeks before the ride. The following weekend my wife and I were flying to Germany for an environmental conference. At the newsstand in Reno airport, there on the front page of the weekend edition, was a picture of me. It was surreal. It was amazing to read about my struggles right there in the airport. I was flying high, figuratively and literally. We bought a few copies and took them to Germany to show people at the conference.

The hotel in Berlin was the last time Marina and I ever made love. I tried a different position, something new for a change, a position we had never worked before and as her body went into convulsions, I knew it had worked for her. I also climaxed soon afterwards. It was wonderful, I thought. But she did not see it the same way. By using a technique she wasn't familiar with, she thought I was having an affair. She became furious. She just didn't say why. I just faced her fury, surprised and hurt. I left the hotel room and went to a cocktail party at a restaurant across town hosted by an international vendor. When I came back, she was silent. It was much later that I found out what she was thinking.

Our flight home Thursday was quiet and the drive from Reno Airport was even quieter. I was mystified. We arrived home Thursday afternoon just in time for me to do short rides in town Friday and Saturday. The Tour de Tahoe was the following day.

My wife moved back into the guest suite upstairs. She was in her 'silent mode.' After the first femoral osteotomy in April 2002 and the corrective surgery in June 2002, she told me to sleep in our suite, back in my own bedroom. No more awful sofa bed. Marina had moved upstairs at that point. Once the hardware had been removed and I was off crutches, I stopped using the CPM machine. Soon after that she moved back in bed with me and we were sleeping together again. But when we returned from Germany in September 2004, that all stopped. We would never sleep together again. I was still mystified what was going on in her head.

Sunday morning I got up really early. I was very apprehensive of the day's events. I had never cycled 72 miles in one day.

I did not have correct cycling clothes at this point, at least not for mountain temperatures as fall approached. I got the first bib shorts in Germany, a T-Mobile professional team pair that was being sold at a discount. But I did not have warm clothing. I had only been cycling at this level for less than four months in the summer. I was naïve to cycling mountains in fall weather. How was I supposed to know it would get friggin cold at 6 a.m.? Why was I cycling at this hour anyway? Oh, yes, I was proving something although hadn't proved my insanity, just yet!

I drove to the start of the race, the Horizon Resort in Stateline, and prepared myself. This was an organized ride so there were plenty of rest stops at certain locations along the way. I left Horizon with some other cyclists around 6:30am. The sun was climbing higher over the east face of the lake but parts of the west face leading to switchbacks towards Emerald Bay were sheltered by trees. It was cold and it took some time for my fingers and toes to defrost.

I climbed the steep switchbacks to the flat portion on top of Emerald Bay Road, Highway 89, and I was feeling good. To the left I noticed a sign indicating 'Photographer Ahead.' I guess one is supposed to smile or wave but I just looked as I continued pedaling. I would use this photograph later when I finish the ride, I thought. I already knew for what.

I stopped in various rest stops, took a quick lunch at King's Beach and then headed east on Lake Shore Drive in Incline Village towards a right turn onto Highway 28 for the ten-mile climb up Spooner Summit. This was not a steep climb but it was long, as I was finding out. My body was beginning to ache and I was growing tired. My muscles were burning at a high rate. My right foot was aching because it was doing most of the pushing up mountains. My ass hurt, my back hurt from being hunched over for so long. Basically my whole body was being beaten to death.

As Alfred Lord Tennyson wrote in his poem Charge of the Light Brigade, "Into the valley of death rode the 600." I was beginning to feel like I was riding through the valley of death, although this was self-inflicted and not some ill-conceived order knowingly given by a Light Brigade officer. As I climbed Spooner, a couple of cyclists passed me, talking to each other. I wondered how the hell they had the breadth and energy to do that.

As I approached the top of Spooner after an arduous pull, my wife passed me, driving with her friend in the opposite direction. I was not expecting that. We had not talked since returning from Germany. I know she did not understand my desire to beat the crap out of my body on a bike, but I had hoped she would care that it was important to me.

She occasionally would pass me when I was on training rides. "Why do you ride so fast?" was all she ever asked. For reasons I never understood, she wanted nothing to do with my cycling heroics. She should have been proud of her husband but she never was. In business, it was the same. I had built up my company from nothing to an internationally recognized and respected scientific company. It was a reputation that I fought very hard to attain. Not once did she ever recognize my accomplishments.

In any event, she saw me near the top of Spooner and quickly turned the car around. There was a rest stop at the top and we met up there.

"I did not expect to see you here," was about all I could muster in conversation. I had no energy to say anything else.

"I wanted to see how you were doing," she said.

There is more to this story, I would learn years later. At the time of this ride, she had already signed on with a lawyer. Perhaps her showing up was to hide the fact she was contemplating divorce.

In any event, I needed to get back on the bike so I could finish. I wasn't being rude to her. I had no energy to talk. I needed to finish but the most important reason was I didn't want my muscles or my damaged knee to cool down. If I stayed too long chatting, I would not be able to get going again.

I turned right out of the rest stop and then took the right feeder road onto Highway 50. It was all downhill now into South Lake Tahoe, or so I thought. It was wishful thinking. It may have seemed like downhill in a car but any change in topography impacted the force and energy required to pedal.

Downhill was easy but sometimes the gradient was steep so downhill was dangerous if speeds were not controlled. Going 50 mph on a bike with one-inch wide wheels was hairy. Immense concentration was required because hitting a stone, rock, or rodent at high speed could spell disaster. It would put a rider in hospital.

As I approached a few miles from the finish line, I was gathered around seven other cyclists. We had a small peloton going. I had migrated or fallen (depending on one's perspective) to the back because I was almost done, physically. Fortunately, the motivational pull was strong from those in front to keep going. Cyclists, I was finding out, are such an encouraging group.

We turned right onto Lake Parkway West going behind Horizon Casino. As the road looped left behind the parking lot, we all turned left into the lot one behind the other. As we went through the finish line one at a time, I heard someone counting

"25th, 26th, 27th....". Then the lady looked at me. "28th".

Wow, I had completed the longest ride of my life from the lowest point of my life in only three and a half months. I doubt anyone expected me to finish 28th. I know I did not.

I looked at the computer attached to my handlebars. I had completed 72 miles circumnavigating Lake Tahoe in four hours forty minutes. I beat the cyclist's time in June's ride by five minutes. I did what I said I would do. I set a goal and I accomplished it.

As I discarded the bike next to my car and walked over to the food and drink offered at the end of the race, a young kid came up and shook my hand. I wore a yellow Tour de France jersey, which to him signified that I had won the event.

"Congratulation," he said. "I want to shake the hand of the winner."

"Well, err, thank you."

I didn't want to disappoint him. I didn't want to discourage his enthusiasm by going into a long explanation. He did shake the hand of a winner. The hand just wasn't from the winner of this cycling event.

Chapter 20

MY FRIEND, JUDY, was surviving longer than the doctors had initially told her. In early October 2004, a year after she had been diagnosed, she sent me an email requesting I come pick up the Sterling before she passed away. That was one of the hardest things I have done. I flew out on a Saturday, stayed overnight with her family in Phoenix and then prepared to drive Puck the 850 or so miles home to South Lake Tahoe. I met their daughter, to whom I promised I would restore her mother's cherished car. I waved goodbye knowing it would be the last time I would see Judy. I was driving her pride and joy away. I felt physically sick.

I found Route 60 and headed northwest out of Phoenix. I passed through a small town called Wickenburg and followed signs for Route 93. Ten miles out in the middle of nowhere coolant sprays from under the hood and splashes against the windshield. Well, shit!! It wasn't good when coolant is external to the engine's closed-loop cooling system. Defeats the purpose, so knew I had to pull over fast.

I stood by the side of the road because there was no phone signal. Fifteen or so minutes later a guy in a beat up truck shows up and pulls over.

"Need help?" he inquires, very politely.

"Yes. A main hose burst and I don't have cell signal to call AAA".

"I will drive you back into Wickenburg and you can call from there." He went on, "I needed help when a truck broke down and someone helped me, so it is a pleasure doing the same."

"Thank you. You are very kind," and then I explained the history behind the car and why I was here.

It was getting dark and light was deteriorating. I was concerned something else would happen to the car but also wondered if AAA would ever find it. We entered Wickenburg and he pulled over in front of a motel. I checked in and called AAA, but not before I was told at which auto shop to drop off the car. It was just down the road from the motel so I arranged with AAA to meet me there once they picked up the car.

That taken care of, I had an hour or so at least before AAA would contact me and I needed something to eat. I walked to McDonalds next to the motel, ordered food (or their interpretation of food) and took it back to the room. New York Yankees were playing Boston Red Sox in the playoffs. The Red Sox were down 3-0 in the series and game 4 was playing that evening.

I knew we had a new hose on another Sterling in Tahoe. The one driven by my brother from Atlanta a few years earlier suffered the same fate. So I would have a mechanic remove it and ship it out the following day. This meant I would be in Wickenburg at least until Tuesday. I eventually had two hoses shipped, one brand new from Atlantic British. The mechanic in Wickenburg installed the second hose (the one shipped from Tahoe failed) but before driving 850 miles home, I drove it around for a few miles and then took it back to see if it was ok. It wasn't. The hose was designed with a temperature sensor glued into it. The glue had melted as the coolant water had warmed up and the sensor was falling out already. It was now Wednesday and I had been here since Saturday and sick of it. I walked over to a local hardware store, bought some epoxy and cable ties, glued the damn sensor in, placed cable ties around it and then went back to the hotel to let it set overnight. I got up that Thursday morning and drove home in one day. That was my nightmare in Wickenburg. I spent six long, awful days there. Wickenburg would come up a few years later when my family lawyer asked if I wanted to save my marriage. I laughed when he brought up a marriage counseling centre in Wickenburg. I had no intention of going back there.

Chapter 21

TOUR DE TAHOE in September 2004 was a magnificent achievement. In three months, I had gone from nearly dead, mentally and physically, to having the strength and stamina to do something I had never done before. Through chronic and adverse conditions, under emotional and psychological destruction, I had trained, and trained hard. I had a goal, and a part of my psych had to set a goal and go for it.

After that ride I had continued cycling into the winter, until the roads were too difficult or impossible to cycle. It was tough to cycle in the snow. If the snow had melted, the side of the road was covered in grit from the snow plows and sanders. All this crap got pushed there which made it very, very dangerous through winter months, even if the weather permitted it.

During my multiple recoveries, I had watched the Tour de France on television. It is one of the most grueling sporting event in the world. The cyclists are machines. They need to push the limits of endurance and mental toughness, exerting pain and suffering on their bodies beyond anything comprehensible. Watching was the easy part. Watching the speeds they reached up the steep gradients was something to behold. I thought it looked easy, until I started to climb up mountain passes. The higher altitudes provide less oxygen. Higher the mountain pass, the less the oxygen content in the available air. As it gets thinner, these athletes push themselves up huge mountain passes, their lungs burning no matter how fit they are. I garnered more appreciation for what these cyclists put their bodies through when I started to train up large mountain passes. I was also about to appreciate the efforts required for endurance cycling.

During the recovery months, and years, I watched Discovery Health Channel a lot. There were several programs about how people's lives were changed by a single event, events that typically came out of the blue. I would lay in bed, watching these people tell how they overcame adversity, how they survived and how they dealt with the aftermath. I wished the show had covered more of their emotional state of mind. With such trauma to the human body comes massive emotional and psychological turmoil. The body goes through a chemical change in which emotions are difficult or impossible to control. I was experiencing that side of it.

My father had a massive stroke when he was only 58, which affected the left side of his body. I would see him try to hide his crying whilst watching movies. It did not matter if they were bad scenes or happy ones. The overwhelming emotional struggle was real. I did not understand that about him until after my surgeries. I wished that I had known back then, while he was still alive. I would have understood him so much better and I could have talked openly and perhaps helped him. I could have better prepared my mother and sister.

All my surgeries had changed me. People, and their hardships, became so much clearer to me. I would just say hello or how are you doing or how is your day to anyone. Just reaching out with those simple words can change a person's day. It would change mine if someone said any of those things to me.

In spring 2005, one of Marina's brother-in-laws approached me with an offer I could not believe and could not refuse. My wife and I were close with her sister and her husband, Douglas. We had been on a Caribbean cruise together in the summer of 2002 after I had endured two massive surgeries.

Douglas was a cyclist. Throughout his youth, he had aspirations of cycling across the US and doing tours down the west coast. He called me in September, right after I had finished the Tour de Tahoe, to find out if I had finished and to congratulate me when I told him I had.

That's when he asked me to train with him for the June 2006 AIDS Lifecycle ride, a mammoth seven-day, 550-mile charity ride from San Francisco to Los Angeles

Douglas had been through medical hell of his own with major heart by-pass surgery. Despite his medical setbacks, he was a keen cyclist. He had recently purchased a touring bike, which he was eager to ride. His touring bike was much heavier and built for carrying equipment. Mine was strictly a racing machine and lightweight.

"Come on, it will be fun," Douglas said unconvincingly. "At least try it," he added, sounding even more implausible!

Man-o-man, 550 miles sounded like a long way. How the hell could I do that with only one good leg?

But there it was, the important factor in recuperating from surgeries. Like the Nike advertisements suggest 'Just Do It'. That was the hammer on the head. I did not have any sanity left so that was one thing I could not lose.

Weather-wise, training for the Tour de Tahoe was relatively easy. The weather in the mountains in summer was incredible so I was not working hard under cold, wet, miserable conditions. But training for the AIDS ride would be something else, I would soon find out.

In the summer of 2005, I started training hard. I would train along routes I was familiar with. Notably Luther Pass, Carson Pass, North Upper Truckee, along Highway 50, Emerald Bay Road. Then I decided to add Monitor Pass on Highway 89.

I drove out to Markleeville and parked my car there. I prepared myself not knowing anything about this mountain. Markleeville was five or so miles from the bottom of Monitor Pass so I theorized that it would allow my muscles to warm up before trying the climb. What did I know? I didn't. I had no idea how big this mountain is.

The road from Markleeville meandered along the side of a river, which was on my right as I cycled out. The terrain wasn't flat and had a few minor ascents and descents before I reached Highways 89/4 junction. Left would take me up the west face of Monitor Pass so I took it. I entered a narrow gorge that the road cut through. On the right was a shallow ravine, the bottom of which was a small stream. The road was narrow and twisty but the gradient remained very manageable. It stayed this way for about a mile and a half. Then I took a slight left turn and the gorge opened up. The road was planted on the left side of the mountain but I looked up and saw where the road was headed. It crossed a ravine and then curved to the right as it headed upwards.

The road was chiseled into the side of the mountain so one side was protected. On the right side as I looked up I saw the embankment drop off into the aforementioned ravine, which had now grown in size and depth. But the gradient was changing drastically. It is tough sometimes to get a read on the slope without any visual aids. There weren't any here. Very little vegetation lined the road and what did had been beaten to death by strong mountain winds. Branches bent every which way.

Confirmation of how steep the pass had become registered in my legs as the energy and strength required increased precipitously, along with a corresponding decrease in speed. The road bent around to the right and I was looking straight up a small section of it. Jesus! As with Luther Pass when I first scaled it, I was left to turn around after climbing a short distance. I could not do it. This was steep and my muscles through the 2004/2005 winter had deteriorated. I had installed a rear-wheel trainer in my bedroom for winter but it was hugely boring and was not motivating. Because of that, I had lost significant strength. Now I was having to rebuild it.

A week later I drove out to try Monitor Pass again. This time I climbed two miles up the slope before turning around. This mountain was huge but perhaps some psychology was at play here. My head was losing a battle it wasn't prepared for.

For the third week in a row, I went out to conquer Monitor Pass. This time I got past a very steep section. Just over three miles up, the road banked to the left as it hugged the side of the mountain. As I cycled around, I saw the gradient change up ahead. That gave me the motivation required to continue on. Now my head was in control and I pressed upwards. As I traversed an animal crossing painted onto the road, the gradient halved as the road banked to the right. I continued on. Four and a half miles into the climb the mountains opened up and I reached an amazing vista. I could now see for miles. I was approaching a height at which most of the Sierra mountains stopped. It was stunning.

I looked off into the distance and saw what looked like the road continuing up the mountain pass. Holy smokes, is that where I am going? I asked myself. I had reached an area where the road went downwards for a few hundred yards or so but then it immediately pointed up and went straight up, snaking its way up the side of the mountain.

After some nourishment, fluids and a short rest, I continued on my quest to conquer my insanity. However, as with Luther Pass a year earlier, once passed the half-way mark, it felt easier to peddle. It might have been psychological but the gradient was a little different which helped. It was steep, around eight percent, but it wasn't ten percent or more, like it was at the lower level. My muscles were pounding and burning on the steeper slope so they were ready for the lesser gradient in earnest. Climbing higher I reached another incredible vista looking west over the huge mountain ranges. I pressed upwards. Three and a half miles more climbing, another short steep gradient change where it peaked at 12 percent and I reached what I thought was the top of Monitor Pass.

It wasn't. The mountain had two peaks and I had reached the first one. I had to drop down into a shallow valley before climbing up the other side. My legs were burning but I was energized. And there it was, the sign that read: Monitor Pass 8314 feet. This was the highest mountain pass I had ever climbed. I was setting goals and I was achieving them. I was getting prepared for the greatest challenge of my life.

Since Douglas lived in South San Francisco, it would necessitate me driving down to the Bay Area often as winter approached. The

UPHILL

AIDS organizers also set up training days so people could train together. I would drive down and meet Douglas to do training rides. I
needed to get miles on my legs. But the Bay Area can be very cold,
especially near the Pacific Ocean.

I was not aware that cycling in the cold would create serious problems for me until I started training. I would cycle 50 miles, drive home
and get really sick with flu-like symptoms. I think it was a side effect
of the surgeries. I also wondered if the chemicals (copious amounts
of anesthesia and drugs) had affected my immune system. Training for
the AIDS ride became a serious problem but it never deterred me. In
essence, I was driving four hours (225 miles) to do a 50-mile training
ride in wet, damp, cold, foggy conditions and then driving four hours
back home. The conditions reminded me of Hull in England. I gave
up training back then. This time I wasn't going to do that.

Following the training rides, I would be sick for days. When I had
recuperated somewhat, I would do the exact same thing again. Each
time though the rides got longer. Each time I would return home and
get sick. I knew this was dangerous but I wanted to train. Soon the
training ride was 75 miles, the longest ride in my cycling career. It
was exciting to push the boundaries so I trained harder and harder.

I was still learning how cycling works, why the correct clothing
was so important, how the angles on the bike needed to be correct
and what were the essential requirements for proper shoes. I would
be taught a valuable lesson later but for the moment, I just kept training and pushing.

On one training ride, I was heading towards a group of cyclists
approaching a left turn at a light. Novices wore special clothing so I
knew they were learning. It was a T intersection and we had merged
into a left turn lane. I had to be careful because of my knee but also
I wanted to limit how many times I needed to stop and remove the
shoe from the pedal clips. Even as I cranked all these miles, I was doing so with limitations and concerns. As I saw the light turn orange, I
peddled faster in an attempt to beat the light. Unfortunately, the nov-
ice in front thought orange meant 'slow down and stop'. As I pushed,

118

she stopped right in front of me. I had to energize my fingers so fast on the brakes not to hit her. The more cyclists on the road, especially ones who had not ridden before, the more dangerous it became for me. I had to be more vigilant because I was taking serious risks.

I built up strength through early 2006, but I was still getting sick. That was something I had no control over unless I did not train, and that wasn't an option.

As the ride week approached, first full week of June, I was getting anxious and nervous. I drove down to stay with Douglas on the Saturday before we set off. I removed my bag, which was rather large, from the car. Douglas looked at me in astonishment.

"What is all in there Geoff? We don't require a kitchen sink. Cooking and food are provided," he said, laughing his head off.

"I tried to limit the essentials," I said laughing along with him. "However, we needed a roll-up mattress, sleeping bag, pillow, clothing."

"Pillow?"

"I have to have my essentials," I said.

Joking aside, I did need my essentials. The body had been beaten up and I would need comfort for sleeping at night.

"Why do you need cologne?" he asked.

I was perplexed.

"Why wouldn't I?"

"We are going to be cycling long distances and we will be grimy" he added.

Being sweaty, grimy, dirty, cycling through rain and immense heat, being lathered in road dust and mineral-laced water wasn't the point. My father wore cologne every day and I worked with a gentleman during my university years that seemed to bathe in the stuff. Both men smelt really good. It was a part of me.

"I know all that," I said. "However, if I crash and head to the hospital, I want to smell good for the hospital nursing staff. Women like men to smell nice."

Clearly Douglas thought I was crazy and just looked at me with a quizzical expression on his face.

"Why so many clothes?" he asked.

"I need seven outfits for the seven days. I don't want to wear sweaty, grimy, smelly clothes on consecutive days. Who knows where we can wash them anyway, or if we can even?"

Add that to the camping gear for comfort, other necessities and clothing for evenings after cycling and the bag had indeed filled up. I had purchased cycling outfits off ebay. I went for pro-cycling clothes and I wanted complete kits. That was me. Cycling under immense incalculable adversity is one thing, but doing so while being well dressed gave me confidence beyond any measure. Looking good added to the feel-good ambience and that was hugely important. This was going to be an immense challenge and any advantage or psychological boost I would take.

My wife had commented on all the clothing I had purchased because of the cost. She took zero interest in this ride and zero interest in the effort and work I put in training for it. It meant nothing for her to see her husband crawl out of the clinical cesspit. I had achieved so much already, but she said nothing. She didn't even say goodbye when I left for the Bay Area on the Saturday before the ride. It was sad and I felt so alone. Once again I was doing this all by myself.

Saturday afternoon Douglas and I drove to the Cow Palace to register for the ride. The bikes were locked and left for departure Sunday. The first leg of the ride would start at the Cow Palace in San Francisco and end in Santa Cruz. Each day, the race organizers would transport our luggage to next destination, ready for pickup when we arrived. It was simply incredible. Huge mess tents would be laid out with the food at each destination camp site.

When we started the ride, news crews and cameras were at the start line. People were being interviewed and big crowds had gathered. It was a media circus. This was a huge ride which, in the end, taught me a staggering amount about cycling, about myself, about pain levels, about concentration and determination, about completing goals.

The bad thing for me was that I put enormous amount of pressure on myself. I entered this ride not understanding the magnitude of it. 550 miles is a fucking long way on a cycle and I had zero concept of what punishment the body would take. I entered the charity ride not to 'do what I can' but to finish it, to complete the ride. Failure in any goal I set for myself was not an option.

Douglas was slower than me. That was an issue. I needed to get into a cadence that was comfortable for me. Too slow was no good because rhythm is important. However, I did not want to leave him behind.

About five miles into the ride, we passed someone already banged up and bloody. I was not expecting that. He evidently hit a pothole on the San Francisco streets. It was easy to do. Never having ridden in a huge group like this before, I was beginning to take note how danger-ous and complex it was. One had to be vigilant at all times because cyclists were so close together, just packed in. One could not see the road underneath before it is too late, as evidenced by the bloody cyclist. I was very nervous.

Later, I was coming down Highway 93 towards Highway 1 inter-section for our first rest stop at Half Moon Bay. The road was busy, which meant cyclists were pushed against the road's curb. I suddenly freaked out as the narrow front wheel of my bike entered a trough formed by a crack in the road surface. I thought I was going to come off. But a few seconds of panic ended when I navigated the wheel out. That was close, I thought, as my heart rate started to subside. I had been going downhill pretty fast. The rest stop was close to the intersection on Highway 1, and as I got down the bottom of the hill, I made a left turn and then a right into the rest stop parking lot. As I dropped the bike off at the staging area, I saw a cyclist sitting on a bench who apparently had not navigated the narrow trough as well as I had. He was bloodied up. Luckily medical teams were there to assist.

Arriving in Santa Cruz late afternoon, we had covered around 84 miles. We grabbed our tents and bags which had been coded and walked to the nearby field to put the tent up. Dinner was incredible. It was phenomenal how this was all catered.

The next day on the ride, I found my rear tyre deflating at the first rest stop, fifteen miles in. I was anxious, which did not help any. This was going to be a long day because we were covering 110 miles from Santa Cruz to King City. I had never done a century ride, which added to my nervousness and anxiety considerably.

I changed the tyre, but for some reason found the next 20 miles a real slog. Not only that, Douglas was quicker than me. He was climbing small hills faster.

"Have you laced your coffee this morning?" I asked.

"No." he replied, laughing.

Clearly I was struggling this section and had no idea why. It wasn't until I reached the second rest stop and dismounted the bike that I knew. I had not properly secured the quick-release wheel clip after replacing the rear inner tube. The damn wheel had moved and the tyre was rubbing against the rear stay. In other words, I had cycled 50 miles instead of 20.

After a lunch stop, we had huge tail winds. This was good until we took left or right turns and became perpendicular to those winds. I had to lean into it to stop being blown off my bicycle. It made the final 20 miles incredibly fast as we sailed straight to King City. My muscles were burning and my body was aching but I had completed my first century ride. My feet were getting sore and tired, and my ass was amassing sores.

I really did not know how to cycle properly and the sores on my ass were getting worse. On day three, the ride from King City to Paso Robles was a relatively short 65 miles. The pain I was inflicting upon myself was getting worse. Arriving at the camp late afternoon, I was exhausted and in agony. My feet were hurting and my muscles were incredibly sore. After talking to cycling veterans, I found out that days two and three are the worst because one is punishing the body so hard. I found out I should not be wearing cotton underwear under cycling bib shorts. The sores were from the cotton getting drenched and then not being able to dry out. The expensive cycling shorts have leather cushions and pads which whisk the moisture away from the body to prevent this from happening. The tight material also helps keep the muscles in place, which also makes a huge difference. For the next four days I would need to find a spot on the saddle and keep my ass fixed so that the pain would subside. I would shift around until I reached a more comfortable position. It was awful and immensely detrimental. I was in pain the next four days.

The other thing I loathed were the racing shoes. My feet were becoming very painful. The rigid shoes made walking around rest stops almost impossible by the third day.

In the end, I had to remove my shoes to walk. The cleats were hard to walk on because they extruded from the bottom of the shoe and so the foot pointed upwards. I was in serious pain. The orientation from the surgical procedures had changed the articulation off the knee. It functioned differently because of the angles it now exhibited. I did not know at the time but my knee needed to be flexible and the foot being rigid in racing shoes prevented this from happening. Not only did I have painful sores on my ass, but the pain in my feet was amplified by the lack of flexibility in the shoes and pedals and because my right leg was doing most of the work. It was a double-whammy. I was immensely uncomfortable for much of the final four days of cycling.

Day four was another century ride. Well, they called it a century but it was 96 miles. Close enough!

The big thing that changed on the fourth day was my muscle aches, aside from the sore ass and painful feet. The muscles aches were diminishing. My body was adjusting to the punishment and doing what it needed to do to compromise. To add credence to this, day five was the easiest day and the shortest. From Santa Maria to Lompoc was 43 miles but I covered those in three and a half hours, including a big rest stop.

My muscles were pounding the rotational momentum and felt incredible. I did not expect this after 400 miles. I thought I would be on a stretcher by now. My ass was still sore, as well as my feet, but I guess I was adjusting to that too. I arrived at the camp on day five before the trucks carrying the essential supplies did. I had to wait around for the tent.

The final day I was feeling quite good, considering. Friday we camped on a beach at Ventura and had a ceremony for all those affected by the AIDS virus. It was quite moving. We left early morning Saturday and then headed north along the Pacific Coast Highway.

Standing in line to use the Port-o-Pot at one of the rest stops, a gentleman and presumably his son approached me. The younger man wore a Cinelli cycling jersey.

"Are you Geoff with the classic Cinelli cycle?" the older gentleman asked.

I was surprised.

"Yes, that is me."

They both started laughing.

"We were told the story from your friend Douglas," who was off in the distance laughing at me, I could see.

It was an interesting story but I didn't think others would find it amusing. My wife positively didn't at the time.

When we lived in Novato I had walked passed a Thrift store and found a classic '80's Cinelli bicycle hanging in the window. I ventured into the store and was taking a quick gander when the store owner approached me.

"That is a classic cycle and worth a lot of money. It has high-end Italian components on it."

He was being patronizing and condescending so I joined in using the same vernacular.

"I am fully aware of what it is. I used to work in a cycle shop in England. The Campagnolo components were top of the line back in those days but not anymore," I said. "Would you consider a trade for the bike?"

I was staring at a beautiful bike. It was like an old Ferrari or some other classic car. In the cycling world, a Cinelli was a classic and I was interested in it. I was back to trading for bikes like I had in England.

"My wife doesn't like our furniture in the home anymore. It is aging and she wants to upgrade."

"I will take furniture."

I told him what we had and then gave him an address where to find me. The following afternoon he came over to my home and we negotiated the terms of the trade. Admittedly the furniture was old and we had purchased most of it soon after getting married. It was showing its age. However, I am not sure she expected me to get rid of it without first buying replacements. I mean, it wasn't as if I had planned this ahead of time. It was purely instinctual, facts I thought would be beneficial in my favour.

My wife returned home to a house devoid of furniture. The sofa, coffee table and aging dining room set were all gone. She was livid and even more so when I showed her the Cinelli. She obviously didn't get it but the bike was a piece of art, I tried to explain. The futility was palpable.

A few days later, there was a knock on the door and she answered it. A police officer was standing there. It wasn't me, I told her.

"The person who bought your furniture lives up the hill across the street from you." He said. "It has been stolen. Do you know anything about it?"

Marina was pissed at this point.

"Why would we know anything about it, officer?" she said.

After the officer left, she looked at me with patronizing eyes, obviously not happy.

"So there is a God!" she said as she walked passed with disdain in the hallway.

What I did not mention was that we frequented furniture auctions a week or so later and bought some stunning Chinese hand-carved rosewood furniture. I made up for my seemingly selfish indiscretion.

Douglas had evidently told the men this story and they were still laughing when they turned and walked away.

We continued on the final day's ride up through Malibu and into the VA Centre on Wilshire Boulevard in Los Angeles. There was one last traffic light before we turned left into the Centre, but I could not stop. The pain and the desire to get off the bike were now almost intolerable and so I ensured the intersection was clear, except for an on-coming car I purposely chose to ignore (I knew I could beat it, hopefully, if I could muster the strength), and then navigated the left turn. Other cyclists were shouting but I could not stop. Douglas was laughing at me but I honestly could not stop. I needed to finish and get off the bike.

The feeling of euphoria enveloped me as I crossed the finish line. I could not believe it. Through staggering pain levels, through immense surgical procedures, through a complication that nearly trashed my rear leg muscle, through unbelievable anguish and personal hardships, through turmoil and complete suffering, I had cycled 550 miles. I had tears in my eyes. This was an immense personal achievement from any perspective. In seven days I had accomplished something quite staggering. I was emotionally drained and physically exhausted.

I pulled into the bike staging area, dragging my bike with me. I had no energy. As I did I heard another cyclist talk about his seven surgeries as he struggled to get off the bike. That's what made this ride life-changing. I saw people on whom I did not think could even ride a bike. They were big, overweight but were pushing themselves to raise money for people they did not know, or perhaps did know. I saw riders who had the AIDS virus with special flags on the bikes to let people know. These people were stricken with a virus that would likely kill them. The whole ride was mind-boggling and humbling. I witnessed humanity at its best.

I had called a taxi which took me to a high-end hotel. It was the closest Hertz car rental place. Affluent people looked down on me, as I was walking around in bright, tight cycling clothes, pushing a bike through the lobby of the hotel. I was sweaty, grimy, dirty, likely smelled, sticky and probably looked like hell. I did not care. They looked with disdain. I spent eighteen months on crutches and two years in physical therapy so that I could do this. Go fuck yourselves, I thought. I had just cycled to raise money for people I will never meet, as well as for my own personal rewards.

I walked to the car rental counter, grabbed the keys to the rental I had made a few weeks earlier and drove out of Los Angeles on the 405 North. I was heading home totally spent. My aching feet and sores on my posterior were something else. It was glorious agony.

When I arrived back home Sunday, no one greeted me. The children were gone and I didn't know where my wife was. What a serious anti-climax to the week's events. I was saddened. It was a massive fall from the euphoria I felt the previous afternoon. The highs and lows, the huge peaks and troughs, they were beginning to escalate in size.

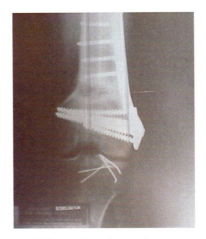

**Taken after the cadaver
meniscus implant in June 2003**

Preparing for a training ride in Tahoe

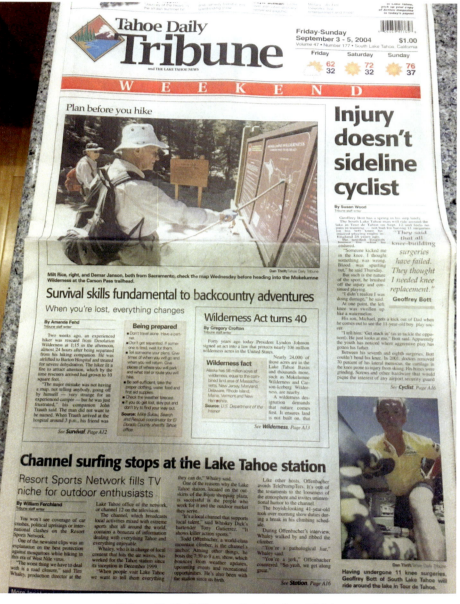

Tahoe Daily Tribune, September 2004

Training ride in San Francisco

Puck, given to me by my friend Judy who passed away from lung cancer

SECTION 3

Chapter 22

IT WAS FRIDAY 13th October 2006, when I had my 12th knee surgery. My surgeon asked if I would be bothered by the date. No, I said, what possibly could be worse than what had already transpired?

Nothing, I thought, nothing at all.

All I knew was my knee was failing and I needed to get it fixed now. What I did not know at the time was that my marriage was also failing, and with it, I was losing my children and my business.

"Another surgery?" asked one doctor. "Why are you doing this to yourself? More surgery is just going to be detrimental. You must be addicted."

But I knew my body very well and I knew there was a problem.

After eleven surgeries, the doctors and medical staff had learnt the hard way that I knew what I was talking about. If I said something was wrong, they now listened. Something was wrong and I could clearly feel it. Perhaps also it was psychological. There had been so many complications and failures up to this point that perhaps I could sense in my psyche something was wrong. Whatever the reason, I knew something wasn't right and I needed to find out what.

The surgery was relatively minor, compared to the last five, but when the surgeon got in there the news was bad. This surgery was supposed to be simple. It wasn't.

I had yet another procedure called microfracture, which helps stimulate cartilage growth and avoid arthritis. Small holes are drilled into the femoral ball and then it is fractured to draw blood to the surface. The blood brings essential oxygen to stimulate some growth.

But drilling holes in one's knee causes the bone and joint to ache like hell. That I expected. What I didn't expect was what the surgeon discovered. Dr. Randy Watson, the world-renowned surgeon at Lake Tahoe who agreed to repair my knee, was speechless and clearly upset. He was an exceptional doctor and we had been through hell together. He took my case, as with all his cases, personally. He saw the anguish and pain in my eyes when he delivered the news.

My knee had rejected the cadaver meniscus inserted three years earlier. It had rejected the implant by dissolving it: 90% of it. The meniscus was gone. It had just disappeared. There weren't even remnants of it left. The dissolved cadaver meniscus was proof that I had rejected the second knee rebuild. My knee was lost. Five re-build surgeries including three corrective procedures, eighteen months on crutches and two full years of physical therapy were all lost. Months of pain after each surgery, and then working hard to get back to the point that I could pump my bike through miles of mountain passes and backroads. I had worked so incredibly hard. God, I worked hard. I started to cry. I was emotionally destroyed. I knew this was the end.

I was only 43! How could I cycle 550 miles on a seven-day charity ride in June and have no knee in October?

I was so proud of the fact I had done things on my bike that no one, none of my doctors or friends, thought possible five months earlier. That obsessive focus, pushing through searing pain with the calming cadence of the bicycle as my reward, was the "drug" that got me through a five-year nightmare. From the surgeon in 2001 telling me to find a doctor close to home because, as he put it, "you are going to need help" to Dr. Orr telling me later in 2001 the knee "is shot". Then Dr Bannar in 2002 scheduling to replace the knee only to change his mind because I was simply too young and active. Then Dr. Watson performing femoral osteotomies in 2002 and 2003 which, as it turned out, is a staggeringly invasive surgical procedure. I endured not one, but two of these, and a complication that nearly lost me my rear leg muscle. During the cadaver implant in June 2003, there was damage to the main nerve which caused me to scream in pain. Then there were three years in physical therapy, with the final two being contiguous, three days a week when I was not traveling.

All that was lost. My body dissolved the cadaver. What was there left to do? Gut-wrenching in the extreme, I was lost and so very depressed. I knew recovering from this surgery was going to be bad, I just did not know how bad.

After so many surgeries, I knew I would be addicted to narcotic pain medication again. That had become normal. I needed medication to numb the throbbing in the joint and to reduce the pain from having a scalpel knife scrape away excess debris and scar tissue. The pain of each surgery was something else, but the depressive side of surgery after surgery deepened the desire for narcotics even more. I needed Vicodin to sleep at night, or at least I thought I did.

Even disciplining myself to take one per day, I knew it was enough to become addicted. Every time I was cleared for surgery, I knew I would have the problem of getting off the drugs afterwards. Narcotics are mind-numbing, affecting my personality, decisions, thoughts, daily life, abilities to function. In addition the medication would cause dizziness and drowsiness. I could not drive in this condition. I could not do much in this condition. When taken long term, the drugs made me short tempered, anxious and depressed.

I took Vicodin mostly to sleep but waking up was awful. The drug-induced hangover felt like I had been drinking all night and I left me feeling like shit for most of the morning. The withdrawal symptoms were simply terrible. Uncontrollable shaking, even in high-altitude summer heat. The chills and fever cycles. Nausea and vomiting, cravings, anxiety, depression, restlessness, bone and muscle pain beyond that which I was already experiencing. It was the discipline, the strength, but mostly the desire to overcome, that I needed to withdraw from drug addiction.

I hated the drugs, but they sent me off into a different world. The drowsiness enveloped me and allowed me to drift away, forgetting reality. They were an escape, even as I hated what they did to me.

Sometimes I needed the escape.

The recent news that my knee had failed hit me hard. But it did not matter. I only had the weekend to recover. I owned my own company and still had to manage the work.

Going back to work was its own nightmare. Just a day or two before the surgery, my PhD chemist from Taiwan gave me notice. I had hired him three years earlier from a university client to operate our isotope ratio mass spectrometer (IRMS) in our lab. But now he wanted to go home. It was a critical position in our company, one not easily replaced. When I moved to the US from England, I had met a world-renowned geochemist whilst working on his mass spectrometer at a major oil company. In 1993, this gentleman asked if I wanted to collaborate. He had left the energy giant a year earlier and had started a new venture. So we did. In 2002, he approached me about expanding the work into stable isotopes. That required a different instrument costing some $175,000. There was already a huge contract from Pemex, Mexico, so we had invested in the equipment and hired the PhD chemist from a client in Taiwan to operate it. IRMS was new technology for the task our company had been asked to do. Unknown to us at the time, it was new to the rest of the world as well. Our chemist was one of the few that knew how to use it because he was incredibly gifted and taught himself.

I was not involved with the day-to-day operation of the instrument. Nor the data production and processing. I knew nothing about it. For the past five years, I had been focused on trying to walk again and build my life back. That took precedence over learning anything new. I left the analytical work to our chemist. So when he left, I had a big problem.

The Monday after my life-changing Friday, the 12th surgery, my primary task was to learn how to operate an instrument I knew nothing about. Then I needed to process data I did not know how to process. Then I had to present that information in software I did not know how to use. And all of this data was vital to energy companies around the world. Screwing up was not an option.

Chapter 23

WHEN I ENTERED my office early Monday 4th December, 2006, my head was spinning. I was heading to Venezuela on Friday and I had that amount of time to figure out the complicated IRMS system. I was recovering from the 12th knee surgery and had just found out my knee had rejected the second rebuild. I was back in physical therapy again but that came to a sudden halt because I was experiencing yet another complication. I thought by this time in my life I could deal with most things that came at me. No longer being able to cycle was not one of them. I was a mess.

I settled in, answering emails, drinking coffee, trying to stay composed. My office manager, Caroline, who had been working for us since October 2003, called me to sign some papers. What could I possibly need to sign? I went upstairs and took a cursory glance at the file. It seemed to be a court filing of some sort.

Then I went numb. The color drained from my face.

My wife was filing for divorce.

Oh my God, this is not good. I had no idea this was coming. I started panicking. She was leaving me. I did not know what to do. Among other issues, my wife did the accounting for our companies. The loss of the chemist had an enormous impact on me personally, but now the business would be in turmoil.

There were many times in our 19+-year marriage when my wife closed up to me. In fact, she was there for me very little during those five tough years of surgeries. She seemed like an empty shell. Yet I was still stunned when she filed for divorce. The minute I got the divorce papers, I went home to see her. She did not want to talk about it. She had this 'condition' that shut her down and clamped her mouth. It was annoying, but occasionally useful if I did not want to talk to her either. But this time I needed to talk. This was serious stuff. I was completely exasperated. I could not handle this now. After all I had gone through, I really was not prepared mentally, psychologically or emotionally for this. I was torn to pieces.

But not talking was all I was going to get from her. I called my brother-in-law and asked him if I could save the marriage. That may have been the most ridiculous question I could have asked him. First he went silent, which told me everything I needed to know. Then he said, "Once she has financial security, then you can go back after her."

I was already aware that she cared only about money. It was a priority for her. I loved her but it was obvious to many she married me thinking I had money. Loss of the knee likely made her believe it was the end of the money train for her. Unfortunately, we had two wonderful teenage children and I just knew this divorce was going to be a mess simply because of the person involved.

When I signed for the divorce papers, I was embarrassed. I thought divorce would single me out. I did not know then that 60% of first marriages end in divorce. Statistics aside, I wanted to keep this divorce as quiet as possible. South Lake Tahoe is a very small town and word spreads fast. I picked up the Yellow Pages and thumbed through divorce attorneys. I found a guy who had a nice ad. His office looked good and he was dressed appropriately and looked professional. He offered a free consultation service to go over the options. He asked if I wanted to save the marriage. At the time, I did not know, but I asked what he could offer.

"There is a marriage counseling centre in Wickenburg," he said.

"Oh, I spent six days there a few years ago."

I was pretty sure I did not want to go back.

I signed an agreement with the attorney to represent me as my family divorce lawyer. Signing on turned out to be a huge mistake.

We agreed to meet up again when I returned home from Venezuela.

Chapter 24

I WAS HEADING down to Venezuela for the first time in my life. I had been invited by the national oil giant PDVSA to work on one of its huge mass spectrometers. The instrument had been sabotaged years earlier after PDVSA employees had gone on strike. Half the work force was eventually fired by then President Hugo Chavez, but no one thought to restrict their access to the facilities. For six months, their security access cards still worked and immense damage ensued. Now I was to fix their large scientific instrument.

I had to prepare for the visit but my brain was anywhere but there. I left Reno on Friday 8th December. It was a long, uncomfortable trip down involving three flights from Reno through Denver, Houston and then to Caracas. The Caracas flight was a red-eye leaving the very early hours of Saturday from Houston. It was awful and I was a mess and didn't sleep well. I was getting pretty sick. My knee throbbed and ached constantly. I could not ride a stationary bike because of another complication that likely would require more surgery to correct it. It still was painful from the healing process after October's surgery. The recent divorce filing and now another surgical complication. I was depleted.

It took a week after my latest surgery to get the leg bent far enough that I could get back on a stationary cycle. Once I could start cycling again I knew it would be the start of true recovery, whatever recovery meant after dissolving the meniscus. As I cycled, a part of the skin around the surgical incision got dragged into the knee. There was a large indentation. It was as if scar tissue had been trapped in the joint and as I rotated on the bike, it got pulled into the knee. The more revolutions, the further it got dragged in. Medical and PT staff would look at it and cringe. It was bizarre. I could only cycle for five or so rotations before I had to stop.

My knee aside, my wife had just filed divorce, and we worked together. My business was in a mess after our chemist departed in October. I was nowhere near ready for my trip and had not slept in days. I had done zero preparation for an international trip to a country I had never been to before. It was all just irrational chaos.

I arrived on Saturday 9th, late morning. I went through Immigration and Customs and then walked out into the arrival hall. A local cab driver saw I was a foreigner and he came over.

"Would you like a cab?" he kindly asked.

"No thank you," I replied. "I am being met by the client."

"Ok, would you like a beautiful woman? I can get you one."

That was my introduction to South America. I liked it already. I had a smile on my face, even if I felt pretty awful.

I was met by Stuart and his wonderful wife, Damaris. Stuart was English but his wife was from Venezuela. They met in England when the government paid for her overseas education. Part of her paid-for education required her to return home to Venezuela for at least two years after graduating. She had to work during that period and help repay her government debt for the education. They were married in England, and Stuart followed her. He was employed by PDVSA. It was a coincidence that worked out really well and we remain close friends today.

As we were driving out of the airport, I saw poverty on a level I had never seen before. Barrios, as they are known in Venezuela, were slums built up everywhere one looked. Yet I marveled at the people who lived in them. They always seemed clean, nicely dressed and happy.

I was booked into the Gran Melia Caracas, which was on the registry of The Finest Hotels in the World. There, surrounded by abject poverty was this magnificent, opulent hotel in a majestic setting in downtown Caracas. It was surreal. I entered the building and my mouth dropped.

After checking in and completely exhausted, I went directly to my room. I work well under pressure, I reminded myself, constantly. This time the pressure was amplified.

Stuart and Damaris picked me up the Sunday morning and took me to PDVSA's facility. There was a party going on. After that we visited an orphanage sponsored by the oil giant. I played soccer on the rooftop with young kids who had nothing. I didn't care about the knee. That seemed somewhat insignificant compared to what I was witnessing. It was sore and painful but these children seemed happy that someone wanted to play with them. I was putting things into more perspective. There also was a beautiful young lady from the US who volunteered there. I got chatting with her for a while.

Monday morning I was greeted by the driver from PDVSA. Stuart had provided me a few Spanish phrases during our time together Sunday. Using those phrases I was able to navigate my way around greetings and pleasantries with the driver.

We sped through the streets of Caracas and onto the road towards one of PDVSA's main laboratory facilities. Barrios were everywhere. People were living in shanty towns built up from concrete blocks. Concrete block houses built on top of concrete block houses, row after row. No windows, just blanket coverings and open doorways. Make-shift electrical connections on some, not all, as wires were strung haphazardly everywhere. No lawyers down here I guess! Presumably running water was there but I did not venture over to inquire. Staggering. Venezuela is poor and people have nothing but they took pride in dressing neatly. They looked happy for the most part.

America is so affluent. People have everything they could possibly want, but they pay little attention to details and are not generally happy. I had worked hard and was living the American dream but my wife was never happy. She always wanted more and more.

We lived in a huge 7,200 square foot home, with two bedroom suites and an indoor swimming pool, located on the fifth green of a local golf course overlooking Mount Tallac. Next to it sat a custom built guest house with a three-car garage we built to match the exterior of the main house. The contrast between how my family lived and how these poor souls lived was startling, and at different ends of the spectrum.

We wound our way out of Caracas, up a hill and towards the laboratory facility.

I spent five long days in the laboratory. I knew the instrument was in trouble but didn't know yet how much trouble. So, standing behind one of the stainless steel housings, I removed one of the flanges. I did not expect the blast of toxic fumes. I had removed hundreds of flanges before and this had never happened. It hit me in the face and I staggered backwards, hitting the wall behind me as I did so. The fumes entered my airway and I sucked them into my lungs.

Over the course of the week, working very hard, long hours, I grew progressively sicker. I got little sleep and I was pretty ill when I flew home the following Sunday. Again, the same long flights only reversed: Caracas to Houston, Houston to Denver and Denver to Reno. They were the worst flights I have ever taken. I got home exhausted and ill. I was in bad shape but I accomplished in Venezuela what I went out to do. For that, I had a great deal of pride.

My personal dilemma was exacerbated by the fact PDVSA employed beautiful ladies. Not only where they beautiful, they were friendly and warm. Despite being incredibly sick, I loved working with the Venezuelans. They were kind, generous and exuded a warm genuine hospitality.

The instrument was being cared for by two local chemists. One might still be the most beautiful lady I have ever worked with. She was funny and helpful, very down to earth, even if she did not understand very much English. I had picked up a few Spanish phrases, but they had nothing to do with science or instrumentation.

I always love foreign business travel for many obvious reasons but getting treated like royalty working in foreign countries is one of them.

Unfortunately, when one's wife files for divorce and one has to think things over, traveling to South America is not a good idea. I would not recommend flying to South America to save a marriage.

I was a foreigner from America. The English accent goes a long way in the scientific community so that helped enormously. My personal life was chaos but Stuart was immensely helpful and provided everything I needed to facilitate the workload.

Why did I need to be controlled by my wife anymore? I didn't need to be treated badly and I was tired of it. I didn't need the domestic crap anymore. I wanted to be treated the same way I treat others.

As soon as I arrived home, I went to visit my lawyer and told him I no longer wish to save my marriage. He looked bewildered but I had made the decision. There are too many wonderful women in this world. Enough was enough. I did not want to watch my wife chase the attention of other men anymore. I was done with it. That was a decision I have never regretted, even if it cost me more than money.

Chapter 25

GONE WERE MY knee and my marriage, and perhaps my children and business. My life was thrust into America's family court, which would turn out to be a bastion of incompetence, stupidity and ignorance. This was the first marriage for both of us, and I was about to get a taste of just how bad the American legal system is, a taste that would arrive very quickly. We had a scheduled court appearance late in December 2006. I had no idea what was going to happen. Little did I know that my lawyer was not about to tell me. Either he did not know what was going on or he did not care about me, his client. As it turned out, it was the latter. But then he was my lawyer and I had to trust him, at least at the beginning, until I knew better.

We arrived in court and as soon as the doors were opened, we entered the room. It was a standard US courtroom with the Plaintiffs' table and chairs to the left, the Defendants' set up on the right and on front of those off to the right was the judge's pulpit. The room was lined in what looked like fine mahogany wood paneling.

When it came time for our case, we were called. As I stepped toward the defendant's chair, a young lady called out my name. I looked over and saw she was a lady I had met weeks earlier, but could not remember where. I had momentarily forgotten her name but she shook my hand.

"What are you doing here?" she said.

"My wife has filed for divorce," I replied.

"I am sorry to hear it," she said but still smiling.

I looked over to my wife who was now pre-occupied with the conversation I was having with a very lovely, young lady. She was obviously wondering how I knew her.

She spent our entire marriage chasing the attention of other men but was always questioning me when I received attention from other women.

Court is all about procedural motions and nothing happens fast. Evidently, in America, it has written in fine print on every marriage license that the wife gets the house and the husband gets fucked. I missed that on our certificate. The judge asked some procedural questions including which person would move out of the family home, but he was addressing that rhetorical question at me.

In this case I was ordered out of the family home. The judge provided a date by which I had to be moved out. I was to move into the guest house that we had built, whether I wanted to or not. It was adjacent to the main house so I did not have to move far.

As we exited court, I ask my lawyer by what date would I have to be moved. My lawyer said the judge never gave a date. I was naïve to the whole process. I thought I remembered a date being given. I was just not listening fully. Neither was my lawyer, apparently.

Christmas arrived and I did what I could under difficult circumstances. After returning from Venezuela, I had taken Michelle and Michael out for lunch to go over what was happening. They were 15 and 13 respectively so were in their most influential years. I knew this would not be good for them. Although they knew their parents had been living in separate bedrooms after all the knee surgeries, I didn't think they knew we would get a divorce.

They knew it was coming, they said. Michelle was always quiet anyway, Michael less so, but they did not say much to me during lunch. I felt as if I was being blamed for their mother's decision.

During Christmas I had purchased tickets to a San Jose Sharks' game. Michelle did not like ice hockey. I drove four hours to see the game with Michael and I came straight home afterwards.

My wife did ask the following day how come I was happy and

enjoying Christmas. I said that just because she was unhappy, does not mean the rest of us have to be. Knowing her temperament, I knew I was not helping myself with answers like that. Clearly she was losing control. I am not sure whether she expected me to fight for the marriage or if my accepting the divorce filing made her crazier.

After Christmas and New Year, we were sitting in the kitchen discussing what was going to happen, according to her fantasy dream anyway. We were going to split the assets but remain partners in the business, she proclaimed nonchalantly. I knew what she was thinking right there. She was going to continue to do the accounting, spending an hour a day in the office, and then receive her big pay check every month. But 19 years of this nonsense was enough. I looked at her and said "I am done making money for you."

She was shocked. Her little fantasy world was not working anymore. In the end, it did not really matter.

Towards the end of January 2007, I was having lunch with my realtor, Joe. We had bought and sold a lot of properties in Tahoe together. I knew the date for moving out was coming up but had no idea when. My lawyer did absolutely nothing, we later found out, so expecting a call from him was wishful thinking, to say the least. I thought he would call when I needed to be out. Well, he did call eventually. Whilst eating lunch that day in late January:

"Geoff, you need to be out of the house in 5 minutes."

"What do you mean? That is ridiculous," I replied.

"Your wife will get the sheriffs involved and have you physically removed if you do not leave the house in 5 minutes. She is threatening to get her lawyer involved and have him show up too."

"This is insanity," I said, "How do I get my stuff out in five minutes?"

I apologized and explained to Joe I had to leave. Luckily we were in a café close to home. I drove home in my yellow Range Rover and backed it up to the garage. I was in a state of panic.

What should I get? How much can I get into the car anyway?

Cycling was my essential necessity, so grabbed my three bikes and all the equipment. I grabbed the cycling clothes and some other clothing. I took an address book, the dual Rolex winder, toiletries and my jewelry. I grabbed a DVD player that was not coded so could play DVD's from anywhere in the world. I grabbed a few CD's, some DVD's and a portable CD player I had purchased in New York City months before we ever met. I was getting pretty upset. I was not used to dealing with authority figures such as sheriffs and cops and my wife threatening to have them show up if I didn't get out in five minutes was disturbing.

I was so angry at my lawyer. How could he have done this? I drove over to the guest house right next door and started to empty the car. I kept remembering stuff I needed or had forgotten but it was too late. I knew I could get back into the house later to retrieve things I brought from England, my personal things, the clothing, etc. My wife arrived home and that was that. Unknown to me at the time, it would be the last time I ever saw the inside of my home. I was never allowed in again. I imagine it is similar to being evacuated from a war zone where one is forced to walk away from everything. In a country that claims to be the best democracy in the world and the land of the free, this should never have been allowed to happen, period. My life in America was beginning to fall apart.

The following day my lawyer called me and said that according to my wife's lawyer, I had removed items that she wanted returned. He mentioned the address book and Rolex winder specifically amongst other items I can no longer recall. It was a dumb question because I owned those things too so I told him to go fuck himself and put the phone down. I was livid.

I plugged the DVD player into the 13" TV that was in the guest house. I went from a mammoth 63" projection TV to a 13" TV. The guest house was 600 square feet and our family home was 7,200.

Life was throwing me a lot of curve balls, and with it some new perspectives. Perhaps I had abused the good life I had worked hard for. We were living the American Dream but that dream was unraveling pretty quickly.

I needed cable TV just to occupy my miserable life so headed over to an electrical store and asked for 50 feet of coax.

"Why do you need 50 feet of cable?" the sales guy asked, his curiosity killing him.

"I am tapping into the cable in the house next door. I need TV"

"Oh, I didn't need to know that", the clerk said laughing.

"No, it is my own house. I am getting divorced and have just been kicked out of my home and now living next door".

"Oh", he replies. "I am divorced and I got kicked out. I lost my home too".

I never again saw the items we bought together or the cherished items I brought with me from England. I never again saw what I had worked so hard to achieve.

Chapter 26

I WAS NOW living in the guest house and was seriously depressed. I was struggling with everything. My wife did the accounting but she wasn't providing me a paycheck. She kept it all. With the divorce filing, we were also now living under court jurisdiction. Things were supposed to be kept status quo but that never happened. She was allowed to get away with anything whilst I was about to be perpetually threatened with contempt of court charges. In any event, the status-quo was purely symbolic and meaningless.

"You cannot do anything, Geoff. You have to keep things status quo," I kept being told.

It was all bullshit.

I had not been cycling, or training, since October and was still struggling with a serious complication. With that, the 13th knee surgery was scheduled late February.

My wife and I were kind of cordial at this point, despite my gradual slide into irritable and angry demeanors. Having monies withheld really precipitated this slide. I had to be cordial. We still worked together. At least she was presenting the impression of cordiality. However, I kept calling the attorney to request my paycheck but nothing happened. I worked out some small transactions which clients paid directly and that kept me solvent but I really had no money to survive.

I was still struggling with 'anesthesia brain'. Memory loss was huge, partial vocabulary loss even more so. Distractions and a diminished capacity to multi-task were huge detriments. I was struggling to deal with all this. Problems at work persisted and I was still having to travel.

Joe, our realtor, called me and said he knew someone who wanted to purchase our guest house. This, to me, was a turning point as we were preparing to commence the asset separation portion. Essentially we were beginning to break up our dream. My dream anyway. Never found out what my wife's dream was.

We signed the sales documents and agreed to split the equity from the guest house in half. The big problem was my forthcoming surgery. I would have to move out soon after. The papers had a closing date for end of February. Luckily the surgery wasn't going to be big so this should not present a problem.

It was scheduled to be done at the Roundhill Surgery Clinic. I had Caroline, my office manager, drive me over since my wife had zero interest in helping me. The surgery was going to be arthroscopic, which would require little recovery.

Waking up afterwards was a different story. I knew then that it was not arthroscopic. I was dosed up and drugged in the recovery room, feeling the normal effects of anesthesia after a lengthy procedure, but the pain around the knee and a feeling an incision had been made suggested something bigger had occurred. Dr. Watson (I watched the video afterwards) had looked inside, saw the scar tissue, saw more problems and decided with considerable exasperation to open me up again. The remaining cadaver meniscus was removed (the 10% that had not dissolved) and then drill-and-fracture was performed on the knee, a procedure I was now familiar with. I knew that from the pain level and bone aching. Jesus... So much for a simple arthroscopic procedure.

Caroline picked me up and drove me to the guest house. To this day I could not understand how a wife of nearly 20 years could turn so cold and nasty. She watched me struggle. I could not do anything. The knee was sheer agony and I was back on crutches. I laid on the sofa without any food in the house. I took a prescribed Vicodin and started to cry.

Prior to the surgery, I had found a home to purchase with the equity split from this sale. I should have rented and kept the money but something told me no. Subconsciously I made a decision that at times I regretted. One cannot predict the future but in late February 2007, we would close on the guest house, split the equity and I would then purchase another home.

Four days after surgery, escrow closed and I moved out of the guest house into the local Days Inn. The house I had purchased belonged to a divorced woman and she wanted to ensure the property closed. We agreed I would not move in for ten days after closure. This would allow her time to move her things. At the time of that agreement, I was anticipating an arthroscopic procedure. I had not imagined the place that I was now. Jesus!

To make the experience even more pleasant, two big snow storms hit during those ten days and I, on crutches, was having to clear my car of snow. It took me years to recover from those ten days or to stay at another Days Inn.

In March, I moved into my new home. I was dosed up on Vicodin again and struggling with addiction and depression. The cadaver meniscus had been totally removed, the knee was done. I had lost that battle for sure. The next surgery would be knee replacement. When I moved into my new house, I made a call to my attorney.

"Get her out of my life," I said. "Get her out!" as I yelled with tears from matrimonial anguish and surgical agony rolling down my face. For the first time in my life I took two Vicodin, which sent me off into a more special LaLa Land. I needed to escape this world.

Chapter 27

A FEW WEEKS after moving in I had to visit a client in Kansas City. I had no time to organize the house nor get acquainted with it. I had simply pushed two pieces of the sectional sofa together so that I could sleep on it. I wasn't sleeping in a bed, or the mattress and box spring left by the previous owner. I hooked up the portable CD player so I could drown myself in music. Wam's Everything She Wants became my theme song and one I would play constantly. 'And everything you want and everything you see, Is out of reach, not good enough. I don't know what the hell you want from me'.. George Michael's melodious, powerful voice bellowing out the all-truistic harmonious words that he could have composed depicting my life.

I was still recovering from the 13th surgery and dosed up on Vicodin every night. I was depressed and in pain and knew I would have to go through the withdrawals again to get off the drug.

Remembering the withdrawals from back in summer 2002, I wasn't looking forward to getting off them for, perhaps, the 5th time. Michael was playing baseball one blisteringly-hot Saturday afternoon in August when it happened again. I was sitting in a chair in the direct sun watching him play. I started to shake, mildly at first, but the shakes increased in frequency and amplitude. It was 90+ degrees outside at high altitude, but I was shivering.

"Take me home please." I said to Marina. "It is starting again and I need to go home quickly."

I need my fix. I needed a Vicodin. I was still in pain after the surgery in June and the addiction had set in. I was driven home where I let myself in and headed straight to the bedroom. I grabbed a pill, swallowed it and laid on the bed waiting for it to kick in. Slowly but surely the drowsiness took hold and the shaking began to subside. The addiction I could handle. I just downed a pill. The withdrawals required some intense discipline and a colossal effort to be able to handle the shaking. As with cycling, I would later learn, the head had to take control and not allow the body to dominate. Taking a pill was an easy copout. Defeating the urge to do so required a discipline I was fortunate to have. I did not want to be dosed up, drugged up, knocked out, have perpetual hangover symptoms and constantly feel like shit. I wanted to function normally.

In order to reach my client in Kansas City, I flew from Reno and then connected to Kansas City via Denver. The flight from Denver was interesting because I was seated on the bulkhead left isle seat right behind First Class. As I made myself comfortable, I saw this huge guy get onto the plane. He was massive and well dressed in an expensive suit. To my surprise, he walked up to my row and motioned that he was sitting in the seat next to me. I offered him my isle seat but he thanked me and refused.

"Middle seat is fine, but thank you." He said smiling.

As he sat down and got comfortable, or tried to, the United personnel were bugging him. One hostess brought her phone so her husband would believe who was on the flight. We got talking and he showed me his Super Bowl ring.

"I played for the New England Patriots in 2001. We won the Super Bowl that year. I then retired and went bankrupt. No one told us how to invest the money because when we retire, it all stops." He continued candidly. "I pulled myself together and got out of the hole I was in. Now I am a motivational speaker. I am heading to Kansas City to give a corporate presentation"

"That is a great story. I am so happy to hear that. What nationality are you, if you don't mind me asking?"

He was Samoan.

"Wait a minute", I said, "Samoans play rugby. I played rugby in England", I explained, "Why are you playing American football? Why didn't you play a real sport?" I said laughing.

"I am first generation Samoan born in the US." He explained, smiling and laughing too.

It was a fascinating conversation and I became his rugby buddy.

I explained my divorce and the 13 knee surgeries.

"Wait", he said, halting our enlightening conversation. He placed his hand on my arm as he pivoted to face me. "13 knee surgeries?" he said with his eyes open wide, shaking his head.

Several years later a second retired professional athlete would share the same expression, looking perplexed and bewildered, when I explained the scarring on the knee. I had just gone through them. It was just a number to me but the shocked expressions on others, even pro athletes, was moving and telling.

It was a fascinating encounter. Before the plane landed, he let me hold the Super Bowl ring again. Wow, it was heavy and beautiful. No wonder women flocked around him.

"Women flock because they want your diamond ring. It isn't your looks or personality." I said laughing so hard.

After he laughed along with me, he signed a book I was going to read on the flight and included his phone number…

The only saving grace regarding the 13th surgery was that it partially corrected the medical complication created during the 12th. After I returned from Kansas City I was back in therapy again but only for a short period. I was there long enough to learn I could get around on the spinner. The indentation still existed, the skin still got dragged into the joint, the pain and discomfort still persisted but only up to a point. I could now rotate on a cycle and that is all I cared about. I needed to continue cycling. I needed to keep going. I had to somehow expunge the anger, frustrations, irritations from events perpetuating in my life without hitting the bottle.

With the abstract chaos and the divorce seemingly heading towards the toilet, I cycled for short rides here and there. I did not do much of it though. I had put weight on, the narcotics were awful and I needed to ween myself off them. I was in a new home and I needed to get it organized, not that I had much furniture to organize.

My wife and I, through our lawyers, had worked out a visitation arrangement for our children. It was amazing anything got achieved with the level of incompetence in my case.

Chapter 28

SUNDAY 24TH JUNE 2007 was an ordinary summer day in the mountains. I usually cycled on weekends but the winds were too strong that morning. I did not venture out. Too dangerous in my condition and it was far too risky. All the surgeries had restricted the flexion in the knee and I didn't want to find out what would happen if I crashed and bent the leg too far.

On this particular weekend, I had Michelle and Michael. That Sunday morning, I decided to take Michelle out and teach her how to drive a manual transmission. I grabbed the keys to the green Sterling 827SLi and off we went to the industrial district where my laboratory was.

The Sterling was Puck, given to me by Judy who had passed away spring 2005. I had been invited by her family to give a talk at her memorial in Norman, Oklahoma. I was nervous and anxious because of my vocabulary loss after surgery in June 2002. My nerves were jangled even more when people who wanted to speak declined because they were too emotional to talk. The pressure increased as a result. I owed it to my late friend and her family whom had accepted me into their lives, even before we had even met. I stood up in church and gave an ad-lib speech that lasted around 45 minutes. It remains the longest public speech I have ever given. A little boy came up to me afterwards and said, "Nice talk. You were funny." I was also thanked by Judy's family. Somehow the anxiety disappeared and appropriate words came to my head at a time they were desperately needed.

As part of my promise to restore Puck, I had upgraded the transmission to a five-speed manual using a donor Sterling purchased from a guy in Wisconsin. The guy's wife was so happy he was getting rid of the car, she came running outside when I showed to pick it up. She had some new Sterling merchandise she wanted to hand me and had this beaming smile. I was her hero taking away the car she evidently didn't like much.

Puck was easy to drive with the manual transmission so it was perfect for Michelle to learn. She spent the next hour driving around the industrial area.

We drove back home around noon. I needed to finally fill up the kitchen cabinets and refrigerator. All three of us headed to the grocery store about three miles away. We loaded the shopping cart and were standing in line to pay when we heard someone say: "There is a fire."

We left Raley's to find ash and debris falling all over the place. There was indeed a fire but where? As I turned around to see where the smoke was coming from, I swallowed hard. Shit.

We quickly drove home. As we were approaching the house, the smoke plume was blowing in the opposite direction. I pulled into the driveway and we ran through the house to get onto the rear deck. The property was on a ridge and looked straight down into Christmas Valley with the mountain ranges off in the distance. Off to the right we could see the trees on fire less than quarter mile or so away. The flames were leaping 200 feet into the air, well above the tree line. This is not good.

I ran into the house to grab the digital camera and started snapping photographs. I ran to the back of the house first and then to the front. The smoke plume was directly over the top of our home by now and was thick enough to partially block the sun.

I had moved into this home three months ago and had nothing except for a few pieces of furniture from the guest house my wife and I sold in February. We needed a water hose so I took Michael with me to the hardware store. We jumped into the car and drove only two houses down before stopping. Our neighbour's garden was on fire.

Their flammable pine needles were a perfect incendiary device for the fire, which was now very close to their spectacular wood-sided home. The fire was getting serious. As I looked down the street, I saw the natural vegetation on fire. People's gardens were in flames. This fire was spreading faster than any of us thought possible. Fire was everywhere, along with the accompanying smoke and embers. As we tried to extinguish the fire, a California Highway Patrol officer came by, instructing us of the mandatory evacuation orders. We were being told to leave.

Luckily the street was a circle, otherwise we would be driving through flames. After grabbing the only things important, my two children and the two cats, I turned right out of the driveway, drove the north side of Coyote Ridge Circle to Lake Tahoe Boulevard, turned right and headed away from the ensuing disaster. As we drove, Michael had turned back and saw a house three down from us enveloped in flames.

He screamed, "There are flames pouring out of the upstairs windows." I just kept going. I needed to get the hell out of here. I needed to protect my loved ones. It was an apocalyptic nightmare. Cars and people were running around everywhere. Embers were flying, the smoke was so thick, I could hardly see. The fire was generating its own wind storm. The sky was grey and washed out with the smoke.

Not knowing what to do, I headed to the family home, which was away from the fire area. My wife would not like us bringing the cats despite the mitigating circumstances. They were brother and sister tabbies and were lovely. We had picked them up from a local shelter but my wife hated animals in the house.

I dropped Michael and the cats off but Michelle wanted to leave with me because she was concerned. I was her Dad and she wanted to know that I was going to be ok. I had no idea myself. I had nowhere to go and had no money for hotels. I was broke. I had few friends that I could call so I was lost in this sea of chaos.

I thought Marina would take pity and invite me to stay in the guest suite for a few days, but obviously that would be a gesture from a person who cared. She simply didn't. We were married over 19 years. She was very happy to see me leave but not happy I took Michelle. I started to see a change in her at this point. I was stunned and heartbroken that she showed no signs of concern or remorse for me. She knew I had nowhere to go. Pain and suffering brought on by failed surgeries is one thing. Pain and suffering brought on by a human being who supposedly loved you once is something else. The former I learnt to handle. The latter just causes heartbreak and emotional distress.

Michelle and I drove around. I finally called a friend of the family to ask if we could stay for a few nights. The people knew my wife so the situation was ugly but we needed a bed. I thanked them and then headed out to an area where we could view the destruction and watch the fire crews. The Angora Fire, as it would be known, ravaging the south part of South Lake Tahoe. The smoke was thick and the winds were howling as the fire created its own wind storm.

Whilst we were staring at the fire, someone I knew told me my neighbors' house, two down from me, the one whose pine needles were on fire, was gone and likely mine too. My heart sank. In the space of five months, I had been removed from three homes.

We were heading to a friend's to stay the night when my wife called, demanding I bring Michelle home. She was losing it.

"I will call the sheriff", she threatened.

"I think there are more important things the sheriffs need to address than some domestic nonsense created by some psycho bitch. Call them! I don't give a shit!!" I responded.

I was losing it too. My knee, my marriage, my children, a failing business and three homes gone in the space of a few months.

Finally at the friend's house, drinking a much needed alcoholic beverage, my English friend called from Texas.

"How is it going, Geoff? Are you involved?"

The fire was evidently making headline news around the country.

"I have just been told my home has gone up in flames," I replied.

"I asked you two weeks ago how things were going and you

replied they cannot get any worse," he reminded me.

"Yes, well, they typically can and do I guess. I will never say that again for as long as I live," I vowed.

A week later my friend sent me a plaque I still have in my home: "CHALLENGES - I Expected Times Like This, But I Never Thought They'd Be So Bad, So Long, And So Frequent."

The following morning, I got a call from Caroline, my office manager. Her husband worked for the local refuse company. They were asked to go in and find out which homes were burnt and which homes were standing. Caroline told me my home was still standing. I might have cried right there, right then, but likely I was too numb.

Michelle was still with me but I had dropped her with a friend. I headed over to the office, which still had open access. However, helicopters dropping water were now operating in the area and I captured a few photos before reaching the office. Caroline walked into the kitchen area where I was making coffee and asked: "How many more hits can you take?"

I looked at her with a pained expression, "I don't know. I really cannot take anymore".

I must have looked shell-shocked. She had been witnessing each disaster as they unfolded and likely wondered when I was going to crack.

My issue now was where was I going to stay. I went downstairs and into my office, put my head in my hands and cried like a baby.

On the Monday afternoon, my wife called again, demanding Michelle be brought home. But my daughter did not want to go home. I had no control over her. She was staying at a friend's house, which did not sit well with her mother.

At that precise moment all my personal belongings were sitting in a plastic bag on the passenger seat of the Range Rover. Toothbrush and toothpaste, deodorant and cologne. That was it. I left the house with absolutely nothing except the clothes I was wearing. Sufficient deodorant, cologne and frequent showers would work for a day or two but nothing further. I had no money to venture into a clothes store. About two minutes after I put the phone down on my scream-ing wife, my English friend Dave, now living in Southern California, called me. He asked if I was involved in the fire and I immediately started crying on the phone. I tried to control myself but I was falling to pieces. We talked for a while and then I clicked off. I needed that call. I needed a reassuring calm voice. Damn, I needed a friend to care.

At some point that day I had noticed a black mark on my yellow car, the driver's door. As we were escaping the fire yesterday after-noon, hot embers must have fallen on the black rubber door seal where the window is. The rubber had melted and dripped down the door. That's when I realized how fortunate we really were.

I had heard about the city hosting a community meeting in the middle school's gymnasium for all those affected by the fire. I headed over early evening. As I was walking to the gymnasium, a local Fox News reporter was standing outside interviewing people who were involved.

"Sir, were you affected by the fire?"

"Yes I was. It has destroyed my neighbourhood," I told him, still feeling shell-shocked.

"Can we ask you some questions?"

When the reporter asked for my story I could not stop. I started to hyperventilate and needed to slow myself down.

I talked for a while and then he specifically asked about TRPA, the local environmental agency that I could only describe back then as a joke. I had already dealt with this agency two years after moving to Tahoe and so had experience with how they operated at the time. It was the TRPA that forbid homeowners from raking up the pine nee-dles in the yard, thinking highly flammable pine needles would be more environmentally sound than bare ground. They stopped home-owners creating defensible space around their property, despite post-ers everywhere telling us to do so. It was madness.

"They want to protect the trees but they need to protect the peo-ple also," I said. Words to that effect anyway. I rambled on a bit more.

A couple of days later a friend from New York called up.

"Hey Geoff, I was watching the local news when this long haired Englishman came on and started talking about the forest fire in Lake Tahoe," he said.

"Was that me?" I joked.

Then another English friend from the San Francisco Bay Area called and said the same thing. I guess my interview had been on national television.

Weeks later I bumped into the gentleman who purchased the guest house from us. He saw the same news report and said I was good and sounded eloquent. I needed that.

After the news interview, I went and sat down for the meeting. A few locals had decided to make it a political event and wanted the limelight. Typical garbage. People had lost everything and were angry at the agency that they believed allowed this to happen. Luckily more level heads prevailed and the meeting was prevented from heading into the toilet. This was national news for a small mountain resort and a lot of locals had been affected.

Then I saw a stunning, young blonde woman walk into the room. She had an expensive camera hanging around her neck so I thought she was a reporter and not a local. She was around 5'2", very slender, dressed casually in tight-fitting blue jeans and a white long sleeve top. God, she was gorgeous.

I turned my attention away from her as the proceedings went on. Then she looked around, saw me and walked over. Turning my head, I could not believe what she was doing. She climbed over the bench in front and sat down next to me on the right.

"Hello. I am Crystal. So nice to meet you. Were you affected by the fire?" she kindly asked.

The events of the past few days disappeared. I was in heaven. We sat and talked for some time. She used to live in Arizona but now lives in Lake Tahoe. Huh, I nearly missed that part.

"You live around here?"

"Yes," she replied.

She was fascinating but I picked up on a few comments that made me believe she was unhappy.

I remembered her name as we said our goodbyes. It had been a monumental evening.

The next day, the blaze continued. No one was allowed back in the fire area near my home because it was too dangerous. Power lines were down and the fire was raging. The fire headed towards the high school, the only high school in South Lake Tahoe. Firemen fought a courageous battle and the school was saved. This was a monumental moment and a turning point for the city. Had the school gone up in smoke, it would have been temporarily catastrophic for our small mountain enclave. After a few days sheltering with friends, I had moved to a Holiday Inn Express. Those were depressing times as I grabbed whatever little things I had and moved into a hotel room. I ended up staying ten days. The insurance companies had set up staging areas around town, and Farmer's Insurance had a mobile unit. They turned out to be good. In fact, they were very good in the end. I had to buy some clothes and shoes and get sorted out just from that perspective. As the week went on, firefighters started to clear areas for property owners to view. We were one of the last areas to be opened and that did not happen until the Friday after the fire, five days later. My children were with their mother but she allowed them to come with me to witness the destruction.

We arrived that Friday and prepared ourselves. I had never seen a natural disaster this local. I was in the Loma Prieta Earthquake in the San Francisco Bay Area in October 1989. This was different. This was more personal because the fire had destroyed my new neighbourhood. A line of property owners drove behind the police car that would escort us all in. We were each given a package containing drinking water, a face mask and other items deemed essential.

"What do we need a face mask for? No smoke anymore," I asked my children.

They, of course, did not know either.

We slowly drove through the mass destruction. I was stunned.

I had tears in my eyes as I saw home after home destroyed. Where homes used to stand, it was a pile of burnt out ashes and debris. Burnt out remains of automobiles littered the lots. The only part of the homes that remained where brick entranceways, stone fireplaces and walls, driveways and twisted metal. Gardens were destroyed. Trees were burnt and their lifeless black shells just stood there. It was as if a bomb had been dropped. We were driving through an apocalypse

Earlier in the week California's Governor Arnold Schwarzenegger had visited the fire zone and was photographed standing on a property one street down from Coyote Ridge Circle. This was a national disaster for a small town.

I was mesmerized at how selective the fire had been. One house was left standing whilst the surrounding area was decimated. As we drove towards our street, I looked over to an area on the right, the west side of Lake Tahoe Boulevard, and it was completely destroyed. No homes were left standing. I later learnt that this was the hottest part of the fire area, one block away from my new home. All of it went up as spontaneous combustion must have catapulted everything into a raging inferno. House after house, row upon row, it was complete, utter destruction. Michelle and Michael didn't say a word. They just stared in disbelief, as did I.

We got to our street and the car in front of me peeled off. I followed. They turned left and then immediately stopped. Their home was evidently the first house on the left as they turned in. It was destroyed. We saw as they exited the car they were already breaking down and crying. My children were with me so I had to control myself but inside I was falling to pieces.

I drove down the street and everything to the left and right was gone. I reached my neighbor's home and it was still standing. The house Michael saw in flames was gone, as was the home in front of my neighbor's. The one next to that, gone. I pulled up outside our home and it looked pretty good, at least from the front. The house on the other side of us was still there but their detached garage was nowhere to be seen. Gone!! The big house next to them on the north side, gone, and the one next to that, gone. Jesus!! I spun around to look for the two homes in front of us. They were gone. All but two homes I could see on Eagle Lane, gone. Piles of grey ash and twisted metal, burnt homes everywhere. My road, Coyote Ridge, was nearly destroyed. Out of 24 homes, 6 remained standing. It was sickening. I wanted to throw up.

Michelle and Michael were speechless. What could we say? I got the key and asked if they wanted to put their masks on. We all declined. What would we need those for? I then opened the door and walked in. The foul and toxic air inside immediately made me gag and I turned around and bolted outside. I bent over and took deep breathes as I tried to get cleaner air inside the lungs. Wow. Now we knew why those masks were included in each disaster kit.

We all put them on and walked inside. The immediate damage was not visible until we got further into the home. The toxic smell was awful. I walked into the kitchen and saw the wooden floor was damaged. Loss of electricity had shut down and defrosted the freezer. The water had warped the wooden floor.

I walked to the rear slider that would take us out on the deck. Debris from fires was everywhere. Even insulation from someone's home was laying on the grass. I saw the house behind us had gone up. Properties in front and behind had disappeared but ours remained. That seemed totally bizarre except we lived on a ridge and I can only believe the embers were taken up and over the ridge. I looked off the side of the deck and saw white plastic trim pieces on the floor. The fire had got so hot at the house, the window pieces had melted and broken the seals. I noticed the deck wooding had shrunk. It was almost too dangerous to stand on but the excessive heat had evaporated all the moisture in the wood. The external decking was trashed. There were burn marks everywhere as flying hot embers had landed on it.

I looked at the brand new deck furniture I had just bought with credit card from K-Mart a month earlier. It was full of burn holes as the embers had settled and melted the material. The bushes close to the home were burnt. The grass along the back of the home was black in places. A wooden retaining wall had been on fire. The plastic windows in the shed were melted and the shed was toast. Pine trees near the home were burnt on one side. The pine needles were brown whilst the back of the trees facing the house were green.

The house was built on the side of a ridge and the deck hanging off the main level was enclosed for storage underneath. Reading up later on home protection material, I believe this was one big reason why my home did not go up in flames. Hot embers landing on the deck above could not get air to ignite them because the wind could not get underneath. It obviously got very hot here. Signs of that were everywhere.

I went back inside and headed upstairs to the master bedroom suite were I slept. The whole house stank. I had my clothes all hanging neatly in the two closets. I turned around, walked over to the bed, put my head in my hands and wanted to cry but couldn't. Michelle had followed me.

"I am sick of moving. I don't want to move anymore!"

Before we left I had gone into the kitchen and retrieved some things. I grabbed a few clothes but they stank of smoke.

We left and I drove the children back to where their mother was waiting for them. This had been a horrific day. It was impossible to purge the scenes we had just seen.

I was assigned an insurance case worker and she turned out to be really nice. I needed nice people around me now.

A few days later, my English friend, Tony, called from the Bay Area. He had a spare ticket to the 2007 Death Ride. Shit, I was coming off two knee surgeries in the winter and I had not done any training whatsoever. Just short rides here and there. My bike was in the garage.

I thought about it for a moment and then said, "I will cycle around the lake this weekend. If I survive, I will do the Death Ride with you".

I went home and brought the cycle back to the Holiday Inn Express. Was I insane?

I had not really done much cycling since the surgeries in October

2006 and the one in February 2007. I had moved into my new home and that required some work and effort to get sorted out. I took a ride here and there but nothing substantial. I could not cycle anyway with the complication in October so I had lost some muscle strength.

Now the forest fire threw another wrench into my screwed-up life. I was depressed. However, I needed to get back on my bike. It was therapy.

Climbing mountain passes were my self-imposed therapy sessions. I didn't need to spend money I did not have on counseling. I just needed to cycle and climb. Climbing mountains, however, with only one good leg really epitomized my life as it stood. Nothing made much sense anymore, not even the cycling. Every time I took one step forwards, something would drag me back two steps. I was heading nowhere except backwards, deeper into the cesspit of hell. Cycling kept me going. It kept my head straight. I took anger and frustrations out on my legs instead of heading to the bar.

The Angora Forest Fire was disturbing and came at a very poor time, if a forest fire can ever come at a good one. Somehow, I kept going. Cycling was the power and overwhelming force behind the desire to overcome. My legs were strong, particularly the right one. I was building legs that boys in their 20's wanted, but it wasn't just that. I was building the drive, the desire to overcome, the tenacity to compete, the power to deliver, the mindset to win at any cost. I was setting goals that were insane for a physically abled person. I did not want people to see they were beating me down little by little. I had to remain strong. I was becoming impervious to the pain thresholds I had to traverse because no matter what I did on a cycle, I had to overcome the pain.

I had been offered a ticket to the 2007 Death Ride. I hadn't even seen some of the five mountain passes on the 129-mile route, a route that would require climbing some 15,000 feet. Sitting in the Holiday Inn Express, I pondered the offer to do the Death Ride. I read somewhere: "Never put off until tomorrow what you can do today because, if you enjoy it today, you can then do it again tomorrow."

Life was crap. I was at a new low but somehow I needed to climb out of this. Somehow I needed to drag myself up out of the gutter. I had two wonderful children who were in trouble. Without knowing what I was doing, oblivious to the ride I was considering, on Saturday morning 13 days after the fire, I grabbed my yellow Giant TCR2 and started cycling around the lake.

Instead of a five hour 72-mile pleasant ride, it turned into an arduous exercise in stupidity. I was not feeling good but I had learnt to deal with pain and suffering. I somehow could partition that into part of the brain not readily accessible. I had made a promise to Tony and if you don't have integrity, then nothing else matters.

I finished the ride but it took over six hours and I was knackered. The insurance lady came to the hotel lobby and we talked about what needed to be done. She was so impressed that I had cycled around the lake but she did not know how I felt afterwards. Perhaps she could see it etched and didn't venture to say anything! I called Tony and told him I had done the ride around the lake and was still alive. Two weeks later I would be involved in my first Death Ride.

The fire was the new low. Cycling was the drive to keep going. Unknown to me then was how cycling was building the drive in me to keep pushing. Never again did I say that life could not get any worse. It can. And it did.

Chapter 29

I PICKED UP the local newspaper shortly after the devastating forest fire and saw Crystal's name. She was discussing her current boyfriend's fight with the Tahoe Regional Planning Agency (TRPA). I remembered her from the citywide meeting held to discuss the fire and its aftermath. In the article, Crystal was asking for people to notify her if they were having problems with the TRPA, a local environmental agency often seen by Tahoe locals as the Gestapo. I had had my fights with TRPA, and even ended up on the front page of the Tahoe Tribune back in 2001. While I had zero interest in pursuing the discussion of the TRPA, I was very interested in getting to know her. The email in the article gave me a point of contact so I wrote, reminding her of the long-haired, crazy Englishman she had met at the town meeting the previous week.

She seemed pleased to hear from me and so we continued a brief email discussion. The fire area had already been opened up so I agreed to take her around and show the devastating destruction. She claimed she was a photographer and wanted to snap some photos. She showed up one afternoon at my laboratory. I think she was surprised by what I did for a living. Admittedly most people are when they see all the scientific equipment, especially in a ski resort town.

I climbed into the passenger side of her Toyota and we headed off through the scene of mass destruction, stopping to take photographs along the way. I showed her where I lived, or used to, but it was emotional. I had learnt by speaking with the property owner behind me that the house next to him, one directly behind my home, had gone up in 20 minutes which likely explained the burnt debris on my grass. He had saved his home, and perhaps mine too, although he did not say so.

It was a good visit to the area. And I admit I enjoyed being driven around by a beautiful lady.

"Would you like to have dinner later?" she said.

"Err, yes, that would be nice," I replied, trying to sound less surprised than I was.

"Good. We can meet around six."

As she drove away, she looked at my orange Mustang with admiration but I was confident it was my debonair charm, witty personality and European good looks helped entice her. The accent wasn't bad either.

I loved the Mustang in a time of desperation and need. It was an impulse purchase made just a month before the forest fire hit. I was severely depressed, lonely and had been kicked out of two homes. I was struggling with the debilitating failed knee surgeries. I was totally lost. It was a stimulus I could not afford but needed. I would make a recommendation to anyone going through such trauma: Find something to distract you, to make you happy, to make you feel good about yourself. It doesn't matter what it is. It might not actually be an object or thing. Anything. Grasp it and hold on. My credit was still impeccable and I bought the Grabber orange Mustang with no money down. It helped salvage some sanity and boy did it ever make me feel good about myself.

Later that day, I met Crystal at a local burger joint on the Nevada side of the lake, close to where she was living. I remembered some of the things she told me when we met at the community meeting, which surprised her. Why wouldn't I? I was enjoying her company and she had no idea how much I needed to be dragged away from reality.

"I have rented '300'. Would you like to come over?" she asked, unexpectedly, after we had finished eating.

"Thank you. I would love that."

Clearly she had planned an evening with me. I honestly doubted anyone had ever turned her down. Not yet anyway. Evidently she was enjoying my company as well. Perhaps she needed an escape from her reality. In any event, we seemed mutually agreeable to enjoying an evening together watching a movie.

We watched "300" but nothing romantic happened between us, nor was I anticipating anything would. The movie was good, not that I was watching, because talking with Crystal was much better.

I was shown a room downstairs and, although not prepared for it, I stayed the night. It was much better than the alternative. I had moved into the rental house where I would end up staying for five months whilst my home was being rebuilt from the fire damage. It was a very depressing time for me, but for one evening I had set that aside and enjoyed dinner and a movie with Crystal.

The following morning I headed to Wells Fargo Bank at Stateline to remove my wife's signature from the business account. While I was there Crystal called but I could not pick up because I was with the banker. I returned her call later but got voicemail.

I never saw her again the rest of 2007. I am not sure why she never returned my call that day. In the end, it did not matter anyway.

I found a house to rent in an area where Michelle and Michael had friends. It was a good choice for them, but a bad choice for me. I hated the area. It was depressing with no views, nothing to look at, hidden by trees that made it so dark. The home was small. I chose the loft as my bedroom, which was V-shaped and claustrophobic, so that my children could have nice rooms downstairs.

I was depressed and hurting. I had no money. My wife was still keeping my paycheck and the lawyer was doing nothing about anything.

When the kids visited on weekends, they went to see their friends. I was left on my own with time to think about things I didn't want to think about. However, we did make some agreements when they came to visit. No more eating in our own rooms. Food would be served at the kitchen table. Also, we would spend quality time by watching TV together. We lived in separate rooms before the divorce filing and that was going to change. We agreed to take turns choosing a show to watch. When it came time for Michelle to pick her show of choice, Michael and I regretted that decision. I had never watched Spongebob before and it wasn't helped when Michael kept looking at me rolling his eyes. We laughed. I learnt to endure Spongebob and benefit from the educational aspects of cartoon characters living at the bottom of the sea.

Chapter 30

IN JULY 2007, I had placed myself in a mess by agreeing to do the Death Ride with Tony. It would be my first time. But I once read in Reader's Digest many years ago: "If someone has integrity, nothing else matters. If someone doesn't have integrity, nothing else matters." I had promised my friend, Tony, that I would accompany him on this year's Death Ride. I didn't want to let him down.

I told him after the forest fire that first I would ride around the lake and if I survived that suicidal mission, I would do the Death Ride with him. I survived that ride around the lake, but only just. I made a promise I had to honour, irregardless of my current mental and physical state. However, I had no time to prepare for this grueling ride and certainly had no training. It was a ridiculous decision if I was factoring in all the variables. I chose to ignore them.

The weekend before The Death Ride, I rode around the lake again. This time I had cramps in my right calf from the start to the finish. Well, that was fun, I thought. I was at a place where I wasn't feeling pain anymore, or so it seemed. Or maybe I was just impervious to it and positively insane enough to try anything. I was punishing myself to see how much more pain I could endure. To see what the boundaries were. To test the borders. To figure out my limitations. Or to see when I would crack.

On Saturday 14th July I drove out to Turtle Rock Park, where the race began, and met up with Tony. A high protein breakfast was provided for the registered riders so we sat and ate that. It was 5:30 a.m.

and time to go. At that time in the mountains at high altitude, it was cold. Damn cold. It was important to ride with the correct clothing.

I made it to the bottom of the west face of Monitor Pass and started climbing. I was overweight, had not prepared and my legs felt like lead weights. I made the arduous eight-and-a-half mile climb, with a rest stop about midway, but I was tired already. Monitor is a big mountain which incorporates steep gradients. After consuming energy food and drinks, I left to continue down the east face of Monitor Pass towards Highway 395.

The problem was I had never been down the east face on a bike before. The decent was fine for the first mile and a half but then I turned a right-hand bend and there it was. Never is it a good thing to see where the drop begins and ends. I could see where the road is going and I swallowed hard. Some way off into the distance and after some considerable drop in altitude, the road snaked down the mountain pass and through a narrow gorge. I didn't need to see that. The road was so faint in the distance that I almost couldn't see it. I started peddling but nothing prepared me for the decent. I had driven this portion of the course in a car a few times. But on a bicycle, it was vastly different. I planted my right foot and started the forward motion. I moved the chain onto the large front ring and the small rear ring using the left and right gear shifters on the brake levers respectively, and took deep breaths for the decent. The gradient was so steep I had to ease off the throttle. The only control on a bike at these speeds is the braking system. God help me if that failed or I had a tyre blowout.

As the gradient changed to eight percent negative (downhill) I could not help the expletives. Shit, fuck, bloody hell and the all-elusive WTF. The road was a two-lane highway but it had sharp curves, tight switchbacks, long drop-offs and cliff-edges along the side of the road, and the damn thing kept on going. It was relentless as the road shed off 3,300 feet of altitude in about 10 miles. I had never been down a mountain pass of this magnitude. At each stage of the decent, I knew I would have to climb back up. I had no idea yet how I would be able to do that without the aid of a gurney and ambulance.

At the bottom was a well-stocked rest stop just off Highway 395 where I could replenish my sanity, perhaps. I didn't see that they provided a package for that and I would have to remain insane for the climb back up.

After some time at the rest stop, I could no longer avoid the inevitable, so I grabbed my bike and started the long 10-to-11-mile haul back up the east face of Monitor Pass. I had to pause for rest countless times, perhaps one stop per mile, I cannot recall. The climb was made worse because nothing grew this side of the mountain. There was no cover and the sun beat down the whole climb. During one of those pauses, a cyclist passes me and looks over.

"I have the wrong gears for this." I simply said.

"We all do," was his funny reply. Damn, cyclists are hilarious.

Finally, I ascended and completed Death Ride pass number two after a two-hour plus slaughter-fest. I received the second sticker put on the rider number safety-pinned on the back of my jersey. Only three more mountain passes to go, but I was physically exhausted and knew this was it. There was no way I could even contemplate another pass. With no training and all the personal strife, I was proud that I had finished at least two. That was a feat in and of itself. I could do no more.

As I parked myself on the gravel to devour the libations from the rest stop, I heard some young people talking. They were volunteers. They were discussing trying it next year. Well, why not, indeed? At least they looked like they had both legs functioning so had no excuse as far as I could tell.

I headed down the west face of Monitor and then took a left on Highway 4 at the bottom. Around two miles or so was the lunch stop. I grabbed my lunch and sat at a table. It was then I noticed riders wearing AIDS Lifecycle jerseys from this year's 550-mile ride, which had been held a month earlier.

How the hell could they do the AIDS ride and the Death Ride within weeks of each other and survive? How did they have the strength? The thought boggled my mind.

So I sat there in the late morning of Saturday 14th July, 2007, knowing that I couldn't continue on and wondered how those cyclists had the strength. It was unfathomable and incomprehensible. My head just could not wrap itself around the idea of completing both staggering rides within weeks of each other. Not in my condition.

Chapter 31

EVER SINCE I was tossed out of my own home, I had been pleading with my lawyer to have my wife removed from my business. I knew she would be decimating it. Her love of money overshadowed everything else. Once again I was told by my attorney to keep things status-quo. My exasperation and irritation levels reached breaking point sometime in July and I did two things to rattle cages:

1) I went to Wells Fargo Bank and had my wife's signature removed from the business account. I was the owner and CEO on record and my signature was already on file. That part turned out to be easier than I had imagined.
2) I opened up my own personal account and transferred money from our joint savings account.

The following morning my lawyer called me.

"Go fuck yourself. I am done with her taking my salary. I keep asking you to sort this out and you have not done anything about it."

"You are under court jurisdiction," he pleaded.

"Fuck you and the court. I don't care anymore. Hold me in contempt." And with that I slammed the phone down. I was done with his incompetent bullshit.

My wife was not happy when I stopped her from signing company checks, nor did it stop her. And the bank kept cashing them, even though she was no longer the signatory. She kept paying herself a large salary and the bank kept cashing the checks. I was livid.

Everyone was in on the act now, including the bank. My lawyer, who was proving to be an incompetent moron, did nothing to prevent this. I was screaming at him to get her out of my company. I sensed now that it was systematically being destroyed. It was likely too late anyway.

At the end of July, we finally had a court date for this to be sorted out. We entered court sometime early August. I was still on my first family lawyer but she was already on her second. I was telling the court that I was paying myself something each month because child and alimony payments had to be withdrawn on a percentage level, according to California Law. We agreed visitation rights with the children based on the presumption that I traveled a lot. I didn't actually, not at that point, but the court seemed to not know or care about reality or facts, I was beginning to observe.

This was a signed agreement that got entered into a court file and accepted by the presiding commissioner. The other thing the commissioner agreed to was having my wife removed from the company we jointly owned. At last she was out. She was livid, I could tell. Her dream of working one-hour days, having me work my ass off and then her giving herself a big paycheck fell apart right there, right then, as I had warned her back in January.

We were to schedule a meeting so that our assets could be distributed. It all seemed too cordial to me. Something was wrong. I left the courtroom happy, but I had yet to look at the company books. While I knew she had to be removed, I did not realize it was six months too late. I went to my office and started to dive into what turned out to be a near catastrophic mess. Whilst under court's jurisdiction, she had decimated our business accounting.

I later learnt that she had been preparing for our divorce since 2004, right after I was told my knee was finished for about the tenth time. Whilst I was learning to walk and talk again, she had liquidated most things. The first letter I looked at was a shut-off notice from the electrical company. The American Express account I used for travel was at a balance of $40K. She had not paid anything except the minimum required. Other American Express accounts were the same but with differing balances. She had been paying the bare minimum, if any at all. I was on the verge of losing everything.

Back in 2004 we had opened an office in the Tri-State area, comprising Connecticut, New York, New Jersey. There was a significant client-base infrastructure there, including major pharmaceutical companies, university laboratories, research institutions, oil and gas. I had flown out on crutches to meet our prospective partner and sales director in this new business venture. I remember that trip because it was bloody terrible. I flew Reno to Denver to Washington DC to Hartford, Connecticut on crutches. We ended up expanding our business with a new entity that eventually employed six engineers and a sales director, all based in the Tri-State area.

We had big aspirations. We purchased an office building in Nyack, New York, 20 miles up the Hudson River from New York City. I immediately fell for Nyack. I never knew a town so nice was that close to NYC. The building was perfect, on a street with a view of the Hudson River. But it was not a time that I should have been starting a new venture, particularly 3,000 miles away. With my head damage in June 2002, I had trouble thinking and found it really difficult to multitask. All those surgeries had beaten me up, and I was exhausted flying coast-to-coast once or twice a month. I was not 100 percent functional. That would have real consequences.

The business entity started to unravel in early 2006. As it turned out, two of the first engineers were on the wrong end of the integrity scale. We were accused of billing for work that wasn't performed. The operator of the instrument had filed the complaint and I had to fly to New Jersey to sort it out. As soon as the engineer told me he had performed the work after 4:30 p.m. one afternoon, I knew he was lying.

Eighteen months later I was getting foreclosure notices from the bank in New York State. My wife had been paying herself the rent from the building but had not been paying the mortgage. She simply kept the money. And property taxes were due. I knew there was a six-figure accounts receivable when we finally closed the east coast office but that was also gone. My companies were a mess and I had employees to pay. I had no personal funds. Less than two months after the forest fire, life was indeed getting worse. It was insane. She had liquidated everything.

She was angry at being removed from the company. She had to go but her temperamental personality meant that I was about to be tossed into the abyss. I knew things were cascading out of control, and cascading fast. We were on rapid free-fall.

Chapter 32

TO HELP ME escape the madness in my life, Dave, one of my partners in the Canadian environmental laboratory, invited me to visit a client in Hong Kong after a conference I was attending in Toyko. That meant August and early September would be busy with international travel, including a company board meeting in Canada and a scheduled visit back to Caracas, Venezuela.

Just prior to leaving, my wife and I met in her second lawyer's office to go over how we would split the assets. The meeting was held so soon after the judge removed her from my company. I had my doubts this would go smoothly. Those doubts were quickly realized. She was clearly livid. She perhaps expected me to save the marriage. I clearly didn't want to and portrayed zero interest in anything other than a divorce. She wanted to remain business partners and do nothing except have me work hard for her large paycheck. She was just removed from the company office by the court so that pipe dream landed. We left that meeting with no hope, other than an understanding another meeting would follow. But one never did. Oblivious to me, plans were already underway to toss this divorce off a cliff.

I flew to Japan for a six-day conference, which turned out to be rewarding and captivating. I had never been to Japan before so this was a new experience and culturally very different. It was exciting and a needed distraction. I ventured into one of the talks about toxic chemicals emitted in forest fires. I had recent insight into a forest fire and thought it would be fascinating. I wasn't mistaken. It was presented by an Australian professor and was an interesting talk. Afterwards I was able to relive with the audience my recent experiences with the Angora Fire in Tahoe.

Just as we were to leave Japan we were warned of a typhoon approaching. It was estimated to arrive around the same time we were scheduled to fly out for Hong Kong. Dave and I arrived at the gate. Boarding did not take long. I could tell the ground staff was anxious to get us up in the air.

As the plane taxied, it was being blown all over the place. Hmm, this will be interesting, I thought. I have flown well over a million miles on United Airlines alone so I have extensive experience with shaky takeoffs. As the plane gained momentum to reach take-off speed, it was being blown every which way. I was actually concerned. Finally, the aircraft reached rotation speed, the nose tipped upwards and we were off the ground. The plane was being buffeted until it gained sufficient altitude and horizontal distance to break clear of the weather. Once that happened, we settled in for the five-hour flight to Hong Kong. I looked at Dave and just smiled but I needed to look for my stomach.

It was late evening in Hong Kong when we landed and it had descended into darkness hours earlier. Fortunately, I was with someone who had been here a few times. This was a new airport built away from the city, so once we grabbed our bags we walked straight onto the train located right inside the airport terminal. Great planning! This took us to Hong Kong's mainland area known as Kowloon where we exited the train and got a taxi to the hotel.

My mind was pre-occupied. I was not paying much attention to the fact I was in one of the best countries in the world. The train had taken us within site of the majestic, stunning and world-renowned Hong Kong harbor skyline but I failed to take note. I checked into the room and sent a message to Crystal, the lady I met the day after the forest fire. 'Hello from Hong Kong,' it said. She immediately responded. I had not seen her for a while and wanted to hear from her.

The following day we walked around before getting a taxi to the harbor ferries. Dave knew exactly where he was going. The ferries took us over to Hong Kong Island. Again, I don't remember the skyline. It was regarded as one of the best cities in the world and my mind had blanked. I vaguely remember a tram ride up to famous Peak Tower. I vaguely remember having coffee in a cafe at the top. I remember nothing of the skyline at all.

Early evening it was still light and our client picked us up and drove us to the bar at Hong Kong's famous rugby club. The rugby club hosts the International Rugby 7 competition each year. The client was an English guy and had lived in Hong Kong a while. The bar overlooked the rugby field. I sat staring at it as we talked and drank beers, not believing where I was. I loved this place.

Later, after the client took us for dinner, something happened that I had never experienced before. He pulled up on Lockhart Road, home of the famous nightclub bars. He dropped us off, told us to enjoy and then left. We walked into one of the bars and found ourselves surrounded by gorgeous women. Almost immediately a young Filipino woman came up to me. She wore a nice top with a short denim skirt and high heels. She was beautiful, had lovely legs, but she was young. I was approaching 44 but what did I care? I simply didn't. I was sitting down on a stool and she stood right in front of me.

"Hello," I said. "I am Geoff."

"Hello, I am Claire."

She was adorable.

I had my legs slightly open as she moved closer between them. I put my hands gently on her legs in a non-sensual way but she softly brushed them off. Ok, I was just testing the limits here. Holding her nicely with my hands around her waist, she got closer again. She asked if I knew what she is.

"You are beautiful," I said, but that wasn't what she meant and I knew it. "Yes, I know what this bar is."

I bought her drinks and we talked. Dave was a big man and he was surrounded by two lovely girls. This place was interesting. No prudish American Christians were shutting this place down anytime soon. I started to touch her legs and she liked that now we understood each other. I learned she is 19 years old.

"You can take me back to the hotel if you are interested", she said.

"I am very interested. How much?"

She told me.

We exited the bar, found an ATM and then hailed a cab. She had no problems displaying what was under her short skirt as she climbed in and scooted over the rear seat to allow me room. Wow. The cab seemed a short ride but time goes fast when one is having fun. It took us under the harbor back to Kowloon but I don't remember it at all. I was fixated on lovely Claire. We cuddled and kissed in the back seat. Her body was so soft and beautiful, not like mine all scarred up.

When we arrived at the hotel, I climbed out and again she had difficulty hiding her pink panties as she followed. She knew what she was doing. We entered the hotel lobby, found the elevator and headed upstairs. I handed her the money as I opened the hotel room door. She was surprised I had given her more than what she had initially asked for. I had no idea what was going to happen but she was sweet and lovely, she was treating me well and she looked happy. The boutique hotel had recently been renovated and the rooms had been freshly remodeled in a modern European style. We walked over to the bedroom which was partially separated from the living room by a low divider. She removed her clothes with one exception and climbed onto the bed. I removed all mine and laid next to her. Her skin was so soft and I was hard already.

Laying on her left I adjusted my position so that my left hand was free to float around. I rolled towards her and gently kissed the neck. I felt her body tingle as I watched her head tilt back and eyes close. She was enjoying this and I smiled. Continuing to kiss the neck area, I brought the left hand up and softly caressed her left breast. It was so beautiful, smooth and delicate. I moved my head down so that my lips could massage and kiss it all over. I then rolled my tongue around the nipple area until it was taught and upright. I heard the light moans escaping through her tender lips as I was loving her body.

Still circling the nipple with the tongue, I moved the left hand down so that I was now touching her beautiful inner thighs. Gently squeezing and massaging the flesh, I moved the hand towards her sexy pink panties. Now I moved over her vagina and used three fingers to softly stroke her. Her panties were getting wet and the moans grew a little louder as her body started writhing. I was paying her to satisfy me but I wanted satisfy her too.

I slipped my hand down the front of her panties and moved my body so that she could touch me. I shifted so I could massage her right breast with my tongue and lips. As I felt her wetness, I grew harder and thicker. I loved her touching me as she wrapped her fingers around and started gently stroking me. Her moans grew more intense. Once I sensed she was closing in on her orgasm, I slipped off her panties, climbed on top and thrust deep inside her. She looked at me with tenderness and sweetness. As she climaxed, the scream she exhaled was intoxicating and I exploded soon after. Once we had finished satisfying each other, I expected her to leave but she did not. She stayed the night which made me even happier. I did not anticipate that at all. Breakfast was included in the hotel room rate so she followed me down after we had a few hours sleep. Dave was surprised to see her, I think, but she joined us for breakfast. We had an appointment to meet with clients at their laboratory, so Claire and I made arrangements to meet at the same bar that evening. She took a taxi and headed off.

We were getting an analytical contract for dioxins and PCB's, so we headed over to the laboratory supplying the work. We talked for some time but my mind was pre-occupied with meeting Claire again that evening. A taxi arrived and picked us up from the laboratory and we headed back to the hotel. I took a shower and got dressed for dinner. Dave and I met in the lobby and we ventured over to a local bar for dinner. All I remember about the pub was it being an Irish Bar and we had to walk down some steps because it was below ground. The sights and sounds or the partying that went on inside, I recall none of it. It was a blank. Afterwards we took a taxi back to the same bar on

Lockhart Road.

I was a tad nervous that evening as I waited for Claire to show up. I grabbed a seat at the bar and ordered a beer. Not long afterwards she walked in and a smile enveloped my face. She saw me, smiled and came over, grabbing the chair next to me. This time she wore tight-fitting jeans and a nice short sleeved shirt. The smile she wore was lovely.

"I have to dress in jeans today," she explained, not that I needed an explanation. I was happy to see her again. "Sometimes these bars get raided and illegal ladies get arrested and thrown out of the country. There is a rumour the bar will get raided tonight." she continued.

"No problem. You look lovely," I said smiling.

My crappy life back home was discarded temporarily as I spent another fabulous evening with this wonderful girl. She was small in height, long brown hair, brown eyes, captivating smile with a young, gorgeous, soft, slender body. She was all natural. Californians waste so much money with false this and false that when natural beauty triumphs it all.

We walked around outside for a while and talked with a couple of ladies she knew.

We grabbed some take-out food at a local store and then headed back to the hotel. She removed her jeans and then proceeded in helping me out of my top layers. She snuggled next to me on the couch wearing only her coloured panties and t-shirt. She was sweet and lovely. I had turned the TV on and selected a movie. We laid out the food and then devoured it. Once done she cuddled next to me and we watched the movie before heading off to the bedroom. Afterwards, with her head on my chest, I wrapped my arms around her and we both fell asleep.

The following morning Dave organized a cab back to Hong Kong Airport. Claire came with us to the airport. It was sad to leave her.

It was time for me to get on the 12-hour flight back to San Francisco and then a flight to Reno before I drove up the mountains to home. It was Sunday morning when I departed Hong Kong and because of the time difference and crossing of the International Date Line, I arrived in San Francisco earlier than the departure time Sunday morning. It was my weekend with the children and back to chaos.

I had already lost Friday and Saturday. I had serious jet-lag and was totally exhausted. But I could not use this as an excuse not to see my children. I drove straight from the Reno airport to the family home to pick them up. We spent the whole day together. When it was time to take them home, I procrastinated. In four days, I was heading back to Venezuela and I wanted to spend as much precious time with the children as I could.

When the perceived 4 p.m. deadline passed, my wife immediately called. I pleaded with her to let me have them for two more days because I had missed the weekend. That was not going to happen, she said. The situation was turning ugly. She was no longer making sense, not that she did before. She wanted to be in control but wasn't. I had serious jet-lag and was exhausted. I did not have the mental capacity to deal with her. Perhaps she knew it.

"I am going to call the sheriff if you do not bring them home right now," she threatened.

Welcome back to America, Geoff, as I was thrust back into the land of stupidity and madness. I stopped giving a toss at this point. My children wanted to be around me and we needed the time together. A few minutes later I started getting calls from the sheriff's office. I knew their number by this point.

"You need to bring your children home right now. They have to be home by 4 p.m.," the sheriff told me.

"Actually, there is no court document that specifies a time they need to be home. I will bring them home when I am ready."

"You need to bring them home right now otherwise we will come for you and arrest you."

"Come find me. I am not doing anything illegal here and I love my children. I will take them home in about half hour, after we have finished our late lunch."

When we arrived back at the house, the sheriff was upset at me.

I reiterated the court document fact I had stated earlier. He did not believe me and needed to look at the documents himself, he assured me. A few minutes later he came out and shook my hand. His demeanor was different and his level of agitation had dissipated.

"I am sorry. You are correct and there is no specified time in which you have to return your kids," he said.

"I know that already. My wife is insane."

"We deal with this all the time," he replied.

This was my first foray into domestic disputes between couples. A few years later, I wondered how the authorities dealt with this on a daily basis. I would go insane. Unknown to me at the time though, my wife was creating a court file which I would later use against her. I returned the children but I was angry. We wanted more days together. I called my lawyer Monday morning and told him I want an extra two days. Much to the annoyance of their mother, I had the children two more days before heading off to Venezuela.

Chapter 33

MY FRIEND, STUART, who worked at PDVSA, Venezuela's national oil giant with the world's largest oil reserves, told me to arrange my next visit over a weekend. I knew there was a lot of work to do on their sabotaged mass spectrometer, so organizing the visit to incorporate a weekend was easy. It would be a long 14-day trip anyway.

I flew down late August and grabbed a taxi to the Gran Melia Caracas. This was the opulent hotel I had stayed in last December, the one listed on the 'World's Best Hotels' registry. I tried to check in but whoever at PDVSA was responsible for making the booking had failed their job. There was no room. I called Stuart and explained the situation. He was livid at the incompetence of some people he worked with. He was on his way to pick me up. As I waited, I called Crystal on my Blackberry from the hotel lobby.

"Where are you?" she asked.

"In the lobby of one of the finest hotels in the world, down in Caracas." I replied laughing. "I have no room so waiting for my friend to pick me up."

Stuart arrived and I spent the weekend with him and his wife, Damaris, at their apartment. They were a very nice couple and we were becoming close friends.

Whilst trying to deal with the mass spectrometer, I was also trying to deal with not having a hotel room. I needed to be settled in order to have my mind focused on the laboratory problems. Stuart had someone at the laboratory organize a hotel for me for the remaining days of my trip. Monday evening the PDVSA car drove me down to Caracas, along with the two laboratory personnel. We pulled up outside the hotel. I grabbed the bags and entered. The lobby area was small and the hotel really did not look like much. The surrounding area was a little suspect too. This was a different planet when comparing it to the sprawling opulence of the Gran Melia. My suspicions were further aroused when I entered the hotel room. There were no coat hangers. The closet was devoid of anything. I walked into the bathroom. It, too, had nothing. No soap and shampoo, an old towel or two. The room was small with cheap furniture. The bedding was suspect but clean, kind of. This did not make any sense to me. I kind of slept and then got up to grab the car ride to PDVSA.

Stuart asked what hotel they had put me up in and as soon as I told him the name, he promptly turned around and headed down the hallway. He was livid. He returned and promised me I was now booked in the downtown Hilton in Caracas. He confirmed my suspicions when he told me the hotel I stayed in usually rents rooms by the hour. That explained why there were no coat hangers, soap and shampoo, I said laughing. He saw the humour but it was not humorous. In hindsight, it was positively dangerous for a foreign national alone to stay in hotels other than noted high-end ones with fences and security. Caracas is one of the most dangerous cities in the world. Staying in a brothel was not funny, although it was, kind of.

I took the PDVSA car down later that day along with the same two lab personnel. We had to stop by the brothel so I could retrieve my clothes and luggage. We then drove over to the Caracas Hilton and I checked in. However, that wasn't before the beautiful lady in the lab had offered her sofa should the Hilton reservation fall through. I was seeking divine intervention in hopes the reservation went sour. But to no avail. Damn it! The Hilton it was.

Damaris and Stuart drove out the following weekend to a resort town on the Caribbean Sea. We left that Friday afternoon, spent a few hours with Damaris' mother in Maracay on the way and then spent the weekend frolicking in Venezuelan beach towns and resorts.

It was an escape I needed and I could not express enough my sincere appreciation. My mind was heavy and I was trying as best I could to leave the problems behind temporarily. On the way back to Caracas late Sunday afternoon we passed a souvenir booth on the side of the road. I saw a Venezuelan cloth hammock I thought would be good hanging in the house.

"Stay in the car," Stuart instructed me. "If they find you are a foreigner, it could get dangerous and the item will cost significantly more."

Stuart negotiated the price and brought it to the car. We continued on our way back to Caracas. What a weekend.

I put the domestic chaos behind me and I worked incredibly hard at PDVSA's lab. I worked long and difficult hours and had their huge VG ZAB2-SEQ mass spectrometer taken to pieces. The whole top bench was dissected as I went through restoring each piece. We had some laughs but it was intensive work. The corrosive oils used when it was sabotaged had eaten through some of the metal pieces. I needed some mechanical work done on the vacuum pumps so this technician showed up in the lab. Immediately he went into a discussion in Spanish and I just stood there watching him. He didn't know my Spanish language limitations so I just let him talk. He was explaining what the pumps required and what he was going to do. Once he stopped talking, I looked at him and said "Que?". Everyone in the lab burst out laughing because no one expected that. They had been looking at me wondering what I was going to say or do as this technician rambled on in Spanish. Even he laughed.

Once the instrument mechanics were sorted out, I started to turn on the electronics. As I did that, some went up in smoke. Many electronic components had aged and required replacement. I knew electronics worked on smoke because once the smoke is emitted, they stop working. Luckily there was a good electrical/electronics department at PDVSA that sourced the parts as I needed them. In the end, through massive amounts of devotion and attention, I was able to restore the instrument. I was able to put aside my personal madness to concentrate on this work. I was good at that as it turned out but the added stress was enormous. I had the instrument turned on and working when I departed Caracas. I could have stayed longer, I wanted to stay longer, but I was exhausted and needed to go home.

In the months prior to the trip to Venezuela, I had been trying to digest the data that was being generated by the IRMS in our laboratory. Most of our clients were from overseas energy companies, some major international companies. What we were tasked with doing was looking at biomarkers in oil and rock to determine several things.

Someone many years ago had researched and developed technology that monitored the isotope of carbon 12. Carbon 13 (deltaC13) is an interesting component in oil and rock biomarkers. Data generated from it helped geochemists, chemists, scientists find oil, and then determine how the oil had been formed, how viscous it is, what essential components are there, how old and how big the oil field is, how many sources of oil are present (Different reservoirs of oil, sources, can migrate through seepage and create a whole new reservoir mixed with those different oils) , and so on. Rock samples are extracted from core samples as wells were drilled during the research process. The results from looking at the deltaC13 biomarkers, when merged with other analytical data, determined if the rock layers have hydrocarbons present. This told engineers if there was potential for oil or gas within that region. Hydrocarbons can only accumulate under certain conditions. If a rock formation is too porous, for example, nothing will get trapped underneath it.

This is a very complex subject and the data being generated was critically important for the outcome. I was shocked when I determined that we had been providing poor data for years. I had refined a technique to simplify data processing. As a consequence, processing hundreds of samples, I was beginning to see various patterns appear as I was staring at thousands of numbers. I was beginning to notice a consistent envelope, or pattern, across the group of peaks I was required to process, from sample to sample, amongst the different class of compounds we were looking at. The envelope could change, as it was expected to, but generally speaking in scientific terms, patterns persisted.

As an example of the importance of biomarkers in oils, after the Exxon Valdez ran aground off the coast of Alaska, studies were performed on the oils collected from shorelines, animals, the sea, etc. From those studies it was found oil already existed on Alaska's coast from previous spills and seepages. Biomarkers can determine the specific area of the world an oil comes from. The results showed oil from areas Exxon had no strategic interest. Alaska already had oil spills not associated with the Valdez.

Another example is the North Sea off the coast of Scotland. Three wells were drilled many miles apart from each other and the oil was studied from each well. Through various analytical studies including biomarkers it was proved the three wells comprised the same oil source. Essentially it was a massive oil reservoir under the sea.

When I started to learn how to process, I was having to manipulate the processing techniques to evaluate data that our chemist, who went back to Taiwan, had been providing. The fact was, after seeing these patterns emerge from thousands of data points across hundreds of samples, the data was simply wrong. The problems were compounded by the fact no one else in the world was doing this kind of work and so no papers or publications were accessible. It really didn't help me that people seemed happy with the data being sent and no one questioned it. We worked with some of the smartest people on the planet but no one could figure out the data seemed incorrect. This should have been brought to my attention long before I figured it out. I did not understand this part. Even when research is performed, they are not strictly blind studies. No one does analytical studies not having some understanding of what to expect. The person doing the research has some inkling of what the data should look like. Someone should have known long before I found out the data was incorrect.

I had to make some decisions pretty fast, but I was not sure how to tell the professor, our client, a gentleman I had become friendly with soon after moving to the US. How do I even broach the subject that years of data he had staked his reputation on was wrong? I sent an email in an attempt to open the subject. I explained that after running many, many samples, I was starting to observe patterns that looked consistent. I told him I had developed my own processing technique and it was beginning to show consistent patterns in the various biomarker groups of compounds. He had also noted some difficulty in trying to interpret the data, he explained but had never mentioned, so we were coming from both ends. The analytical end and the interpretive end were generating data that was conflicting and difficult to understand. I am an engineer, not a geochemist, so I had zero understanding of what the data all meant. I was just coming from the logical mindset of an engineer. I was flying into San Francisco from Caracas on a Thursday and so we arranged to meet when I got off the plane.

He picked me up at SFO and we ventured out for dinner in South San Francisco. He and I discussed the observations and I presented alternative processes for the data. As we left, we agreed that I was going to run some data and process it the way I believe it needed to be processed. The patterns would be left as I saw they were being generated.

After dinner, I stayed in the San Francisco area before driving home that Friday morning. I was physically, mentally and emotionally exhausted from the long trip and the immense amount of work I had just completed. And, oh yes, the chaos didn't help.

Chapter 34

MY FAMILY LAWYER had called me whilst I was in Venezuela. I was scheduled to meet with him the following Monday afternoon. He was turning out to be a fucking incompetent idiot and I hated him. It was now early September 2007. He gave me no details on the phone, except that he had a matter to discuss. That Monday I showed up and the whole office was quiet. We walked back to his private office and he said "Your wife has a new lawyer and they just filed a default judgment against you."

"What? What is a default judgment?"

By definition, a Default Judgment is a binding judgment in favour of either party based on some failure to take action by the other party. It continues, most often it is a judgment that favours the plaintiff when the defendant has not responded to a request, summons, failed to appear in court. The failure to take action results in a default.

I had no idea that my lawyer had been doing absolutely nothing on my behalf, until now. I mean nothing at all. His incompetence and negligence had resulted in my wife's lawyer filing a Default Judgment because he had not responded to her request to assist in separating the assets. She was desperate for her money since that is all she cared about.

The pertinent point to make about a Default Judgment is that it still has to follow rules of law. The judgment may still favour the plaintiff but laws cannot be circumvented or ignored, even if the judgment was by default. Shit could not simply be made up.

That did not happen here and the rules of law got tossed into the lake. Shit was made up...

"Your wife in the judgment has listed the things she wants and listed the things you get."

"Huh? Before I left the country I thought we had started to do the asset separation process with her second lawyer."

Little did I know and nor was I told what was really going on. I was oblivious to everything. My lawyer had told me nothing and the judgment blindsided me for obvious reasons. I had been so preoccupied with my knee problems and with trying to save my company, paying employees' salaries. However, I had a gut feeling that my wife seemingly being cordial last month felt a tad bizarre.

He continued, "I have gone through it and it looks like you get what you wanted."

That was obviously an absurd statement and underlined his incompetence even further. The defendant doesn't get what they want in a default judgment. It typically favours the plaintiff.

"I am trying to see it from your point of view, but I cannot shove my head far enough up my ass!" I replied.

He started to tell me what she wanted, which was ridiculous. She had made a lot of it up and had transferred mortgages, lied about property values, created a number for my salary, missed out debts and awarded herself a huge cash payment... Wow, I was stunned. I felt physically sick. My heart sank and I put my head in my hands. I kept my composure but really I wanted to punch this guy, my lawyer, and toss him out of his second story office window. It would have been better had I done so as it turned out.

Whatever life I had before was shredded in that very document. The default judgment was complete fabrication. It was fraud, all of it.

I drove home with my head spinning. I had to think. How could this happen?

I called my corporate attorney, James, late that night and left a message. I had no idea what else to do. He returned my call that evening.

"Hello Geoff. I figured if you are calling me at 8 o'clock at night, then something is seriously wrong."

His perception was one hundred percent accurate.

"I just had a Default Judgment filed against me in the asset separation portion of the divorce. I am lost, James."

"Do not worry, Geoff. This can be handled by your lawyer. He can file a California Code of Civil Procedure 473(b) and have the judgment vacated."

As has always been the case throughout knowing James, a call from him changed everything about my mental state. He was good.

This code, when presented to a judge, permits the court to relieve a party or his or her legal representative from a judgment, order, or other proceeding taken against him or her through his or her mistake, inadvertence, surprise, or excusable neglect. A request is enhanced by an Affidavit of Fault from a legal representative if it was indeed his or her fault that caused the judgment, in this case. It is also of note that a court order denying relief is scrutinized more carefully.

"Really, James?"

"Yes, it is used to vacate an erroneous judgment brought on because of a lawyer's mistake. He goes to court and tells the judge it was his errors and omissions that created this. The judge then vacates the judgment. The court has determined it would be grossly unfair for someone to be badly damaged financially, or any other way, from an error and omission made by a lawyer. The court, therefore, allows that to be corrected. In the morning you tell the idiot to file California Code of Civil Procedure 473(b)."

Immediately I felt some relief but James did not know my lawyer. Nor did he know the local judge who would become personally involved. I picked up the phone and called my lawyer the following morning. It was now Tuesday.

"You can use California Code of Civil Procedure 473(b) to have the judgment vacated," I told him.

"Ok, I will look into it and get back to you."

"Yes you will," I answered and put the phone down.

The previous month we had ratified an agreement **in court** and had filed a document that pertained to my income and the amount of alimony and child support I would be paying. I thought that had been taken care of. The judge had signed off on it and the paperwork legally filed.

I looked through the judgment and it was awful. Now, only one month later, the judge was about to accept the Default Judgment, which claimed I was paying myself more than three times the amount we had already agreed I was paying myself. The court was about to hold me accountable for a salary three time more than agreed to without any evidentiary supporting documents. No tax returns, nothing. The reality was I was paying myself nothing. I had nothing and was left nothing. The company accounting had been decimated months earlier. It was all fraud and I was heartbroken, dumbfounded.

After I told my lawyer to file the California Code of Civil Procedure, I flew back up to Vancouver for a board meeting with my Canadian partners. I was shell-shocked and likely looked like hell. I certainly felt like hell. We were all sitting in a bar adjacent to the Hampton Inn in Surrey where I usually stayed. My third partner was Jean, who had built up a Canadian environmental laboratory company of his own. He was fantastic man, very successful. He was also very generous with his knowledge and passed that along in Board Meetings. I learnt a lot from him. Jean sat next to me as I was relaying my plight and discussing the judgment. He moved closer and put his arm around me:

"Geoff, we are here for you. Let us know if you need anything. We are here for you."

The warmth this gentleman emanated in that simple passage of words was astounding. It is a moment I will never forget. I needed it. Damn, I was rapidly losing faith in humanity, but Jean jabbed me on the heart to let me know real people still exist.

Late 2007, my lawyer filed a motion to have the judgment vacated and set aside. It is heard in court January 2008. First, my lawyer's wife was up on the stand in front of the commissioner claiming that my lawyer was an idiot, basically. Next my lawyer admitted negligence, and that his errors and omissions caused the judgment to be filed. It was a simple plea, and correct, according to California Law. His negligence directly impacted me financially. It should have been vacated right then and right there. It was simple. 'A court denying relief is scrutinized more carefully,' I read.

"You have not proved your case. The judgment will not be vacated. It is, therefore, filed and now law," said the judge.

Huh? This made no sense. No one could figure out why it wasn't vacated. The case was simple and the Affidavit accurate and precise. Now there was a good chance I was about to lose everything I had ever worked for. The ruling set me back. I was gutted. It was clear the judge hated my lawyer. Detested him.

How I kept my cool and remained focused goes beyond understanding. I called my corporate attorney, James, and he told me to come to San Rafael in Marin County and meet Cora, the family lawyer in the same office building.

"There were legal ramifications in how we proceed from here, Geoff." James continued. "It has to be done the right way."

So, one afternoon soon after the judge refused to set aside the judgment, I followed James' advice and drove down to his office where I was introduced to Cora.

"Well, this looks like a mess, Geoff," she said.

"That is an understatement. My lawyer did nothing. He did nothing at all."

"Yes, I can see that. It is obvious he took your retainer and did nothing for you after that".

Cora and I discussed what we needed to do. We had one more shot at my lawyer to correct the error and have the judgment vacated, but we had to move fast. He had to file another motion and have it on the calendar within six months of it being recorded. It was recorded and entered 17th September, so we had until 17th April 2008 essentially.

"How are the children doing?"

Cora's question rocked me. I had been staying composed but I was right on the edge. That was it for me. The question turned on a faucet. I put my head in my hands and sobbed like a baby. Cora knew it was coming, I suspect, and she left me to compose myself. She didn't say anything whilst I regained whatever dignity I had remaining. It wasn't much anymore.

"I apologize Cora. I was ok until you asked the question. I can deal with most things but I cannot deal with what is happening to my children. No one cares; not their mother, not the lawyers, not the court system, not the judge. No one. I am dumbfounded again. I don't honestly know how to handle that part."

"I understand, Geoff. No need to apologize. You are a good man, I can see. You have been through a lot already and I am not sure how you are dealing with it to be honest. Clearly this is affecting you. Let's deal with one thing at a time here. This is a mess. I have never seen anything as bad as this."

We discussed the next phase but clearly things had to proceed in an organized fashion. I could not fire my lawyer yet because that would set off a timetable we would not be prepared for. It would shorten the length of time we would need to prepare.

After several months of convincing him, we finally got my attorney to file a second motion to vacate the judgment. It got filed on the last day allowed by the 473(b) law in April 2008 and we appeared in court soon after.

To the shock of everyone, it got rejected.

"Motion denied," the judge said.

I was livid. 'Motion denied' meant I must be heading towards bankruptcy. I could see no mechanism for not losing everything I had worked for. The blood drained from my face and I could hardly walk. At that moment, I could not see a way out of it. I would need to file bankruptcy. It also meant I was now officially divorced. Contained in the judgment was the official divorce proclamation.

Cora had driven up from the Bay Area to observe the hearing. She was stunned. James, my corporate attorney, was shocked when I notified him. They couldn't see why the commissioner refused to vacate the judgement.

Cora and I left the court room ready to prepare for what was next. I could not fire my lawyer yet until the next phase was in place.

"Your lawyer told me he didn't care about your divorce." Cora told me as we exited the courtroom.

"He said what?" I replied in a higher pitched tone than I really wanted to.

"He told me in court he did not care about your divorce."

"He actually said those exact words to another lawyer?"

"Yes." Cora replied.

It was a dark period. I would stare at the four walls of my office and then go home to cry. Sleep deprivation was massive.

On the list of assets she retained was my beloved 1999 Land Rover Discovery Series II TReK edition. It was #7 of around 12 made.

The TReK event was organized by Land Rover and was an off-road competition for the top forty dealerships in the country. It was designed to build camaraderie between employees in each dealership, build team spirit but also to show them what a Land Rover product is capable of. In 1999 it had been hosted by the dealership in San Rafael, Marin County, very close to Novato where we lived back then. The event took place on a custom-made off-road obstacle course in Bodega. The dealership in Marin was going to be given one of the 12 and the rest would be spread around the country. I talked to the sales lady there and she put my name down. A few months later she had called me to say I was on top of the list. We would be getting #7, she told me.

When we went to pick it up, I could not believe it. My wife told me we could not afford it but Land Rover's financing people said we could. Who was I to believe? I was invited to the off-road course in Bodega the following year, 2000, and I took Michelle with me. We both loved it. Now it was part of my life. Marina hated the thing. It brought too much attention in orange and black, covered in decals and off-road equipment. I loved it.

I had written four articles about our Land Rovers that were published in Land Rover Enthusiast, a world-wide publication printed in

England. I was a true enthusiast.

Now my wife had awarded herself the Discovery in the default judgment because she knew how much it meant to me. I was gutted.

I kept the Discovery for a few weeks after the judgment was finally filed in court in April 2008. I did not want her to have it. In the end it did not matter. I grew weary. People told me my ex-wife had been seen around the industrial neighbourhood. She was stalking me. Eventually, one day in late May, the sheriffs showed up at my office.

"I am here to pick up the Discovery awarded your wife in the divorce." He said.

"Go fuck yourself." I replied full of venom.

"You are under court order to turn over the car".

I watched as she appeared and drove away my favourite automobile. Another rock bottom. I didn't know when it was all going to end but end it must. My office manager asked the day after the forest fire in June 2007 how many more hits could I take. In the end, it did not matter because they kept on coming. I had to page my office manager to drive me back home.

"I need to get my Mustang please." I said.

"I am truly sorry, Geoff," said Caroline.

She was watching a strong, healthy man being slowly beaten to death. I was withdrawn and my face must have looked awful.

"My ex-wife is a suckopus" I said.

Confused she asked what one of those was.

"A woman who sucks the life out of a healthy male." I replied.

Angora Fire, June 2007

House in front of mine gone

Smoke Plume over my home

The house behind me went up in 20 minutes

200 foot flames taken from my rear deck

The remnants of the house that Michael saw on fire as we left

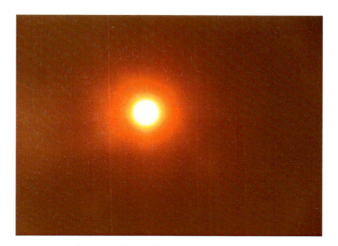

The sun filtered through the smoke

Helicopters dropping water

The 2007 Mustang GT that really made me feel good at the time

The yellow Range Rover

SECTION 4

Chapter 35

IN AUGUST 2007, my wife had been thrown out of my company and only then did I realized (much too late) the financial damage she had left in her wake. In September 2007, the Default Judgment was filed as a result of her anger and my lawyer's incompetence. Life had entered a very dark hole and I needed a distraction to keep me moving forwards. In the fall, Douglas, my ex-wife's brother-in-law, called me to discuss doing the AIDS Lifecycle ride again the following June. It would require serious training. I told him I was signing up to do the Death Ride in 2008 also. I was not at all confident about doing both. Actually, I did not feel good about doing anything. But something inside made me determined to do it anyway.

"Doing the AIDS ride will prepare you for the Death Ride," he said.

"Err, the Death Ride is mammoth. The AIDS ride is 550 miles in 7 days. That trashed my body in 2006 and I needed a long time to recover."

I am legally disabled. How could I possibly complete both? Cycling relatively flat terrain is completely different than climbing huge mountains.

But with all the strife in my life, my mindset was different now. If I started something or challenged myself, I wanted to finish it. I did not want to do 300 miles on the AIDS ride and then only finish with three passes on the Death Ride. Those would not be accomplishments. Those would be failures and would only make me feel worse.

I could not accept half-assed approaches to any of this. Failure was not an option. If I was going to train for the 2008 AIDS Lifecycle Ride with Douglas, having already signed up for the 2008 Death Ride, I would want to complete both rides. But how? My life was cascading into stupidity, so I may as well set stupid goals. I was amassing so much pent up anger and frustration that I needed something to take it out on something. I needed something huge.

I saw Dr. Watson at some point and discussed my desire to complete the Death Ride. He laughed and thought I was crazy, but not in a bad way. At least I didn't think so.

"I will send you over to a psychiatrist if you do," he said laughing. I left his office smiling. I wondered how good the psychiatrist would be.

I talked with Dr. Bannar about the Death Ride and he told me to go for it. Cycling is incredibly good for bad knees because there is no impact and it builds up muscle to strengthen them.

"Just climb passes. Just keep climbing mountains as much as you can, but remember to hydrate and eat frequently," was the advice he gave.

After I failed to finish the 2007 Death Ride, I was even more determined to do so now. My life was shit, I was depressed and I needed some goals to set for myself. My head needed something to keep it from exploding and my life needed something to stop it imploding. 2008 Death Ride was set and I then added the 2008 AIDS Lifecycle Ride to it. Why not?

I grabbed my bike and just started cranking. As the summer months were ending and the cold ones were moving in, I just cycled and cycled. I started to train up mountain passes. I would drive out to Markleeville and park the car, get the bike and cycle towards Monitor and Ebbets on Highway 89. As before I would use the five-mile section of road that meandered along the side of a river before it split off at the base of Monitor and Ebbets to warm my muscles and get my legs pumping.

The west face of Monitor was the first pass I started to train in earnest. I was in a serious mode now. The passes were staggering. I was beginning to develop a thought process for big mountain climbing. Once I conquered the lower levels, I deemed finishing the easier part. I was beginning to notice something in my muscles. Climbing required some effort, obviously, but sometimes the muscles would not turn on until after a mile or so of climbing. I would struggle for the first few miles and then the muscles would turn on. Once they turned on, I was able to climb better and faster. It was weird. It was also a head game. I struggled psychologically many days.

One time I got six or so miles up Monitor. It was hard work. Why am I doing it this way? I am disabled, so I had to rethink strategy. I did not want a three-ring, front-end chain set and to this day don't possess a bike with one (out of the five I currently own). That was purely psychological. At the time, I did not want aids that helped me propel up mountains with only one good leg. I wanted to be and feel like a normal cyclist. Why was that? Ego? I do not know. That day six miles up Monitor, I stopped, turned around and went back to the car in Markleeville. I drove immediately to see Kent at Wattabikes in Tahoe and asked him to help. He removed the largest ring on the back block, 24, and installed a 28. Next time up Monitor things felt different, a little easier and better.

Some days I would leave the house and cycle out on Highway 89 instead of driving to Markleeville. This would take me on Highway 89 up Luther Pass north face, down Luther Pass south face to Pickett's Junction and then west on Highway 88 to climb Carson Pass. These passes all started at 6,300 to 7,000 feet so the climbs were shorter, relatively speaking. But on a bike, a mountain is a mountain.

One thing was becoming very evident. The stress on my right leg was enormous. The pain would be unbelievable at times and I would go home in agony. I was in agony when I completed the AIDS Lifecycle ride in 2006 but had no appreciation for why that was. I just thought 550 miles in seven days was the reason. It wasn't!! Well, it was but not the whole story. My right foot would be awful and the left was in pain at times. The pain was not equally distributed. I thought it was the stress of mountain climbing but it turned out to be more than that in the end.

I just dealt with the pain but it was hard work. Pain was a detriment to my muscles and head working in unison. It was a constant battle but damn I worked hard at it. I was fortunate that my head was so full of pain by now that I just wanted more. I may have been addicted to pain. My head pushed and pushed, I wanted to achieve my goals, but the pain as I did more climbing, cranking out more miles on longer and longer mountain passes, just became deeper and deeper. I had learnt to partition off some of the pain into a compartment of the brain not readily accessed. The same compartment my common sense was in I suspect. My feet and muscles would just burn.

I would come home, discard my clothes and lay on the bed naked. I could not move. Why was I doing this to myself? I wanted to achieve those goals, yes, but my life was utter chaos. I had been ripped to shreds. I was losing everything I had worked hard for and I needed an avenue to vent. I needed the impossible escape to match the impossible chaos. As my life fell deeper into the cesspit of hell, I needed to apply Newton's Third Law of Motion. It states that for every action, there is an equal and opposite reaction. Consequently, the deeper I fell, the harder I wanted to push to escape. The longer I fell, the higher I had to climb. Every time the stress and bullshit increased, the stronger I became. But there was more to it, I think. There is an English phrase: Don't let the bastards wear you down. I wasn't going to let them. I was determined to fight back.

One ride in early 2008 I had conquered west face of Monitor and was now trying for Ebbetts. Monitor was an eight-and-a-half mile climb but Ebbetts turned out to be a whopping 14-mile climb to 8,700 feet altitude. I had to be careful and mindful in the mountains because there was no one was around to help. An occasional car would pass or even a cyclists. But, generally, if something happened requiring an emergency, I would be on my own. The phone signal in mountains as big as these was spotty at best. As a result, I had to carry sufficient water and nutritional supplies, extra clothing, spare inner tubes and tools. Cycling in mountains in the middle of nowhere was a totally different proposition, I was finding out quickly. A 20-mile ride outbound required 20 miles to get back in. Downhill meant cycling back uphill, and vice versa. Bonking, as it is known in cycling, could be hugely dangerous in mountains on your own if one had not planned things correctly. Bonking is the total loss of energy. To bonk simply meant one cannot push one pedal forward. This happens for several reasons but the most common is the lack of proper nutritional intake and lack of hydration. It is so important to stuff the body with the proper electrolytes, chemicals and hydration.

Climbing east face of Ebbetts for the first time I was starting to struggle. The pain was incredible and was beginning to interfere with my head. I had done Monitor west face already and had cycled from Markleeville so I already had 20 miles or so with significant climbing. After about 5 miles into Ebbetts I had to make a decision to stop. I climbed off the bike and laid on the side of the road. My feet were in agony, particularly the right foot. After five minutes, I climbed back on and navigated the return trip back to the car in incredible discomfort. I un-clipped the front wheel, put the bike in the back of my Range Rover, climbed in the front seat and went home. After half hour or so of settling down, I went to visit Kent again at the local bike shop. I needed flexibility on the shoes. The racing cleats did not provide that. They were rigid and formed. With the articulation of the left knee so radically changed, I needed freedom to move. Also, because my right leg was doing significantly more work, I needed comfort over form. I no longer needed to look like a racer. I needed to be realistic and pragmatic.

Kent suggested I change out the pedals and try mountain bike pedals instead. Those pedals and cleats would help facilitate my feet to flex, to move and not be rigid, he explained. I thought this would be a really good idea. Not only that, but mountain bike shoes have the benefit of the cleats being recessed. They don't protrude from the bottom of the shoe. This means walking around would be easier and more comfortable. I would no longer be articulating the foot to accommodate the cleats, which added strain on the bad knee. It was a simple solution but made a world of difference. I began to play with angles of handlebars, length of the handlebar stem, position of the seat, how high it was. I started to make small differences in the comfort level on the bike. I wanted to try anything because doing all this cycling was bloody difficult and painful.

Winter training is impossible in the mountains so I used a rear wheel trainer in my bedroom. I purchased warm clothing which made a world of difference during the rare times I could cycle on the roads. I was learning quickly that comfort was essential climbing passes.

One training ride up Ebbetts I watched the dark clouds amass. As I got closer to the top, the clouds grew even darker. It was going to be a race to see if I got to the top first or it started raining first. In my mind, if I did not see the green marker posts at the top of each respective mountain that named the pass and its' altitude, then the climb would be a failure. On this ride, I was very close to the top of Ebbetts but not quite there. I wanted to complete the 14 miles, 3,200 feet of vertical climbing. I did not want to 'quit' so close to the top. I knew I was close, perhaps less than a mile, when the heavens opened and it started to pour down. Ebbetts has a lake very close to the top on the east face. I passed it. I wasn't going to quit. I kept going, clawing my way up the final few feet to the top. When I got there, I knew this was bad. The top half of the mountain was very steep in places, with huge drop offs on the sides. Some were 500-to-1000 foot cliffs that just dropped at the edge of the road. The road had many switchbacks with sharp turns with no protection from those cliff edges.

One California Highway Patrol Officer I knew asked why cyclists who climb mountain passes bother to wear helmets. "If they go off the road, which they frequently do, why bother with the helmet? The body is broken up so badly that we only hope they are dead before we get to them."

"The helmet is required for cyclists who have wakes," I replied. "At least the head will not have to be reconstructed when the casket is opened."

"Good point," he said, looking at me funny.

I put on a wind jacket, which was waterproof, and started the long descent down. As the rain splashed against my fingers and toes, my appendages started to freeze. Rain is very cold at this altitude no matter what time of year. As my fingers froze, I had difficulty braking. Steep mountain passes required perpetual braking to slow the bike to controllable speeds. I did not fancy flying off the edge of a cliff. With wet wheels, more pressure was required. With my fingers falling off, braking was painfully difficult and my hand muscles started to ache. I took one switchback at a time, but with the road getting wetter and the braking harder.

The front wheel started splashing water against my body, including my shoes. The cold, wet air shooting past as the bike descended the mountain cooled my body further. My sweat, generated from climbing so hard, now turned into very cold moisture.

I saw two cyclists being picked up by someone in a Jeep Cherokee. But I wasn't going to chicken out, I thought in one of my stupider moments. This was a valuable experience. Note to self, avoid going down a huge mountain pass in freezing rain, you dumb shit!!

I was also mindful of the left knee. It had limitations in its flexibility so always wondered what would happen if I crashed. Riding in the rain down a mountain would increase the likelihood of it happening. It was all stupid. What was I risking here?

Fortunately, I made it down. The relative warmth at the lower altitude made things easier. However, my toes were still falling off and both hand muscles were numb and cold but ached from the relentless braking forces. I had to concentrate coming down mountains, perpetually scouring the road for debris, including rocks, small stones, holes, rodents, wood, trees, etc, etc. Descending at high speed is inherently dangerous. Downhill sounds fun but it was very difficult and hard work that required intense concentration. It was made worse by the size of the passes I was training on and doing it in pouring rain was madness!

I made it to Markleeville, drenched and cold but alive. I climbed in the car and drove home.

What the hell was wrong with me? Was I insane? Well, that was a rhetorical question. I have become insane. Why was I trying to kill myself? With so much pent up anger and frustration at the system, it needed to be vented to alleviate the stress. As the definition of stress goes: The confusion created when one's mind overrides the body's basic desire to beat the living shit out of some asshole who desperately deserves it.

During the winter months, when timing permitted, I was also driving back to the Bay Area again to train with Douglas. One thing for sure, the level of fitness I demanded and needed at this level required significant time and dedication. It was absolute work.

Chapter 36

THE FIGHTS WERE constant and the battle to keep my life going was immense. I was mentally exhausted. I had to run a business with employees but had no cash. There wasn't any. The reserves had been taken. Whilst all the personal nonsense was perpetually ebbing and flowing, I had to keep my head down and keep working for my company.

The IRMS data had been an issue from day one but no one knew. From the time our Isoprime was installed in 2004, the data being generated was erroneous. Yet no one had questioned it. I was determine to correct the problems on an instrument I knew very little about. We were trying to provide data clients could use. They had to make decisions, perhaps some huge monetary decisions, based on the information we provided. The professor I worked with told me the interpretive process was difficult because of the data quality. No one knew why at the time. It should have been questioned but wasn't. I was deeply exasperated.

After meeting with the professor when I returned from Venezuela back in September, we left it that data would be processed the way I thought it should be. I started to re-run previously-run samples and compiled the data sets. It would then be sent off for some comparative interpretative studies.

"The data you are generating now is starting to make more sense. I can interpret it better and the numbers are starting to align properly," the professor told me a week or so later. "Now we need to re-run the last two and a half years of samples," he said. "We need to present these new findings to clients that have the old data sets."

How was I going to finance this? I had no money. I had to bring in money and business, not run samples for free. This was not good news, not good news at all, but I knew it had to be done.

"We can spread the work out so samples do not have to be done all at once," the professor said. "When we present the new data, you are going to have to write a letter to each client explaining the reasons behind the incorrectly calculated results."

Huh! Why me? Clearly there was shared fault and I didn't have the technical or literary skill to compose letters of this magnitude. We were talking about PhD chemists, who were heads of geochemical departments in multi-national global energy giants, and academics who were the tops of their fields. This was going to be difficult for sure. Not only that but PhD chemists and professors are immensely eloquent in their literary skills. They can read between lines of bullshit, as I found out very early on in this profession. The letter would have to be both technical and factual, but ultimately it would need to be credible. I would need the help of a dictionary **and** thesaurus!

The re-run of samples was a major effort. The accompanying letter was eloquent and factual and sent to the respective heads of departments, along with the new data results. We lost some major clients because of this. It was a huge mess for sure. At the time, the work we were doing was not being done anywhere else in the world. We were collaborating on some proprietary analytical separation techniques. What a cluster-fuck this predicament turned out to be. Observing important patterns in biomarker carbon 13 (C13) data under insatiable, absurd, immense pressure and stress was a significant accomplishment. It should have been a pinnacle in anyone's professional career but it wasn't. All I was doing was correcting problems others had created or failed to notice. If I had been involved when my company started doing this work in 2003, things might have been different.

Unfortunately, that did not happen. 2003 was a medical disaster and I was simply incapable of direct involvement. I spent most of

2003 dosed up on narcotics, suffering through three major knee surgeries, struggling with immense pain and hobbling around on crutches. My mind was simply screwed up and floated around in LaLa Land for extended periods. In any event, we hired a PhD chemist for this purpose. The poor data was a financial and professional debacle but someone should have known this.

Chapter 37

ALMOST FIVE MONTHS after the forest fire, early December 2007, I was able to move back into the fire-repaired home. I could not wait. I had been so depressed in the rental property. The house was small, no views, and was dark inside. I had picked the place because it was close to my children's friends so when I had them for the select weekends the judge had agreed on, they could visit their friends and be happy. I was left to be miserable on my own. I needed back in the home badly where it was my castle. A home is an Englishman's castle. I desperately needed a sanctuary, somewhere warm I could escape to. A private place I trusted.

Repairs to my home had stopped in September but no one had bothered to call me. I found out it was my mortgage company's fault.

The following day I called Wells Fargo Home Mortgage' Claims Department and explained what was going on. The lady pulled the file.

"We had a question for you before we could release the second payment." The lady said.

"Well why didn't you call me?" I responded. "Winter is approaching and I need to get this finished. I want to move back into my home."

"We couldn't call you. This is an in-call department only. We cannot call out."

"Pardon?" I was furious. "The phone was invented some time ago by Alexander Graham Bell. It works in both directions. It is an amazing device when used properly," I said as sarcastically as possible.

"Well this department doesn't allow us to call out sir."

That resolved, I was going to move on a Monday so I spent the weekend packing my things. I had boxes and suitcases but there wasn't much since I had not purchased much. As I needed items I would drive to the fire damaged house and retrieve what I needed. Each time I went, my neighbour would see my car and immediately knock on the door.

"Are you moving in yet?" He would ask.

"No, Tom, not yet. The house isn't finished. Soon, I hope."

Monday came around and I loaded the Range Rover. I was so happy. I needed to get into my own home. When I parked on the driveway, exited the car and walked towards the front door, I had this huge smile. Finally! At last!!

I opened the door and immediately a musty smell enveloped me. Oh shit. I knew that was the smell of standing water that had been there for a while. Then, as I walked further into the home, I could hear the sound of running water. The house was built on the side of a hill in three levels. As I approached the stairs going down to the lower level, the smell became more intense and the sound of running water was louder. When I looked down the stairs, I could see a few inches of standing water. My heart sank. What was going on now?

I went downstairs to survey the damage and entered the master bedroom on the left. There were about four inches of standing water. The noise of the water was coming from behind a wooden panel in the wall so I removed that. As I did, I saw the damage. A water pipe had cracked. Sigh! More shit!

I knew where the main water shutoff valve was so I clambered behind the downstairs closet and reached for the valve. Once turned off, the water stopped. Unfortunately the damage was done. It was later determined the contractors had turned off the heater before they left the previous Friday. That weekend turned out to be the coldest of the early winter, causing the pipe to freeze and split. The walls were wet at the bottom and the carpet was soaking. The water had traveled down the small hallway but luckily not all the way into the fourth bedroom I had added on during the reconstruction. It was bad but could have been worse.

I called my insurance company who told me which company to call to fix the mess. I made that call and got Thomas to come out to assess the damage. Two feet of sheetrock had to come off the walls. The carpets were removed. The Wayne's coat in the bedroom was gone and so it was removed. I had to find yet another $3,000 for the deductible, but the carpets the insurance company didn't want to replace after the fire now had to be replaced.

Despite the damage, I refused to leave my home again. The water did not distract me from the desire to get back home. I emptied the car and filled a room with a small number of boxes and suitcases. I didn't have much. The divorce saw to that. 2007 had been a very bad year and now, as it was closing out, I had water damage to contend with. Fire and water claims in one year, and I had not owned the house eight months yet. I wanted 2007 to go away fast.

Chapter 38

ONE DAY IN late February 2008 I decided to make someone else happy despite my misery. I ordered flowers and had them sent to Crystal. It had been six months since we last communicated so I thought it would be a surprise. I had not messaged her since the call from Caracas. Nothing happens for a day but then she called me.

"Geoff, did you send me flowers? You are the only person who sends me flowers."

"Yes," I replied. "I was having a bad day and wanted to cheer someone up."

I think I made her happy in that moment. It was all good. When the chips were stacked against me, I still wanted to make someone else happy. I still had it in me to stay calm (kind of), be kind (kind of) and be there for someone.

In March 2008, it was the annual Fireman's Ball, a big winter charity gala in Harrah's at Lake Tahoe, and I invited Crystal. It would be our first date, kind of. She wore a tiny black dress. She had gorgeous legs. In essence she was a Barbie Doll with blonde hair, voluptuous lips, toned and tanned slender body with breast enhancements. Everything I never had before. She looked stunning and I was happy. I had arranged for a friend of mine to accompany a friend of hers and the four of us departed for the Fireman's Ball.

While I was dancing with Crystal in the middle of the dance floor, I saw him. It was an enormous moment. I hadn't seen him since the surgery in February 2007 after we had been through hell together. But there he was. Dr. Watson looked at me from across the dance floor and, at that moment, we were telepathically engaged. It was pretty emotional. Then we were in the middle of the dance floor, hugging each other, oblivious to anyone or anything. I had struggled for so long while Dr. Watson had kept me going. After many seconds, we let go and then hugged again. I then introduced him to Crystal.

"You know I am divorced now, right?" I asked him.

Without any change in his demeanor, he answered me in a matter-of-fact tone that surprised me. "Yes, I heard. Sorry Geoff. When families go through what you went through, nothing can keep them together. We see it often in the medical profession. You had a very tough time, which your wife could not deal with. You came through and I am very proud of that."

The evening came to an end and I took Crystal home with zero expectations. I was invited in. She is out of her dress immediately and headed toward the bedroom wearing only her tiny black panties. What a beautiful sight! I had an erection brewing intently. I followed her, discarding my clothing along the way. I was surprised to see a twin bed as I entered her bedroom but it made the rest of the night interesting.

Chapter 39

IN APRIL 2008, Douglas and I signed up for the Party at Pardee ride at Ione in the California foothills, close to Jackson. My divorce had degraded to a new low. Michelle had been kicked out by her mother so she was living with me. At 16, she could not drive and she worked later in the afternoon. I had to be home at a specific time to pick her up. The organized ride was relatively short at 65 miles, with around 3,000 feet of climbing. I wanted to get my legs warmed up after winter stagnation.

One notable event occurred on this ride which changed my cycling. I saw a rider wearing a Death Ride shirt so I cycled up to him.

"Have you completed the Death Ride?" I asked. Cyclists are generally friendly people.

"Yes," The nice man replied.

"I am doing it this year."

Without even prompting him, he looked down at the gearing on the bike.

"You will not finish it with the gears on your bike. I recommend you do something because you will need lower gears for the mountains."

"Well, thank you. I appreciate the advice."

"It is hard work so try and make it easier on yourself," he said smiling.

At the lunch stop I told Douglas I need to get home so I departed on my own. I made the last 20 miles in one hour, pedaling really fast.

My muscles were burning at this point but I drove home with urgency to get to Michelle on time.

I then went to visit Kent at his bike shop and explained what the guy had said on the ride. He thought for a while. Putting three rings on the front would be expensive because everything would have to change. Gear levers, chain, derailleurs and front chain set would be expensive. Kent then had an idea.

"What if I install a mountain bike derailleur on the back? It will retain the current layout with the two rings at the front but nothing much would have to be modified. You would retain the 53/39 teeth ring on the front but add a 34 teeth ring on the back. It would make a significant improvement."

"Ok, sounds excellent."

I wanted to keep the bigger ring on the front because I reach immense speeds coming down the mountain passes. I would fly down and needed, or wanted, the big ring at the front. His suggestion sounded really good.

I left the bike there and a week later I retrieved it with the modifications described. The Shimano XT rear derailleur made a massive difference. Before, I was slow going up mountains. Now, I shot passed my neighbours. It was so different and I started cranking the miles even harder.

I was preparing for the 2008 AIDS Lifecycle ride. I just kept pedaling and pedaling. One weekend I did 25 miles on the Friday evening, rode around Lake Tahoe from my home and back which was 80 miles on the Saturday, and then cycled up both sides of Monitor on the Sunday. That was 160+ miles in three days. I was smoking and the new gearing made a huge difference.

Chapter 40

IN APRIL 2008, soon after the judge failed to grant the motion to vacate the default judgment for a second time, I fired my lawyer. I wanted to fire him earlier (and beat the crap out of him) but we were on a set timetable and things had to be done in order. I was about to file suit against him.

My new lawyer, Cora, and I were now on a tight timetable to get things sorted out. She was working really hard behind the scenes, but I wasn't fully aware of what she was doing or how she was doing it. My newly-fired lawyer's liability insurance company was now involved because they knew litigation was forthcoming.

Cora was trying to get the insurance company to pay some of the alimony and child support that I was in arrears. The Department of Child Support Services (DCSS) continued to harass me, but the real crippler was when they suspended my driver's license. How could I work without a driver's license? As an engineer working in a scientific world, the DCSS logic here left me perplexed.

The things I never understood with DCSS were their priorities. Their job was to protect children. The family court's number one priority, as I understand it, is the children. But I never got the impression that was their mission. Not at any time did I feel they were protecting my children. Not once. My ex-wife had already thrown one of our children out on the streets, but that did not diminish DCSS' persistent attacks on me. It was relentless.

James, my corporate attorney, told me that he had never seen an insurance company pay alimony and child support, ever, and he had been a divorce attorney for years. What Cora was doing, he went on, was unbelievable. I think she threatened them with losses beyond the insurance limits. If they went to court and lost, and it was determined an event beyond normal errors and omissions had occurred, the judge had the authority to remove those limits. This was not simply some error my lawyer made. This was tantamount to gross negligence beyond any capacity, and it was intentional.

Cora had contacted San Francisco's top appeals court lawyer. He only took on cases based on merit. Cora called me. "Geoff, you need to call this lawyer. He will interview you as you go over the details. Be precise and accurate. He is preparing to accept the case based on what you tell him."

I was in a client's lab in West Sacramento when I had to make the call. I explained everything in precise detail. I went through it piece by piece until I had finished.

"Looks like a good case here. Rules of Law were not followed and the judge made a personal judgment that was in error," the attorney said.

I was beginning to feel good as top people were taking control. Everyone was optimistic and thought an appeal justified. The Appelate Court should put a stay on the default judgment, I was told. It was a common theme amongst my legal team: we will win the appeal.

Once we filed the motion to appeal the default judgment in the Appelate Court in Placerville, we could do nothing but wait. It would be at least a year waiting period, I was told. Oh my God.... I had to live this life for another 12 months, at least. I wasn't sure how I could. Until the appeal was heard, the default judgment should have been put on hold. Only part of it was. With the filing of the appeal, and since the judgment contained the divorce decree, the divorce itself was officially put on hold. Essentially I was still married but this point wasn't made clear at the time. Or perhaps it was and I had chosen not to listen. I could have chosen to ignore what somebody must have told me.

We waited and waited. DCSS was still after me. They knew I didn't pay myself what the judgment claimed I did. They knew we had filed an appeal but they simply did not care. This made no sense. An appeal was filed which meant the judgment was on hold, I was still married and yet DCSS still went after me.

I was still behind on alimony and child support payments, even though an insurance company was now involved. DCSS still suspended my driver's license. It was absurdity elevated to new levels. Nothing made much sense at this juncture. They put on hold one part of the judgment but not all if it. It made no sense at all.

Chapter 41

ON SATURDAY AT the end of May, 2008, I drove down to Douglas' house in South San Francisco to prepare for the AIDS ride, which started the next day. It was similar route to the ride in 2006 so I knew where we were going.

But several things had changed on this ride. I had become much quicker and my speed and cadence increased. That meant leaving Douglas behind each day. I had adjusted to a cadence I was comfortable with. That was so important for extended rides. Slowing for someone took the rhythm away and made it harder. Douglas was ok with that because it meant I arrived at camp early and put up the tent. The site was all prepared when he finished his rides.

This time I knew how to wear cycling clothes so the agonizing sores on my ass disappeared. My ass hurt after seven days on a bike but it was manageable. The change to mountain bike pedals and cleats made a monumental difference. My feet still hurt but nowhere near as much. I had gained strength and experience.

I crossed into the park on Wilshire Boulevard on Saturday, the 7th, feeling really good. I had achieved Goal #1 for 2008, the AIDS ride, and it had not wiped me out. As I did in 2006, I headed off to a hotel, retrieved a rental car and drove back to South San Francisco. Douglas flew home, and I still beat him.

When I drove back to Lake Tahoe on the Sunday, Crystal was there to greet me. She was really excited and proud that I had finished. She didn't know me that well and certainly didn't know I was an avid cyclist. She had a congratulatory card for me and I felt good arriving home.

A couple of weeks later, her mother and stepfather visited from Arizona. The Saturday we were going to meet up, I was out training again in the mountains. This time I was going to try and complete both sides of Monitor and east face of Ebbetts. I had never done three huge mountain passes at one time. It took some serious effort but I felt strong and climbed to the top of Ebbetts feeling good, although I was whacked.

I went home and got ready to meet her parents. I drove over to Crystal's apartment on Kingsbury Grade and had dinner. The following day they came over to my home and we all sat outside drinking beer. Whilst Crystal's parents were in town I had quietly asked her mother for her daughter's hand in marriage. She hugged me and gave me her blessing. I called her adopted father and put forth the same question. Both were very happy for us.

The 2008 Death Ride on Saturday, July 12th marked several accomplishments for me that year. I had completed the AIDS Lifecycle just a month earlier. In 2007, at the same event, I never thought those two rides, separated by just weeks, in the same year was remotely doable.

I was living two different lives. In one, I was being destroyed by my wife. In the other, I was in a kind of fantasy land where I could cycle like everyone else. The differences from reality and fantasy were mind-blowing. I was angry and took my immense anger out on my legs instead of the person who desperately deserved it.

Cycling 550 miles for the AIDS ride and, a month later, cycling 109 miles with over 15,000 feet of vertical climbing through five mountain passes, with only one good leg was a remarkable feat. Actually, I would have said it was impossible. The transition from the 2007 Death Ride, just after the forest fire and two major knee surgeries, to completing both the AIDS ride and Death Ride a year later was magical. It was ridiculous but it exemplified my desire. It was testament to the effort I exerted but, like Newton's Third Law of Motion, it proved action and reaction are equal and opposite. I completed the two goals I set myself. I didn't see it as a mammoth and colossal feat for me. I saw it rather as a reflection on how bad my life had sunk. Completing the AIDS and Death Rides within weeks of each other was exactly what I needed to achieve in order to keep moving forward.

I learnt something important on 2008's Death Ride. The first two mountain passes were pretty easy, once my muscles started working. East face of Ebbett's Pass was a struggle because it is huge. I was beating up my muscles. The west face was a seven-mile, seven percent climb straight up. There was no change in gradient and no rest area per se. I pushed the whole way.

Half way up mountain pass number four, the west face, my body changed. My body had wanted to stop a long time ago but my head refused the overpowering urge. Half way up my body stopped fighting the urge to quit. At that point it started working in unison with my head. Head and body worked as a team from then on out. It was a remarkable transition. Crystal and Michael waited for me in Markleeville, after I had completed the fourth pass, expecting me to be on the verge of collapse and requiring medical attention. I simply wasn't. As I rode up the small climb into Markleeville, I was talking to an HP employee doing his first Death Ride when I spotted Crystal.

The easiest climb was mountain pass number five. Once I had crossed that barrier of the body fighting the head, the cycling took on a new dimension.

A week after the Death Ride, Crystal and I drove down to Folsom Shopping Mall and I purchased matching engagement rings. I was so happy. She wore this 50's style flowered summer dress that was low cut on her breast implants and flowed out above her knees. Dinner was with her adoptive father and his wife in celebration of our engagement.

Then I drove back home. I parked and we started making out. I pushed the button to bring the front passenger seat down. She seemed happy too. I brought my left hand down and started to caress her lovely soft legs. I could feel movement in my pants. I moved my left hand up her inner thighs, massaging them until I reached her panties. She was wet and ready. Damn, she was gorgeous and I could not believe it. I slowly removed her lace panties, unbuttoned my jeans and climbed on top, easing myself slowly inside of her. I was in heaven now. Whatever was going on in the background didn't matter at this point. Crystal was stunning and we were happy.

Chapter 42

CHRISTMAS 2008 WAS significantly different than the year before. Crystal and I were now engaged. We were all happy. Many presents were laid out under the tree. I had installed Christmas lights on the front of the house, which added to the festivities. Everyone was enjoying life, except, it seems, Crystal. Something wasn't clicking with her. She enjoyed Christmas but faded rapidly after that. She was struggling with a bad shoulder from shoveling snow, she said.

My guess is that she was beginning to feel isolated. She didn't work. I bought a Toyota Highlander off her last boyfriend so she could have a car. But I too was struggling financially, which didn't help. In fact it just burdened me with added stress. I could not involve her with the company because I had suffered a bad experience with my wife controlling the finances. Perhaps we had jumped the gun getting engaged but we loved each other, I thought. I was wrong.

She was taking Zanax, which I learnt too late, and drinking wine. She was coming from bad relationships, including an ex-husband who was abusive, bad childhood, unhappy life. I did not know how to handle it at the time. I tried but I was failing.

Despite the struggles, Crystal and I had a commitment ceremony at a local wedding chapel. Crystal wore a gorgeous white dress and I wore my white Italian linen suit. It was wonderful but we signed no marriage certificate. We couldn't, luckily, as it turned out, because of my appeal.

Her shoulder problem grew worse and she underwent surgery in February.

I tried my best to make her feel wanted, loved and cared for. Damn, I loved and adored her. I cooked my famous homemade macaroni and cheese because it was easy to swallow. She laid in bed upstairs as I brought it to her. She had been prescribed both Percocet and Vicodin for the pain relief. I could take one Vicodin a day and get addicted. She began swallowing these in huge doses. The first 30 Vicodin went pretty rapidly so I suspected she was taking two every 4 hours. I grew concerned. She was petit, 5-foot-4, weighed around 110 pounds. There was absolutely no way her body could accommodate nor metabolize the amount of narcotics she was digesting.

Her demeanor was changing and she was becoming weird and bizarre. I knew drug addiction would change her. It changed me. She was becoming more withdrawn, more distant, more depressed. Her behavior was unpredictable and erratic. She waited to come to bed thinking I would be asleep. She had anxiety, was agitated and irritable. She wanted to spend less time with me. I saw the writing on the wall, but I could never have predicted what happened next. My mind doesn't operate down at that level and it hit me like a speeding bullet train.

On Wednesday afternoon mid-March, we went to an appointment to look at her shoulder. It was heavily bruised but was progressing as expected. The surgeon seemed happy with the progress but I noted all the bruising. As we drove home, we decided to have early dinner at a cafe right off Highway 50. It was around 3:30 when we sat down. We ordered drinks and food as we talked. It did not take long for the conversation to turn weird. Crystal started saying strange things, well strange for her anyway. I ordered another double 12-year-old Glenlivet and she had more wine. Then things started to take a sharp turn in the conversation.

I was oblivious to what was going on behind the scenes and I had no idea what she was conspiring to do.

After five hours, I had had three double whiskies. I was feeling ok.

No idea how much wine she had consumed but I knew that was mixed with narcotics. Not a good combination. My Range Rover was parked outside but she had already asked the bar to call a cab. I didn't drink enough to warrant a cab but she insisted. I continued to protest lightly. It didn't matter. I was going to drive home no matter what she told me.

As I walked outside a police officer showed up. What was he doing here? I asked myself. He walked over to me and involved himself in our conversation. The yellow cab arrived but I wanted to drive home. I never drink enough to warrant a cab, just a rule of thumb I have adhered to for years.

"If you get in the car, I will arrest you for DUI," said the officer.

I was shocked. Why was he even called to the restaurant and who requested his presence was more to the point?

"I don't drink so much I cannot drive home, Officer. Never have. I am fine," I pleaded but with no success.

"I suggest you take the taxi otherwise I will arrest you." He was polite but something was happening here I did not understand. As it turned out, it was all a cover for what Crystal had planned.

We climbed into the yellow cab and went home. I opened the front door and we walked into the kitchen. She was in a strange mood now. I don't like fighting or arguing.

After the cab dropped us off, she tried to start another argument. I didn't play that game, so I went upstairs to the bathroom. The combination of greasy food and the three double whiskies made me feel awful. I put the toilet seat up and promptly discarded both the food and whiskey. As I walked out of the bathroom and into the bedroom, two sheriffs greeted me.

"We are here to arrest you," obviously predicting the question about to escape my mouth.

"Arrest me for what? I have not done anything."

"For domestic violence. You hit your wife on her shoulder. Please turn around because I am going to cuff you."

"What?" I was stunned. "I didn't hit my fiancee. Where is the evidentiary support?"

"We don't require evidence to arrest somebody. She is on her way to the hospital in an ambulance."

America doesn't require evidence to toss someone in jail? It also doesn't require evidence in divorce default judgments either. It was all bullshit.

I must have gone into shock because the next few minutes were blank. I don't recall leaving the house or being put into the squad car. None of it. Michelle later told me I was crying and an ambulance was taking Crystal to hospital. I didn't even know Michelle was at the house. It was complete and utter pandemonium, she added but I don't recall any of it. I was in shock. I had just been accused of hitting a woman (I don't hit women) and hitting her on her bad shoulder. With my surgical history, that scenario was preposterous. With zero proof, I had been arrested for domestic violence.

I was taken to jail. I was asked to remove my watch, jewelry and wallet, which were all placed in a plastic bag. Bail was set at $8,500, which would mean I could get out if I posted $850 bond. Once I was put into the jail cell I saw a bail bondsmen advertisement on the wall around the phone. I looked at the advertisements and found someone I knew. Our children went to the same Catholic school as his. I placed the call and got an answer straight away. I needed to stay in jail overnight to calm down. I was livid. As I lay on a concrete bench in the cell trying to sleep, I vowed to make better choices in my life. The legal system was insane and bordered stupidity. I was bailed out and driven back to my car still parked outside the front of the restaurant.

I went straight to my office and was talking with my office manager when a call came in from Jerry. Jerry was a pastor at a local church. Crystal had me going back to church. He called me totally out of the blue, evidently, that Thursday morning.

"I am coming over Geoff. Let us go out for an early lunch."

I was grateful for his intervention because he learned I had just been released from jail. I was not myself and felt as if I had been beaten hard across the head with another baseball bat. I liked Jerry. He took time out to help people.

"Crystal called me this morning. She was upset. I asked her to explain what happened and so she did. Geoff, why don't you tell me what happened?" he said in a calming voice.

I explained everything, item by item. Ten or so minutes later, Jerry responded. "You have almost described word for word exactly what Crystal said."

I just sat in stunned silence. I could feel my body changing inside.

"She is supposed to be a Christian. How could she do this?" I asked.

I was stunned, heartbroken and mystified. I had never been around someone so damaged before. I could not go home because of the restraining order for seven days, even after she had moved out. I ended up staying with a tenant from my building.

That weekend a snow storm hit Tahoe. The Range Rover was parked outside my tenant's home. I needed to go somewhere so cleared off the snow so I could climb in, turn on the engine and press the 'Program' button on the front dash of the car which turned the car, windshield and rear window heaters on. The car was facing forwards in the driveway so once I was ready and the windows were clear, I sat in the car, pressed the gas pedal and selected reverse. As I drove backwards off the driveway, snow on the roof slid forwards on to the windshield. I immediately heard what sounded like gun shots as the snow slid onto the glass. I rapidly swiveled my head, looked around and then dropped below the window height. I heard a few more pops and wondered who was firing at me. My heart rate was sky high. What the hell was happening? Then, after a few seconds had passed, I lifted my head and realized what it was. The windshield had cracked big time. I knew I had a small crack in the lower right corner that had progressed from a stone chip. Now the windshield had enormous cracks along the top, bottom and middle. The snow had rapidly cooled the hot glass when it fell on it. The popping sound was not a gun but the windshield splintering. I really needed to improve on my personal decisions. I was bloody good in my professional life. Why could I not handle the personal life as well? I really didn't need all this drama nonsense. Nobody does! Nobody needs this crap.

After seven days, my criminal lawyer told me to request a civil standby before I legally entered my home. Crystal was gone and she let the authorities know she had left the house. I was, therefore, allowed back in. A female police office showed up and entered the home first. The house had been mostly emptied. Crystal had removed her stuff and the house felt empty. The reality of the situation hit me at that point. I was walking around half dazed, observing the aftermath of my engagement. My life was once again in tatters. My home was once again devoid of life and most furnishings. I had been cleaned out. It was all surreal now. My body went numb, my mind emptied and I just sat, dropped my head into the cupped hands and started crying. I went into shock and would remain that way for five very long months

Chapter 43

IT WAS VERY difficult for me to function properly after the false arrest. My mind was blank and I was walking around in a clouded haze. I still had to run a business, travel to client sites and take care of analytical work in the laboratory. But I needed an escape. Where else would I go but my trusted yellow Giant TCR2 bike? The first opportunity that I had after I was released from jail, I took it.

Late in March 2009, the roads in and around South Lake Tahoe were clear. I filled up a water bottle with powder mix one Saturday morning, put on the appropriately warm attire and started off on a 22+ mile circuit. I was well familiar with the route around South Lake Tahoe because I had done it many times. It was my warm-up sprint route after the winter blues. I had a speed and time window in my head in which to perform under. Outside of that window, I would deem it a poor ride. My fastest recorded averaged sprint time was 19mph.

I circumnavigated this once and then sat at the end of my street. I cycled that pretty fast considering it was the first road ride after winter. I slipped the water bottle out of the carbon fiber holder on the bike frame and gulped some electrolytic-laced fluids.

I was livid, angry, upset, disillusioned, numb, in shock, and did I mention angry? I drank some more powder mix to restore some of the nutrients lost and contemplated doing the circuit one more time. I ended up doing two circuits with the one stop for water. I was livid beyond any measure and I vented the only way I knew how.

In the end, I had the longest contiguous ride of my cycling career. Anger pushing the pedals, pain to push away pain.

My daughter and I were having issues because times were rough. She had been living with me for a year. I decided one day she needed time away. I wanted to send her away to England to stay with her cousin who was one year older. Michelle needed this part of her life purged and forgotten.

So, late spring, off she went. I changed her phone plan to include international calling in case she needed to call. And one day, she did.

"Dad, I want to do a stud in my belly button."

I went silent for a few seconds.

"Ok, if you do that, then I am going to have an earring done."

Now silence the other end.

"Are you serious, Dad?" she said in a slightly elevated tone.

"Of course," I said, laughing.

She came home from England thankfully without a stud in her belly button. What a lucky escape for me.

She had a tremendous time with her cousin and she needed it.

"I was centre of attention because I am from America," she said as she was reciting some tales. "I could drink in bars, go to parties and meet people. I was the foreigner."

I already knew how that worked, being a foreigner in another country. It was the best thing she could have done. She returned a different person. We were all struggling with events unfolding and her trip overseas gave her some modicum of confidence. Money well spent, even if I did not have it.

Chapter 44

AN EX SISTER-IN-LAW called soon after I was released from jail. She had evidently heard the story. She wanted me to meet a friend of a friend of hers who lived in San Francisco. Tamara, a beautiful name, was Jordanian, a few years younger than me.

One Saturday in April, I drove to have our date at The Cliff House in San Francisco. It was close to where Tamara lived. I knew Arabic women were aware of clothing and styles. Some of the finest linens, cloths, cotton, rugs, carpets come from the Middle East. Arabs can dress impeccably, most notably Arab ladies. I chose a black Italian pant with pleats and cuffs, a white cotton shirt with French cuffs and a burnt orange Italian double-breasted jacket. Added to that was a pair of black leather dress shoes. It all complemented the orange Mustang I took down - not that I dressed to match my automobiles - very often.

Tamara opened the door to her apartment. She was beautiful. She was typically Middle Eastern which, to say, meant she looked exotic with her olive skin, dark brown eyes, shoulder length black hair. She was slender and wore a silk cream dress, which was partially see-through, in an elegant, modest way. I knew she had three children but they were back in Jordan.

She had a bubbly personality and we got on straight away. I don't know what she thought when she saw the Mustang but she liked that too. I opened the car door for her as she stepped in to the passenger seat.

After dinner I drove her back home as we talked more. I walked her to the front door but I was not expecting anything further. We agreed to meet up again soon, hugged briefly and I left.

We started dating but I knew I was different. Jail had changed me. I was nervous. I had to be very careful how I approached her. Now I knew someone could call 911 just like that. It made me timid and very apprehensive. It was difficult for me to trust any woman.

We became close over the few months we were together. She came to Tahoe one weekend but I could not handle it. She was beautiful and she loved me. She knew how to cook and look after a man. She loved sex. But for me, there was something missing. I was terrified of a relationship.

Anxiety encapsulated me and I had to run after only a couple of months of dating. I could not handle a relationship. I was petrified. She would have made a first class girlfriend or wife but I could not handle it.

Jail was not funny. Tossing innocent people in jail to help curb the escalating domestic violence problem is not an answer. It changed me.

I have met several men who have been tossed in jail by their spouses and they say the same things. They are bitter and angry. They are changed men. I see it in their emotions when they talk about it. I could tell by their choice of words what jail meant to them being innocent.

Chapter 45

AFTER THE LONGEST contiguous ride end of March, I started training really hard in the mountains again. I cycled and cycled, pushed and pushed, trained and trained, through pain, sun, rain, cold, exhaustive heat, more pain. Anything to get my mind away from reality. I once did east face of Monitor, the colossal 11-mile, insatiable eight-percent straight-up climb, but was exhausted and had no energy. I did not understand why until another cyclist told me it was 105 degrees. I was climbing huge open-road passes in 105 degree heat. Madness, all of it. It did not matter. I was angrier than I had ever been. I needed to vent.

I ended up completing The Death Ride a second time that July which no one thought I could do. Not only did I finish the five passes, but I cycled back down to the camping area where my car was located. I had done the 129 miles. I cycled up to my Highlander and just sat on the tailgate in complete and utter disbelief. I felt better than I thought I would. Those 129 miles remain the longest cycle ride in my life. Only a hand full of people thought I could finish in 2008. No one thought I could do it twice. It was mind-blowing.

A few years later I went to listen to David Zabriskie give a talk at a small theater in Marin County. He was coming off a strong Tour de France showing and during the question time, someone asked why he did so well. He explained that he lives in Utah and his home was broken into. They stole all his cherished trophies, awards, memorabilia, most things that could not ever be replaced. He was angry. He did a strong tour because he was angry.

I could relate to that because I completed my second Death Ride in 2009 because I was angry. I was beyond angry. I was livid at being tossed in jail for being guilty of nothing at all. I was livid at the Appeal against the fraudulent default judgment taking so long. Not only did I finish the ride, but in places I conquered it. Climbing up east face of Monitor, the second huge pass, 11 miles of it, I met someone at the bottom and we talked the whole way up. I was hauling myself up mountains and talking at the same time. The first time I completed the Tour de Tahoe in 2004, I could not comprehend how someone could do that. I was mastering it. East face of Ebbetts pass, which was the third huge climb, 14 miles of it, I was talking to a college kid out of Colorado as we both climbed. He was early 20s I am estimating. I left him behind. I was fucking livid and needed to quench my anger. I took it out on my legs.

August 2009 rolled around and I needed something other than my bike to help me. I needed to be satisfied sexually. I needed a lady to help me get through this. I found a telephone number of an escort agency and I made a call one Saturday morning. To me it was not necessarily the sex that I needed but someone for companionship, someone I could talk to and be comfortable without any commitments or expectations or emotional attachments. Requesting a specific type of lady though is always a crap-shoot with an agency. However, we made the arrangements and a lady named Casey was going to contact me later that afternoon. She would not be off work until around 4:30pm. Ok, I was fine with that.

Casey finally called and told me what time she would be showing up. It is a fascinating experience, always, because one never knows who is actually going to show. Around 5:30 the doorbell rang. I had already seen the black Mercedes C class drive up. I looked at Casey. She was mid 20s and she was gorgeous. Slender, around 5'6", long brown straight hair that was parted off-centre so one side flowed over the side of her face, hazel eyes and gorgeous with very tender, moist, natural lips. She wore this simple black dress that buttoned up the front with black high heel shoes. The dress was just a touch above the lovely shaped knees.

"Hi Geoff, I am Casey".

"Welcome to my home Casey. Please come on in. You look beautiful and thank you for coming to visit me".

She walked into the house and gave me this lovely hug. I had showered and put my favorite Chanel cologne on. She had a big smile on her face.

I appreciate it must be tough for women who do this work. And I don't think they expect someone like me requesting their services. At least that is what I have been told from time to time. Why are you doing this? some would ask. Simple, because it is much easier with less headaches, no complications, limited expectations or zero commitments and, of course, no drama.

"You are very handsome and smell nice. I love your accent," Casey said.

"Thank you," I replied, with a beaming smile.

I knew already this was going to be a good experience. She was friendly, beautiful, voluptuously elegant and professionally dressed. She had a bubbly personality and a gorgeous smile. She walked into the kitchen area and immediately sat herself on one of the breakfast bar stools. We quickly got the business end of this transaction sorted out and then continued to talk. She sat with her lovely smooth legs crossed and I could see at the lower end of the dress that it was open, partly revealing her amazing thighs. Oh boy... My body's numbness was diminishing, I was feeling again. She had little make-up on, simple and stunning.

"I just came from work. I am sorry. All I have are my dress and panties", she said.

"That is fine. You don't need anything else. You are sweet and beautiful. All we need to do is this."

As I was saying that, I proceeded in unbuttoning two bottom buttons on her dress which revealed even more of her legs. She seemed comfortable with me doing this. "Thank you," she replied as

I performed that task. I was being careful to help her feel comfortable with me.

We talked more, laughing often. Then it was time for her to entertain me. She excused herself and off she went to the bathroom but not before she told me to go sit on the couch and make myself comfortable. A few minutes later she came out in just her black panties. OMG. She was stunning. My mouth fell open. She was all natural. Everything appeared real. Her body was smooth, full of youth and it was slightly toned in texture and colour. Her breasts were perfectly contoured, the small nipples complemented them. She could have been a model.

As I sat on the couch, she danced for me and then a few minutes later she removed her panties. I was now in heaven. She sat on the coffee table with her legs slightly parted. She was completely shaved. She got up, gently removed my shorts and t-shirt and sat on my lap as we talked for a while longer. My hands were gently massaging her beautiful body as she was touching me. She then asked where my bedroom was. Watching her beautiful naked body, I took her upstairs.

What an amazing experience. She was so lovely but there was also a chemistry between us at play here. It added to the wonderful, liberating experience. We kept talking through most of being together. She loved my body also. Women loved the strong legs even though it was a by-product of my anger and my upper body was still toned with smooth skin. As I removed my jockeys, her eyes opened.

"I need to be paying you, I think," she said, laughing. At a time when my life was in the toilet, she was precisely what the doctor had ordered. Two women had tossed me to the sharks but Casey made me feel so special. Yes, I was paying her but chemistry is chemistry. I knew the difference.

She made sure I had her number before we parted and I also made sure she had mine too. A few months later I got a text message totally out of the blue:

"Hi Geoff, I have moved to Reno and I want to see you again. Want to meet for a drink? You are different than most men I meet and

I would enjoy having a drink before going back to your place."

Well, how do I answer that?

I continued to see her for several years after the first encounter. Casey moved back to San Diego area and I went down a few times to rendezvous with her. I could deal with her. I wasn't scared because it was a different kind of relationship whose boundaries had already been defined. We both knew exactly who we were and what we wanted.

One time we planned to meet in a hotel in La Jolla overlooking the Pacific Ocean. I had spent an afternoon arranging flowers for the table at the restaurant that evening. She was so special, so nice, so beautiful, so bubbly. We walked into the restaurant adjacent to the hotel and there were the flowers waiting in the middle of our table. We had this chemistry which was so important and added to the ambience of being together. It was like a girlfriend experience without the commitment and pressures.

Before she left for San Diego I had told her I want to see her. I booked dinner at a nice restaurant, added a flower arrangement on the table in her favourite colour and then booked a room in a local resort for afterwards. We spent hours together that night. Time with her was so wonderful. I am not sure she had a client treat her so special, but she always complimented me and made me feel good. That was vitally important for me at that time. I needed someone to make me feel good about myself without the commitment. Jail changed me. It was an experience I would not wish on anyone, not even my enemies!

Chapter 46

MY ORTHOPEDIST, DR. Bannar, told me about a cycle race around Lake Tahoe on a weekend in September, during the Lake Tahoe marathon. He brought it up when I was visiting his clinic. I doubt he was expecting me to sign up for it, unless he too thought I was sliding enough into insanity.

But signing up for the September 2009 race is precisely what I did. In preparation for the race around the lake, I, in my infinite wisdom, had decided to do a race beforehand. It would provide much needed experience as I had never raced before, ever. The local Alpina Cycle Club out of Carson City did regular races during the season. I signed up to participate in April's event in Diamond Valley, near Woodfords. The closest I had been to racing was in England when I cycled with my friend David to Bridlington to watch cycle races near the beach.

I drove out to Diamond Valley and registered to race that evening. The lady at the registration desk looked at me.

"What group are you in?"

"I have no idea. I have never raced before."

She looked down at my legs and must have seen the muscles on the right one, or wrong leg depending on one's perspective.

"I will put you in Group B" she said

As I paid and turned away, the guy behind me had a sly grin, as if he knew something I didn't.

Good luck he said. Clearly I had no idea what the hell I was getting myself into. However, that hadn't stopped me so far.

My legs were big and they were feeling good too. The lady picked the wrong leg for the group I needed to be in. We were doing two and one half laps of a circuit that is 12 miles long. I was going to race 30 miles. Hmm.....

When we started the race I was doing ok. On a very shallow descent, soon after the start, I was keeping up and even led the pack for 30 or so seconds. But once that stretch of road was finished and we turned right to head up a small hill, that was it. I did not have the power in the left leg to climb fast up hills so Group B disappeared pretty fast. I could have been disheartened but I wasn't. At least I was trying.

I came second to last and my muscles were sore. I did not come last because someone who raced for University of Nevada, Reno's cycling team had a mechanical failure.

The race in April around Diamond Valley wasn't too good but it motivated me to train harder. I had zero desire to embarrass myself. When Dr. Bannar had mentioned a race around the lake, it captured my attention. After I signed up for September's race, I reminded my-self that I didn't set a goal that I didn't have the intention of finishing.

I was also training to complete the Death Ride in July so I knew I had to crank the miles and altitudes. I knew I had to climb mountains and build strength. Everything, all the anger, frustration and despair in my life, went into each mile, and I pushed into and through the pain. At this level I had achieved, there was always the pain.

Chapter 47

2009 CONTINUED IN the same vain as 2008. The default judgment was still on hold because we had filed an appeal. My life continued in chaos and I was surrounded by abstract madness.

DCSS continued their assault on me, which made no sense. If the Judgment was on hold, why did they continue to hound me? My driver's license kept being suspended and I had to drive, even if it broke the law, so I could work and make money. Once the second appeal to vacate was denied, Cora got onto the liability insurance company assigned by my first family lawyer. They knew our lawsuit was coming so they were preparing. They had started paying child support and alimony but kept delaying payment which took the account into delinquency. I had to keep calling Cora to deal with it. The absurdity and bullshit kept escalating. The paradigm kept shifting and I kept having to make adjustments.

In the summer of 2009, I was returning home from Sacramento. I was being careful how I drove and kept my speed at the limit (the legal limit). My license was once again suspended due to arrears in child support and I was greatly concerned about being thrown in jail again. I was driving the Mustang, which is like a beacon with cops. I was traveling east on Highway 50 towards South Lake Tahoe and had just passed Sierra at Tahoe Ski Resort on my right. I was traveling behind a short convoy headed by an old truck. The truck was struggling. Even with a passing lane, I retained the speed of the convoy being set by the slow-moving camper. It was dusk so light was fading. As the road flattened out on Echo Summit, I looked in the rear view mirror and saw a police car racing up the hill behind me, his lights flashing. I gulped a little and my heart rate took a turn for the worse. Surely he wasn't after me. I wasn't doing anything.

To my astonishment, he pulls up right behind me. I find a place to pull off the road. I dropped the passenger side window with a cursory push of the button. The officer headed towards that side of the vehicle.

"Do you know why I pulled you over?" the officer said.

"No, officer, I do not,"

"You were speeding. I caught you doing 65 as you were passing Sierra at Tahoe."

Now I was agitated and pissed. Clearly the officer was lying, but I had to be very careful because of my suspended license

"Officer, I was behind a newer model X5 and he was behind an old truck pulling a camper. We were in convoy so I could not have been speeding. The truck was struggling up the mountain at this altitude."

By describing the cars in front of me, I was trying to portray the environment I was driving in to demonstrate my awareness. It did not seem to work on this guy.

"I have you speeding."

"I did not see you by the Resort. Where were you?"

"I need your license and registration please."

I knew he was lying but there it was. Now my heart was pounding. I was pretty confident driving on a suspended license was illegal. Whilst he was back at his police car, I was trying to gather my thoughts to determine what would happen next. I thought an arrest would be coming, and my beautiful Mustang impounded. I would be off to jail. I saw him coming back.

"Here is your license and registration. I have written up a ticket for speeding....." as he proceeded in telling me the court date and my options.

"I will see you in court," I said. Traffic officers never like those words.

I was clearly agitated by this ticket, but when I realized he wasn't going to arrest me, I became bolder. I rotated the key and cranked the 4.6L V8 engine. The Magnaflow exhaust spurred into life with a melodious thunder. God I love the sound of American V8 engines. I dropped the clutch, shifted the gear lever into first and vacated the area, somehow overcoming the immense urge to spray gravel all over the officer and his car.

I had dodged a bullet but why did the system put me in that position in the first place? I didn't understand any of it. It just left me more bitter and even more angry.

Chapter 48

IN MAY, I sold a high-end mass spectrometer to a new laboratory in Vancouver, Canada and it required installation. I realized too late that my passport needed to be renewed so I filled out the appropriate paperwork, took the necessary photos and expedited them off. To my astonishment, the package was returned with the renewal being denied by DCSS in California because of delinquent child support payments. This was getting pretty serious and I was getting angrier and angrier. Without a passport, I could not travel internationally. That was my work, I travelled overseas. This was total insanity.

Cora called the insurance company and once again got them to tender payment for child support arrears. With the insurance company paying the child support in arrears, the way was cleared for renewing my passport.

The trip up there was an opportunity to escape but it ended up being really educational, fascinating and funny. I always revel when an opportunity to learn something new is presented and international travel definitely facilitated that. The company buying the equipment was owned and operated by Russians. They had a contract to study hydrogen as a source of fuel for automobiles. However, or luckily, take your pick, those involved in this development realized early on that driving around with compressed hydrogen in the trunk of a car was not a good idea. This company would be studying the effects of using a catalyst to generate hydrogen right at the ignition source.

It was also fortuitous that on a recent trip to University of Hawaii in Honolulu I had developed a method to perform a similar study on a very similar instrument.

I pulled up to the laboratory, which was a small commercial condominium set amongst a small strip complex. The building was just wide enough to house the instrument once installed. Next door was an auto body shop and outside sat a '90's Nissan Skyline GT-R that was damaged.

"Who owns the Skyline?" I inquired with Igor, the instrument operator.

"No idea. It has been there for a while."

"That car is worth a lot of money. I want it," I said jokingly. I had no money.

"Why would you want that? It is damaged and not worth much."

"No, Igor. That is worth a lot of money. The Skyline wasn't made for left-hand-drive. Only grey market cars escaped Japan. These are collectible and have a cult following," I explained.

Once I showed him on the internet what they sell for, he was shocked.

As I was removing the instrument from the 24-foot Penske truck I had driven to Vancouver in, a beautiful white Lexus LS400 with custom rims drives up. The windows were blacked out. Out stepped a Russian-looking gentleman wearing a very nice suit. He introduced himself as the owner of the company and we shook hands.

"Dohbreyh dehyn." I said, which means good afternoon in Russian.

We talked for a while and when he left I said pleasure to meet you, and then goodbye using the more formal Russian vernacular.

"Ochen priyatno. Dohsvedahnyah."

I was chuckling to myself the whole time. Would I return home alive, I thought.

It was like watching a scene in a Russian movie play out. The fancy car, the well-dressed Russian business man, the small alley for the unscrupulous business to be hidden from view, the British foreign national mixed in with all this. I was half expecting to be tossed in the trunk once installation was completed, never to be seen again.

The installation was quick and I managed to escape the Russians without incident, by leaving early one morning and driving home.

Chapter 49

BY THE SUMMER, I was really tired of dealing with court and all the other nonsense. I did not have the time to keep wasting on motions and procedural protocols, particularly with the criminal court. It was incredibly consuming and travel had to accommodate repeated trips to the court room. The Appeal against the judgment filed in the divorce was still holding firm. This was also taking forever and I needed resolution on something.

I called John, my criminal lawyer, as I worked on a site in Columbus, Ohio.

"How do I get the false charges removed or dropped?"

"You have to agree to do something Geoff. They cannot be dropped even though you did not do anything." He replied.

He provided a couple of options so I chose counseling. I had to go to counseling to get the charges dropped and my criminal record expunged. I was recommended a therapist near Woodsford for anger management counseling. When I walked into her office soon after, she took one look at me and told me I don't need anger management.

"I will discuss anger management for a few minutes but clearly you need to find a way to choose your partners better. I will counsel you on domestic violence instead."

I was shocked at what I learnt during those ten sessions with her. Simply amazed. My family was told years ago that my mother tossing pots and cups at our father was a sign of a healthy marriage. It clearly wasn't.

UPHILL

The error I apparently made was that I thought I could help Crystal. That was a mistake in judgment I paid for dearly. People, I was told, have to help themselves first before someone else can. They need that desire to want to change their life and move on from past experiences.

Soon after I completed the court-mandated counseling sessions, I went to have the charges dropped. The district attorney looked at me as if he was doing me a favour. John told me he would do the necessary paperwork to have my criminal record cleaned up.

A few months later, cannot remember how many, I was flying back home from another trip to Vancouver and going through US Immigration in Canada. The officer scanned my passport. He looked at his computer monitor and told me to head off to a different room for further processing and questioning. What the hell. I ventured over to where he had pointed and walked into the office. I stood behind a counter and waited for someone to come forwards. A young man approached his desk and asked for my passport. When he scanned it in, he looked at me.

"You have a restraining order on here. Were you in some sort of trouble?" he politely asked.

When I told him what happened, he started laughing. I didn't prompt it.

"Yes, most of the young women are screwed up in this area also."

I could not stop laughing. The guy was funny. I explained the record should have been cleared up. He chuckled, handed me the passport back and ushered me on my way, but not before he said:

"Stay away from the crazies."

I looked at him with a grin.

We were two men from two different countries expressing our matching sentiments about a predicament that is common. From a woman's perspective, I am coming off as insensitive but women talk about the exact same thing about men when they are together. Damaged people exist from both genders and some of the reasons for the damage are not funny at all. From my personal perspective,

260

tossing an innocent person in jail because your life was bad is a ludicrous concept. A legal system that allows that to perpetuate is even more ludicrous. One cannot extol the virtues of a free society when events like this are common.

A year or so later I am stranded for a few days in Grand Junction, of all places. A Penske truck I had rented to transport some equipment had broken down and needed to be repaired. I entered the mall across the street from the hotel and headed to a Columbus outlet. Walking around the store holding an orange sweater, a lovely young assistant walks up to me.

"Can I help you?" she kindly asked.

"Only if you are a trained psychologist." I replied.

She burst out laughing claiming she wasn't one of those and walked away, smiling. I put humour in the place of anger in an attempt to slowly move away from the horrifying and life-changing events.

What was happening to me wasn't funny. However, in a foreign country going through Immigration, I had to find ways to blow through my palpable frustration and irritation. I do international travel and having false claims on my record is quite demeaning and incriminating. Scanning my passport, some countries may elect to not let me in for example. It was utter madness and absurd beyond any calculable measure. I had anxiety going through any immigration port and it added stress I didn't need nor deserve. International travel for work is difficult enough without the added nonsense.

Chapter 50

THE TAHOE MARATHON weekend started Friday 25th September, 2009. The race itself was on the Saturday morning. I was told it is quite an event with police escorting the riders on one lane of a busy four-lane highway through the middle of South Lake Tahoe. It sounded pretty exciting and intense.

My friend, Kent, at Wattabikes recommended Perpetuem as a nutritional product to use for racing. If I were to drink a bottle every hour, then I would not require solid food. That makes it easier.

The morning of the race, I was up early. When I got to Zephyr Cove, the start of the race, it was a hive of activity. One lane was coned off and police were there. It was a real event and my adrenaline was pumping. I was pretty nervous. I don't like failing at anything so I was taking this pretty seriously, even if others were not. I had no idea what I was capable of doing. All I was going to do was do my best, whatever that was.

Cyclists are generally a friendly bunch of folk so I got into conversation with a few at the start line. Laughter was good and lightened the nerves, but not by much. The faster cyclists were herded to the front of the group. The only warm clothing I wore above my normal cycling clothes were long fingered gloves, a wind-breaker jacket and arm warmers. I just hoped at 7 a.m. on a late September morning in the mountains, my toes would not fall off before the sun came up enough to warm the area.

The police were ready and we set off. The professional cyclists had disappeared very quickly. Damn! I put my head down and cycled to the best of my ability. I had no idea what I was in for but just continued as fast as I could.

My first stop was the top of the climb just after Vikingsholm parking lot. I removed my wind breaker and arm warmers. I had cycled 20 or so miles pretty fast. I just kept cranking.

I liked the west side of the lake after Emerald Bay, the hills are relatively small and generally more downhill than up, descending around 1,000 feet of elevation. That part was fast. At one point I looked down and I was over 20 mph on a flat portion. As I hit Tahoe City people were lined up on the right of the road to hand out water bottles.

I wasn't sticking to the plan of one Perpetuem-filled bottle per hour and I would pay later. I kept pedaling. King's Beach arrived and I knew there was a rest area and toilets with water fountains. It would be a good place to stop and fill the water bottles. That was my second stop. Around 55 miles into the 72-mile ride. I had no idea what time I was doing. And I didn't know until I finished that it was important to know that.

There is a short climb up Brockway Hill after King's Beach. Then after a few more miles I hit Lake Shore Drive in Incline Village. Now marathon runners were on the right side of the road but heading in the opposite direction. The natural order for cyclists was to pass them on the outside. It was safer for the runners, but one motorist in particular did not like cyclists being in the road as they were making way for runners coming in the opposite direction. She started blaring her horn and shouted through the open front passenger window. I hate stupid people and I started to chase her but several cyclists slowed me down and calmed me.

At that point I started to bonk. To bonk in cycling terminology is to run out of energy. I had to slow. I had to drink copious amounts of Perpetuem-laced water. I had some Cliff energy chew bars, so ate some of those. As I neared the end of Lake Shore Drive I felt some energy coming back. This was good to feel because once I turned right onto Highway 28, I would have that ten-mile, 1,000-foot elevation climb to Spooner Junction. I needed all the energy to climb that in a racing situation.

I climbed Spooner pretty well and felt good at the top. I was talking to other cyclists as I climbed and even met two female cyclists from Alaska who talked about darkness, time differences, short summers, etc. I could not find a reason to live in Alaska after talking with them.

At the top of Spooner I turned right onto Highway 50 and pedaled downhill towards the lake. This was a fast portion and brakes were required to keep speeds below 50 mph. A few miles later I was almost home. As I turned the last short left hand bend, I could see Zephyr Cove Lodge off in the distance. It was a short downhill section and then a short climb to the Lodge. My muscles were pumping and I was feeling good as the adrenaline and endorphin rushes were climaxing. The uphill gradient was small but I didn't care. I needed the downhill to gather momentum for the final push home and the adrenaline was kicking in. I had raced 72 miles around Lake Tahoe with only two stops. I felt good but I was very tired. As I approached the finish line there was this huge clock which posted cyclists finishing times. I saw the clock read around 3 hours 55 minutes. I was elated no matter what the time was. I had done what I had set out to do and the time seemed irrelevant.

I got off the bike and walked towards my car and the activities going on. Then some guy came over and told me congratulations.

"Well done. You finished in under 4 hours. That means you will get a medal."

"A medal. A medal for what?"

"You don't know?", he said. He saw me shaking my head so continued. "Cyclists who finish in under 4 hours get a medal."

So, I cycled as fast as I could not knowing I could get a medal. It really didn't matter had I known because I could not have done any more than I did.

The two ladies from Alaska also received medals and they looked much better out of their cycling clothes than in them, I thought, smiling. Perhaps Alaska isn't all bad.

Another mammoth event I had finished. I went up to receive a package which, along with the medal, also included a trophy simply for entering the race and a license plate surround that said "I cycled Lake Tahoe Under 4 Hours'.

Later that year I met Dr. Bannar at a charity wine and food event at Harrah's Casino. I told him I had finished the Death Ride a second time and had raced around the lake in under four hours. He was speechless but the look on his face was priceless.

Chapter 51

MY ATTORNEY, CORA, called in late fall of 2009.

"We lost the Appeal on the default judgement in a 2-1 decision Geoff," she said.

Somehow reading my mind over the phone, she continued. "I know you are upset but we have to deal with it. The higher courts try to protect the lower court judges. They have to. Also, this is only someone's divorce, so no one really cares."

"This is my life," I said. "I will be bankrupt within two years. Everything I have worked for will be lost."

I may have cried at that point but cannot remember. This would mean I would be in yet another fight to salvage what remained of my assets and my business, whatever little was left by now anyway.

"Not only did the appeal get tossed out, Geoff," Cora continued, "But the appeal and the file will be sealed from public records. In other words, your appeal doesn't exist."

The three appelate judges had decided to seal my appeal file from public records. It does not exist. Is that even legal? Does that affect my civil rights? In a free society, I did not get it. The only conclusion I could draw was that the judges didn't want this appeal to be case law. They did not want other divorce lawyers to access the file. I should not have been surprised at the judges' verdict but I was surprised at the appeal being sealed.

I felt vindicated to some extent because I had been saying all along the judgment was fraudulent and illegal. By sealing the appeal file, the three-judge panel had essentially agreed with me. The legal system would not be allowed to access my case file in future divorces which was good, otherwise the divorce system may have collapsed.

I was dumbfounded. The loss of the appeal was huge but we had to deal with it.

Now I had to deal with my corporate attorney, James. Because the appeal was tossed out, this validated the lawsuit against my first family lawyer. This, however, became more difficult as my lawyer had filed for bankruptcy protection in the interim.

Now I needed to find a bankruptcy lawyer to remove the stay on the lawsuit against him. I found one in Sacramento, which brought the number of lawyers on my payroll to six. Could it get even more ridiculous?

The stay was eventually removed and the lawsuit was allowed to proceed in earnest, but not before another bombshell hit me in late October 2009.

I was looking through my emails and found one from a Wells Fargo Bank in a suburb of Sacramento. Without my knowledge, I had been assigned someone to deal with my case. In the default judgment, two mortgages on property awarded to my wife had been transferred to property awarded me. This was an illegal transfer. The banks would never allow that to happen. It became a massive mess.

In hindsight, I should have stopped paying the mortgages from when the judgment was filed and gone into bankruptcy. That would have been the smart move. Unfortunately, I made my wife's mortgage payments to protect family assets. A big mistake. In the end Wells Fargo Bank, one of the lien holders, didn't want anything to do with this mess so they sent me an email. I was told to stop making mortgage payments because the properties were going to auction.

The auction date had been set for some time in February 2010.

The lawsuit was terminated within hours of the auction, but not before I had gone mentally insane. I am bound by law not to divulge information pertaining to any perceived settlement. The case was closed. I was given about three minutes to list personal items

I wanted in the divorce. I was given those three minutes parked at the side of Highway 50 as I was driving to Sacramento from Tahoe. I guess I was lucky I had phone signal. Remembering what I had and what I wanted was impossible.

Never again did I see the inside of my home after being removed January 2007. I can no longer recall what I used to own except on occasion when I get reminded by something or someone.

I have a plaque on the wall in my home: "Things turn out best for those who make the best of the way things turn out."

Once the Appeal was lost, the divorce became official. At least I won that battle.

Just before the final rest stop at Pickett's Junction, Death Ride 2008

Approaching the staging area at the top of Carson Pass

A monumental moment; the fifth round decal being planted on my cycling
bib number at the top of Carson Pass. The fifth and final mountain climb
of the infamous *Death Ride*

SECTION 5

Chapter 52

IT WAS OFFICIAL, finally. I was divorced. It only took three years and two months. The judgment was never vacated and remained in force. The assets had been finalized and split, but not without tremendous loss of value.

Cora called me one day.

"Geoff, I am going to recommend another family lawyer. I am exhausted mentally. I am done and cannot adequately provide the continued support you require. Your case depleted my resources."

The lawsuit was settled and most assets had been distributed. Unfortunately, there were two remaining issues that needed some attention. One I had to deal with and the other someone else took control of.

I was on a job site in Klamath Falls, Oregon in March 2010 when I gave my third family lawyer a call. I sat behind the large instrument I had been asked to work on so the clients could not see me. I had tears rolling down my face as I explained the story to John. I needed to have the child support and alimony changed to be more reflective on what I actually paid myself according to tax returns and my current status. What I was still paying was absurd. John agreed to take on my case and we would meet up when I returned from Oregon. Unfortunately, I had no understanding of what it would take to have alimony and child support payments reduced.

I had to deal with a forensic accountant to look into my personal and corporate financials. A huge dossier was meticulously crafted and then filed in court.

My ex-wife had no idea this was coming. I was looking forward to this. They would have to present documentation that justified the number they put down in the Default Judgment as my salary. This would also make the judge not look too good. I was fighting back, slowly, but it was time consuming and required massive effort.

Late in July, I was playing around on the internet. A few years earlier I had found a third party Land Rover dealer in Alabama that would get some one-off Land Rovers. I would check the site occasionally, when bored or I needed motivation. There she was: TReK #3 from the same event in 1999. It was identical to #7 my ex-wife had taken from me. I immediately called the sales guy and found it was available. A week or so later, it arrived on the back of a trailer from Alabama. The paint was no longer a bright orange. It had faded and was rough and milky, as if no one had ever waxed or polished it for fear of damaging decals. I spent a long time in my garage over the winter hand polishing the paint. I was amazed at how it came out. It looked showroom again. I added or replaced damaged/missing decals and it was starting to look really good.

Unfortunately, two weeks after receiving the Discovery, it ended up in court documents. She was pissed that I had purchased the TReK #3. That was another win for me. I had one or two wins, not many, but enough to keep me going. There was a mind game going on. I had been beaten down and I kept having to scramble and grab things to keep me afloat, metaphorically speaking. Anything positive no matter how trivial kept me moving forward. The alternative to not moving forward wasn't pretty.

I mounted the 'I Cycled Lake Tahoe Under 4 Hours' license plate surround onto the rear of the Discovery. It seemed appropriately suited to the Land Rover.

Chapter 53

IN THE SPRING of 2010 I was back out training again. During the winter I had not used the indoor trainer much at all. I had elected to drive off the mountains and get on my bike. It was significantly better. I was contemplating doing the Death Ride again but didn't have a ticket yet. My thought would be to drive out the Friday afternoon before the ride to see if they had any left. After the rides in 2008 and 2009, I was still feeling pretty strong. Some, but not all, of the financial pressures from the divorce nonsense had dissipated and jail a year earlier was a fading memory. The change in me was still there but I wasn't so angry.

The winds in the mountains can be pretty erratic, changing direction quickly and radically. A lot of the passes ventured into gorges, canyons and ravines where the winds get tormented and flustered. One can have a tail wind and then just from going around a corner it can turn into a head wind. They are unpredictable and incredibly strong, powerful and, unfortunately, dangerous.

I was fast coming down mountains. Very difficult to observe speeds with the little computer I had fastened to the handlebars. I had to keep my eyes glued to the road in front when cycling at speeds in excess of 40 mph but I could access maximum speed later. I loved the adrenaline. The speed rush was a drug and scintillating. It got the endorphins all juiced up and feeling happy. It was a feeling very difficult to articulate and impossible to understand. I just needed that rush. I needed the excitement, the danger, the living-on-the-edge feeling.

In the years leading up to this particular day, I had not experienced anything to cause concern or cast doubt. I loved speed including fast cars and fast women.

One Saturday morning I climbed Monitor Pass and was returning down the west face. I was attempting to see how fast I could go. At the top half of the mountain I had attained speeds I had never reached before. When I needed to change the gearing to execute the Death Rides, I wanted to keep the 53/39 set-up at the front. 53 is a big ring and it allows for real pace. Later I found out I had reached 55mph this particular morning but what happened soon after changed my cycling for many years.

The lower half of Monitor Pass west face is steep, around 10-12 percent. The road enters a canyon that gets narrower as the road drops in altitude. As I was speeding down the road, a gust of wind, like a shear blast, hit the front forks. Immediately they went into violent oscillation as the handlebars steered right, then left, then right, then left at a frequency hard to control. I had never experienced this shimmering before. Jesus, I was fighting with the handlebars just to hold onto them. Instinctively I wanted to let go, as the force of the brutal and rapid shifts threatened to rip my hands off the bars or, worse, snap my arms. My life depended on either of those not happening.

I must have been coming down the mountain at 50+mph. I was at colossal speed and my heart rate skyrocketed. I grew scared very fast. I was on the right side of the road as it hugged the mountain face. The mountain disappeared and a deep ravine entered the fray with huge boulders everywhere. I was panicking as I tried to force the bike to slow down. I could not control the oscillations, they were too strong, and I pummeled the brake levers, trying to activate them like an ABS braking system. If I applied full braking force too quickly, I would lock the front wheel which would then send me cartwheeling over the handlebars and into the ravine, but not before sliding along the road first. I did not fancy being vulture meat that morning. I saw the huge boulders. I saw the deep ravine. I thought I was going over the edge. I thought my life was ending right here.

Even with the front forks still in the oscillatory mode, I was gradually applying enough ABS-style braking to slow the bike down. But it wasn't slowing down fast enough. Nor was my heart rate. This was the most hair-raising event I had ever experienced on a cycle. Even big trucks going past with inches to spare were less scary. I was petrified and panicking.

For a period of time I thought it was all over. I thought I was going over the edge, smashing into an object that would have remained fixed, despite the high speed impact. I may not have been found in days, although I had learnt from training in the mountains on my own that I needed to tell someone where I was just in case. I learnt that lesson quickly because cycling in mountains is pure isolation, and inherently dangerous.

Slowly the bike came under control. It seemed to be taking forever. Finally the oscillations slowed down and I was eventually able to control the forks with the strength in my arms. Once they were controlled, I could slow the bike down, eventually grinding to a halt at the side of the road. I removed both feet from their pedal clips and planted them firmly on the ground. I bent over the handlebars and took deep breaths. Bloody hell.

That event triggered a change in my cycling for five years. I slowed down coming down mountains. I never reached speeds above 35mph for several years. I was more aware of the winds and what damage they can do, having nearly been blown off a mountain.

I have felt the same wind forces on the forks since then. I experienced those oscillations again a few years later but I wasn't going 50+mph that time. Now when I feel strong winds affecting the forks, I slow down.

Chapter 54

ON FRIDAY JULY 9th, I drove over to Turtle Rock Park just north of Markleeville. This was the staging area for the Death Ride. I walked up to the registration window and inquired about no-show ticket availability.

"Yes sir, there are some available," the woman responded.

Fantastic. I was now entered for tomorrow's ride.

The ride was strong and uneventful, but I was slower coming down the passes. Unfortunately, I saw a lot more crashes than usual and there seemed to be too many ambulances around. One guy crashed in the same area where I nearly got blown off on Monitor. I wondered if he had suffered the same fate with the wind.

My yellow Range Rover was parked just past Turtle Rock Park on the right side of the road as I cycled up to it. It stood out like a beacon. I did love that thing.

I had completed four passes at that point and I really didn't want to scale up through the canyon to do Carson Pass. I was feeling really good and my head was in a better place. I could have done the fifth pass but I was ok with stopping. I did not have to prove anything to anyone anymore. I gently rested the bike up against the car, dropped the tailgate, sat on it and stared off into the yonder. As I sat there, a cyclist I had been talking to earlier peddled past me.

"I don't blame you," he said laughing.

"I feel good but I am done. The 30th Anniversary Five-Pass shirt is ugly this year. Why bother?" I replied, laughing.

After a short rest, I placed the bike in the back, climbed into the driver's seat and off I went home.

Chapter 55

SOON AFTER THE Death Ride a court date came up for a hearing regarding the change in alimony and child support. I detested court with a passion. The lawyer for DCSS was also there. My lawyer, John, went through the procedural motions, discussions and formalities in presenting our case. I was tired of all this nonsense. It wasn't as if we had cash coming out of our ears but I knew what I had spent on legal fees. I had no idea what my ex-wife had spent. It was lunacy on a different level. In the end it did not matter. That was the last court date I would ever have with my ex-wife. A few months later, after more documents had been filed and another ten thousand dollars or more had been spent, we would eventually settle. The absurdity would stop and it came in a manner befitting such level of stupidity.

Around late September, early October I receive a fax at work. My ex-wife is done and wants to settle on alimony and child support, it read. After the shock had dissipated and my heart rate had settled, I gather my thoughts and immediately notify John. I was anticipating a battle and I was tired of court. Money I didn't have was being tossed away. It was a simple one-page fax containing a few brief sentences. I was stunned. Why wasn't the rest of the divorce dealt with this way? In the end alimony was to finish but child support had to continue until Michael turned 18. I breathed a big sigh of relief. Nothing made much sense in the end, except somebody wanted their money. The divorce was finally over but its aftermath and consequences would linger on perhaps until I die.

I signed the official documents a few days later and we were done. I had ten or so more months dealing with DCSS. Now I had to rebuild what was left of my shattered life...

Prologue

IT WAS THURSDAY 26th November, 2015. I sat on the Dragonair flight from Kaohsiung, Taiwan and laid back in exhaustion. I had just spent 12 or so days with a client I love being with. He treats me like a brother whenever I visit his laboratory. It had been my third visit to Taiwan and I love it. Now Hong Kong was only an hour away and I was getting excited. I was going to arrive on Thanksgiving Day around 1:00 pm. I was exhausted because Werner, my client and now one of my best friends, and I had been out in Kaohsiung most nights until 5 am. I would drop off the hotel key every morning before heading out for work. The first time I show up at around 5:30am to retrieve the room key, the night manager is a little confused. Then he laughed and got me the key. After that, he got used to seeing me show up in the early morning hours. Werner and I were never drunk but we would meet people and friends throughout the evening hours, which then extended into the early morning hours. Bars seemed to stay open until the last person left. But we had amazing chemistry and talked for hours. Karaoke is a big cultural phenomenon in Asia and I got to sing in bars. I sounded good, I thought, but I had been drinking. It was fun and rewarding.

The final weekend in Kaohsiung Werner sends me a message from his home town Taipei via the social app Line.

"Grab a taxi and get on the High Speed Rail (HSR) early Monday morning. I will meet you at the main station in Taipei and take you on a tour of the city, including Taipei 101 tower."

Wow, what an invitation. Early that Monday I followed Werner's instructions and grabbed a taxi to the train station. I then purchased a business-class ticket on the HSR linking both ends of Taiwan. We spend a fantastic day touring the historical city before driving to Kaohsiung late that evening in his scintillating RS4 Avant. I first visited Taiwan in 2004 but a recent earthquake had shut down Taipei 101. I never thought I would be back.

I got off the plane in Hong Kong and went through customs. I was staying in a hotel only one block from Hong Kong Harbor in a district of Kowloon. It was a five star hotel called The Kowloon Hotel. I hailed a cab. It was a nice drive over amazing bridges and roadways toward the world famous skyline of Hong Kong. Two blocks west were the ferry terminals that could take me anywhere, even mainland China. I wanted to explore Hong Kong and finish a period of my life. I vaguely remember some things from my trip in 2007. The ferry, a trolley-climb up a steep hill, a bar we went to and of course the night life were all vague memories, with the odd exception. The first trip was at the onset of my divorce and I don't remember much of it at all. Now with my life calming down and the pain becoming second nature, I was ready to break out and seek new adventures.

I had changed. My life had changed. I had lost most things I had ever worked for. Now I just wanted to live and be happy, whatever those entailed. Furthermore, I wanted to retrace what I had missed in 2007. It would prove to me that I was slowly recovering from the traumatic events and that I was on the right path.

Thursday afternoon was bustling in Kowloon area and I was happy to hang around the hotel and just walk around the area close by. When it got dark I ventured over to the water front and observed the spectacular night skyline. Jesus! I didn't remember this from eight years ago.

Friday morning I knew I was going to take the ferry across to HK Island and try to locate the famous tram tour. I meandered across the street and in the general direction of the ferry terminals. The ferry was a short ride but took a course directly across the famous skyline. What an incredible experience! I was savoring every moment and taking it all in, digesting as much as I could at each moment.

The ferry docked and I walked over to find a taxi outside the terminal. I had no idea where the tram was located. I vaguely remember getting a bus in 2007 but not this time. I thought it was a long ride but I expressed to the driver where I wanted to go and he immediately sped off in the direction he knew. Five or so minutes later, we were parked outside the tram stop. I saw the line was long so this was going to take some time. I paid the cab driver and I stepped out and walked over to stand in line as it weaved around the building, all carefully roped off for the visitors and tourists. I must have waited at least 90 minutes.

Once everyone was seated, the tram set off up a steep incline. A few minutes later it arrived at the top. I stepped off and looked around. I don't remember the huge lookout building nor the vast array of shops at the top of the hill. I was thirsty so headed over towards the café. As I walked in a sense of déjà vue came over me. It was a very strange feeling that would repeat itself later that day but in a more powerful way. I grabbed a coffee and a pastry and sat down to take in the staggering view above the majestic Hong Kong skyline. It was climactic, absolutely awe-inspiring and stunning. Where was my head in 2007?

Eight years earlier I was in chaos. I had been tossed into a sea of man-eating sharks with both my arms and legs tied. I had been sinking fast. Eight years later, as I stared at one of the most awesome sights in the world, my head was at peace. With energy I mustered from somewhere deep down, I had survived. There were long periods in my life when I had cried every night. Now, as I climbed many steps and made my way to the top of the viewing area above Hong Kong harbor's skyline, mesmerized at the stunning views, I was at peace with myself and with the world. I sat and stared at the 360 degree views in awe and then the emotions and memories came flooding over me...

I had somehow pieced some of my life back together. I had moved away from the many court cases, the jail experience, the loss of assets and homes, the forest fire, the decimation of my company and the loss of the knee.

Settling alimony and finishing with child support were huge. It meant the personalized relentless attacks on me by DCSS had come to an end. It also meant the court system could no longer attack my bank accounts. For over two years I had to keep my personal accounts at zero dollars. It was an absolutely insane way to be forced to live. Now I could access my bank accounts anywhere in the world without fear and interruption. Being able to access my funds via ATM's was a huge breakthrough and allowed me back into the 21st Century again.

I was rebuilding the business. We had sold some mass spectrometers to Werner's new laboratory in Taiwan and I had been out to install them back in 2014. I had done an analytical project for one of the largest energy companies in the world and the data was brilliant. No one thought we could isolate and show differences between two oil sources from the Bakken Oil Field that were almost identical in composition and formation. My processing technique showed distinct but small differences. I continued to travel.

In September 2010 I once again raced around Lake Tahoe on my bike. This time on a brand new carbon fiber Felt that Kent had sold me that summer. The angles were different, the gearing was slower but I circumnavigated the lake in 4 hours 7 minutes. It was an amazing achievement and quite rewarding, despite being half dead at the finish. I was only 7 minutes off another medal but it did extol the virtues of having a cycle correctly set up. Something I had eventually found out through thousands of miles of self-inflicted pain and suffering.

In 2011 we were forced to sell our partnership in Canada. I had visions of me moving up there and helping it grow but the divorce ended that little pipe dream, as it did most things. My partners had no interest dealing with the divorce fallout and I didn't blame them. No one would have. I love Vancouver though and don't need an excuse to visit but the loss of the partnership cut deep. The perpetual trips up to Canada were exciting and rewarding.

Land Rover of Sacramento invited me to an off-road event in the summer of 2011 at their property in Carmel, California. I showed up in the recently-purchased TReK Discovery Series II. Land Rover representatives, some of whom remain friends today, and participants fell over backwards. The pressure was on and I ended up winning that event. It wasn't the winning that was important but the rebuilding of a tattered life and the making of new friends.

I didn't really appreciate nor understand the risk I was taking with my cycling until one late August morning in 2012. I always wondered what would happen if I crashed and bent the left leg beyond the post-surgical limitations. I found that out one early morning when I was heading to Reno Airport for a cross-country flight. I walked out of my home and slipped on ice created by a lethal combination of sprinklers and a cold night. My right leg went from underneath me and the left leg bent and took the weight. I leaned forward and forced myself off the deck to alleviate the pressure, but I was too slow. I felt and heard the pop followed by immense swelling and pain. Subsequent X-rays showed I had snapped the knee cap in half. I deemed myself lucky though because the broken patella repaired itself without surgical intervention. Had it not, Dr. Bannar would have replaced the knee. He proclaimed during examination that he wouldn't screw the patella together if it failed to heal properly. He would just replace the knee. Scared and frightened, I escaped yet another knee replacement.

Unfortunately, this time the damage was also psychological and it took three years to mentally recover from the injury. My cycling slowed, climbing mountain passes was different and I was always pre-occupied with what might happen. I had been made aware in no uncertain terms what could happen if I crashed. It wasn't until the spring of 2015 that I gained my confidence again and started to really climb. Then, soon after, I rolled my right ankle because I am always having to concentrate on the left knee. Coming down small steps after washing my car I didn't notice the thick hot water hose under the steps. My focus is always on protecting the left knee and so I stepped on the hose with my right leg and violently rolled the ankle, breaking it. The outside tendon was ripped from the bone, but the tendon survived. The roll was so vicious that an anchor point for one end of the tendon had been ripped away from the main bone.

Four months after breaking my ankle, I did the Tour de Tahoe again. This time I completed the ride in 4 hours 41 minutes. I pushed hard because I wanted to, not because I was angry. I dragged people up Spooner Summit which was remarkable all by itself since I had done little training that year.

Having been diagnosed legally-disabled by a qualified doctor in 2005, I was finding out it isn't just living with a disability, but how it impacts other aspects of one's life. It certainly does that. One has to make adjustments as one moves forward in life.

But I had survived all that. I had navigated my life around abstract chaos and insanity created by others. It still wasn't clear why a divorce should tear someone to pieces, or why the court system should allow it to happen. A sealed divorce file proves my point and should have never happened in a free democracy. A judge becoming personally involved speaks for itself.

The knee was my problem. I created it because I was an incredibly gifted athlete and wanted to excel in sports. The accident playing rugby seemed innocuous and was unfortunate but no one could have predicted the surgical complications and failures. I dealt with those too, somehow. The surgeries themselves would have finished off most people but what came after that shuck my core and tore me to pieces. I wasn't prepared for any of it.

Despite all the nonsense, lies, turmoil and adversity, one email still rattles around my head. It came from Jean in Canada soon after the sale of our partnership up there in 2011. It went like this:

> *Throughout all the trials and tribulations in your life, I learnt something about you Geoff. I learnt that when everyone around you was losing their minds and going insane, you kept your head. You kept focused and kept your integrity. That I will never forget.*

I read the email a few times and pondered what he had written. He was right. I kept my head. Who knows how is a question that will never be answered. I am proud to say I can walk into any room and hold my head high. There were a few people associated with my divorce that cannot say that. I could have elected a different path but I had children to protect and I didn't want to stray from what I had worked all my life for. We have nothing when we enter this world and all we have when we depart is our integrity. The words from Jean will be forever etched in memory.

As Winston Churchill once said: If you are going through hell, keep going.

I wasn't aware of time passing or of the tears slowly rolling down my face. The memories will forever haunt me and the emotions are only one thin layer of skin away from being punctured at random times. I looked at my watch. I had been sitting at the top of the look-out platform for over two hours. It was time to finish my trip.

I carefully made my way down the vast number of stairs, grabbed the tram back down and secured a taxi back to the ferry terminal. Another ferry back across the bay to Kowloon whilst passing the amazing harbor. That part of my journey was now fulfilled.

I was hungry after analyzing my life so I went looking for an eatery. Then I saw it. I walked right passed a sign for Delaney's Irish Pub. An Englishman finding an Irish pub in a foreign country! What were the chances of that? It was below ground and required steps. I walked down the stairs and once again I had a feeling I had been here before, only this feeling was more profound, more powerful. Thousands of miles from home and I randomly select a bar I felt I had been to before.

I sat down, grabbed a beer and ordered fish and chips, of course. What Englishman wouldn't? I left the bar and went to fulfill something on my Bucket List. I wanted some custom-tailored clothing from Hong Kong. I locate a place not far from the hotel and order a three-piece suit, three custom shirts with French cuffs and two Italian linen jackets. I organize shipping to my home once they are done.

I decided I wanted one more beer at Delaney's before I left Hong Kong. I walked in and sat down at the bar, still marveling at how familiar the place looked. When I returned to the hotel I emailed Dave, now my ex-partner in Canada, to inquire about Delaney's.

"Did we go into this bar, Dave? How about the café?" I asked.

"Yes, of course, don't you remember? The bar was hopping and we were watching the Australian Rules Football final. Next to us was a couple cheering for one team and we were cheering for the other. Remember?"

"No, I don't, Dave. I don't remember much about HK in 2007."

"You remember the Philippine lady you were with two nights, don't you?"

"Claire? Of course I do. She took the taxi with us to the airport."

The next night, I spent venturing into the nightlife on Hong Kong Island. It was time to find Lockhart Road. I took the metro under the harbor. Two stops later I walked off and followed beautiful ladies since, presumably, they were heading to the famous bars on Lockhart Road. I was right.

For the first half hour I just walked up and down the road, looking and observing. Often someone from a bar would grab my arm to get me into that particular bar but I just brushed them away. The bars were full of gorgeous ladies talking with men.

Finally I walked passed a bar called The San Francisco Club, something like that, and I eventually accepted the grabbing of the arm to get me in. When I walked in I was immediately met by two incredibly beautiful Filipino ladies. They were gorgeous. The owner of the bar came over and discussed the arrangement. I could buy them drinks, all would be happy. If I bought better drinks, we would move off into a private room. Deal done, drinks bought and off we went.

They removed all but their panties. We were talking away and enjoying ourselves. The ladies moved off to one side when the owner came back in.

"What would you like to do?" she inquired.

"I do not know. I am just here to enjoy myself."

"Well, I can offer you several arrangements. You can have the two girls for an hour, for two hours or you and I can arrange for the whole night. They can go back to your hotel," she casually added.

Stunned, I asked, "Can I pay with a credit card?"

"Of course," the owner replied.

They went off to get dressed. One came out in shorts and a nice shirt and the other followed in a lovely short dress. All three of us grabbed a taxi to take us under the harbor to Kowloon and back to my hotel.

I jumped into the shower as the two ladies washed and cleaned me up. We were laughing and joking the whole time. Their English was ok, at least good enough to communicate on a basic level. One of the ladies wanted room service so I found the menu and we sourced some food. Half hour later there is a knock on the door.

"Hello Mr. Bott. Your room service delivery," said the smartly dressed older gentleman.

He thought I was on my own but I obviously wasn't. The two lovely ladies had jumped on the bed and slid the covers over most of their bodies. With their bare arms and shoulders showing, it was evident they were partly naked.

"Thank you. Please, come on in."

The room was small and the hallway was narrow as it passed the bathroom area. Once beyond the bathroom, it opened into the bedroom. The look on the guy's face as he saw the two ladies was hilarious.

"Oh," he blurted out.

He quickly placed the food cart in the room, opened up the lids and then departed. We ate the food before watching the "Minions" movie in bed.

Sunday morning I paid for the two ladies' taxi back to the island and then I headed to the restaurant for an exceptionally different breakfast. Well, the food was the same but my head was somewhere else. In August 2007, I had visited one of the most incredible countries and could not remember most of it. Today, my life was peaceful.

My head was clear. I had fulfilled numerous fantasies on this trip both in Taiwan and Hong Kong. I walked out of the hotel lobby and got into a taxi.

A few hours later I collapsed on the United Airlines flight 862 back to San Francisco. It was surreal. I was dazed. My trip to Hong Kong was incredible.

My Discovery Series II TReK #3 at the Land Rover off-road event in Carmel, the event I won

Taipei 101 building

Hong Kong Island

View of Hong Kong from the Peak observation platform

Hong Kong